All About
ASSET
ALLOCATION

SECOND EDITION

RICHARD A. FERRI, CFA

New York   Chicago   San Francisco   Lisbon   London
Madrid   Mexico City   Milan   New Delhi   San Juan
Seoul   Singapore   Sydney   Toronto

1 2 3 4 5 6 7 8 9 0   DOC/DOC   1 9 8 7 6 5 4 3 2 1 0

ISBN   978-0-07-170078-8
MHID   0-07-170078-1

This publication is designed to provide accurate and authoritative information in regard to the subject matter covered. It is sold with the understanding that the publisher is not engaged in rendering legal, accounting, securities trading, or other professional services. If legal advice or other expert assistance is required, the services of a competent professional person should be sought.

—*From a Declaration of Principles Jointly Adopted by a Committee of the American Bar Association and a Committee of Publishers and Associations*

McGraw-Hill books are available at special quantity discounts to use as premiums and sales promotions, or for use in corporate training programs. To contact a representative please visit the Contact Us pages at www.mhprofessional.com.

This book is printed on acid-free paper.

* * * * *

To my parents, with love and admiration

* * * * *

CONTENTS

FOREWORD

In the fall of 1929, Alfred Cowles III had an ordinary, if rather large, problem. Ordinary because, like many other Americans, he had been badly hurt by the recent stock market crash. And large because, not only was he the heir to the *Chicago Tribune* fortune, but he also managed it.

A highly intelligent young man, he took his charge seriously, consuming as much written analysis from the nation's brokerage houses, insurance firms, and financial commentators as he could. Alas, it was in vain; none of them warned him of the impending crash. How could the country's brightest financial stars have been so uniformly wrong?

Cowles's response to the catastrophic stock market decline that wiped out nearly 90 percent of the stock market's value over the next three years, and the Great Depression that it ignited, has thundered down through the financial markets to this very day. Modern investors ignore the lessons learned by Cowles, and those who followed in his footsteps, at their own peril.

For what Cowles and his followers did was nothing less than remove finance from the realm of ignorance and superstition and place it on a scientific footing. With the help of the nation's foremost economists, he founded the Econometric Society, and, along with the legendary Benjamin Graham, who had been similarly affected by the 1929 crash, he began to collect and analyze financial data in the most detailed and thoroughgoing way possible. In effect, he, and those who have followed him in the seven decades since, took investing away from the astrologers and the charlatans and gave it to the astronomers and physicists. (This is, in some cases, quite literally true: many of the finest minds of modern finance began their careers in the physical sciences.)

Unfortunately, when you pick up a financial magazine, watch CNBC, or call your broker, you've just traveled back to the pre–1929 era. In fact, you've just accomplished the financial equivalent of betting the farm on the daily horoscope or of taking a rare cancer to a doctor whose main source of recent medical knowledge is *USA Today*.

Like most intellectual revolutions, the modern science of investing is highly counterintuitive. Do you think that it is possible, through careful securities research, to reliably select market-beating portfolios? Wrong: the data show that although many investors do so, in almost all cases this is purely the result of the randomness of the markets—in simple terms, dumb luck. People have also gotten fabulously rich buying lottery tickets; they have also gotten off scot-free without ever wearing a seatbelt. That does not make either activity a good idea. Do you think that, by choosing a portfolio of only a few stocks that you hope will score big, you are maximizing your chances of becoming wealthy? Indeed you are, but by doing so, you are also maximizing your chances of a retirement of cat food cuisine. And make no mistake about it: the object of this particular game is not to get rich—it's to not get poor.

All About Asset Allocation will bring you back into the modern era with a comprehensive, yet readable, exposition of how to apply to your investment portfolio what seven decades of financial research have taught us about investing.

Building an asset allocation is much like putting up a skyscraper. You will need blueprints—what asset classes to buy, which ones to skip, and how much of each to use. You will also need the construction materials—which building blocks to buy, and whom to buy them from. Rick Ferri provides you with both of these, in spades.

Unfortunately, in building your financial skyscraper, there is one thing that neither Rick nor I nor any other financial expert can do for you, which is to provide you with the nerve to stick to those blueprints when you find yourself 30 stories up in the naked girders in a howling wind. But with *All About Asset Allocation* by your side, you'll know that you're executing a sound design, using the best materials, and wearing the best safety rope that money can buy.

William Bernstein

ACKNOWLEDGMENTS

I am particularly thankful to Dr. William Bernstein for writing an enlightening foreword. In addition, many thanks to to noted authors and investment experts Scott Simon and Bill Schultheis. A special thanks goes to John Bogle, former chairman of the Vanguard Group and founder of affordable mutual fund investing. Appreciation to all those at Vanguard, Morningstar, and Bloomberg for their help in gathering and organizing data. A warm thanks to my cyber friends on the Bogleheads.org for the helpful suggestions over the years. Credit goes to my coworkers at Portfolio Solutions, LLC, who did an excellent job of reviewing the manuscript. Finally, I wish to thank my wife, Daria, for her love and never-ending support. The Texas ranch sure is nice.

INTRODUCTION

"Is asset allocation dead?"

"Has the past decade changed the way I should invest?"

"Can I trust the markets to meet my financial needs?"

The short answers are no, perhaps, and yes.

The first decade in the new millennium was a challenge for all investors. Unprecedented shocks caused extremes in market volatility over the period. The decade began with the deflation of technology and communication stock expectations, followed by two attacks on U.S. soil that lead to two wars fought halfway around the world, and finished with a housing price collapse that brought too-big-to-fail global financial institutions to their knees and massive government bailouts.

The events of the past decade have shaken the foundations of investment knowledge and have forced people to rethink their own investment strategies from the ground up. People are questioning the validity of modern portfolio theory (MPT) that had become well indoctrinated into portfolios. Do the markets still operate efficiently? Is a buy and hold investment strategy dead? How does a radical shift in the global economic power affect my portfolio? Is the U.S. dollar in a long-term decline? What new asset classes are available, and should I invest in them? These questions are all valid, and they all deserve answers.

In your quest for information and solutions, you will find no shortage of people willing to help with answers—any answers— even bad answers, and there will be people trying to sell you products that go along with their answers. If it isn't one person pushing you into gold or commodity investments, it's another saying you should invest in the Chinese real estate market. Everyone selling a product has an answer to volatility in the first decade, and most are selling products that you'd best avoid.

Deep down, I believe that everyone knows that the future is unknowable, which means that you cannot pick one sector or one investment and count on it for financial security. But this does not stop us from wishing we did know, and this is why people pay good money for the advice of experts. But, which expert do you believe? Which one are you going to rely on for advice?

Block out the gurus who say that they can tell the next move in the stock markets, interest rates, or the price of gold, because *they don't know*. Focus instead those advisors who recommend developing a long-term investment policy using a diversified asset base, and then implementing that policy with diligence, dedication, and discipline.

IT'S ALL ABOUT ASSET ALLOCATION

The investment strategies outlined in this second edition of *All About Asset Allocation* provide a no-nonsense, businesslike approach to getting a tough job done. They offer an investment solution that is easy to understand, rational in its approach, and just plain workable. Simply stated, spread your investment risk across many different securities while keeping costs very low and controlling for risk and taxes. Don't try to out-guess the markets because you will not be successful in the long term, and it will cost you dearly. Control what you can control: costs, taxes, risk. Then let the markets take care of the rest. This approach has the highest probability of financial success.

WHAT ASSET ALLOCATION CAN AND CANNOT DO

A prudent asset allocation that is followed by discipline will increase your chances for reaching and maintaining financial security over your lifetime. That being said, no investment strategy can protect your portfolio all the time. You must be prepared for some bumps in the road. There will be poor months, quarters, and occasionally years. There is no getting around this fact.

Unfortunately, there is also a large market for financial fraud. Many unethical and unscrupulous investment experts will say that they have found a risk-free road to wealth. They are lying. High returns do not come without risk. Many experts who said that they had the secret to success in the markets went to jail in 2008 and 2009. Bernard Madoff was the most famous person, followed by many other less famous crooks.

There is no free lunch on Wall Street. There is risk. This risk can be controlled to some extent through good investment policy and prudent execution of that policy. Disciplined investors who follow their well-defined investment policy will come out far ahead over those who drift aimlessly from strategy to strategy, hoping for a lucky break.

The lessons in this book are simple. First, allocate your investments across multiple asset classes to reduce overall portfolio risk. Second, invest broadly within each asset class to eliminate the specific risk of owning any single security. Third, keep your costs as low as feasible, including taxes. Fourth, rebalance your portfolio periodically to keep your risk on target with your investment policy.

Asset allocation is a simple concept to understand and yet extremely difficult to implement. You can select asset classes easily, decide on the percentage target for each asset class, choose low-cost mutual funds to represent the asset classes, and perhaps intend to get your portfolio on track.

Yet, despite good intentions, many people have great difficulty implementing their strategy fully or maintaining it after the initial allocation. There are too many distractions. You don't have the time, the market doesn't look right, the talking heads are saying something else. and so on. To top it all off, a friend or family member was just hired by a brokerage firm, and you promised to listen to his or her novice sales ideas. Procrastination has killed good intentions.

Rebalancing is often the most difficult part of an asset allocation strategy because it is counterintuitive. Rebalancing requires you to sell a little of the investment that went up and buy more of what went down. Can you imagine buying stocks in early 2009 when the market was more than 60 percent below its high and every expert on television was predicting lower prices? That is exactly what the strategy required, and the only investors who were rewarded with excess returns by the end of 2009 were those who rebalanced religiously.

The temptations to deviate from a simple investment strategy are great. I know from my years of experience that many people are not able to stay the course. There is a solution. If you do not have the discipline to manage an asset allocation strategy yourself, then hire a competent, low-fee advisor to do it. You will pay for this service, but at least the job gets done fully and efficiently.

THE CONCEPT OF TOTAL RISK

Do you know how much portfolio risk you can handle? I will tell you that it is not all about market risk. There is a lot going on in your life besides your investments. What happens outside your portfolio can affect how you react to your portfolio. For example, if the markets are down, typically the economy is slow or slowing, which means that consumer confidence is low, and perhaps your job at risk. These outside influences create stresses in your life that may affect the way you invest your well-thought-out strategy.

Your asset allocation should take into account potential stresses that may not seem to have direct impact on the asset allocation process. I spoke with one person in late 2009 who said she sold stocks at the bottom of the bear market. Now she wanted to go back in at the same 60 percent stock allocation. My reaction was that she was investing above her tolerance for risk in 2009 and that going back in at a 60 percent in stock was a mistake. It was my opinion that she would only make the same knee-jerk emotional mistake again during the next bear market. She insisted that she would not because last time she had just been through a messy divorce, her mother took ill and she had to move in to help, and her dog died.

The loss of a job or any other loss can cause investors to abandon their investment policy even if the portfolio was set to the right risk level for the investors based only on their future financial needs. A change in health can make people feel as though they have less control over their life, and this may cause them to over-compensate in an area they can control, such as changing their investment portfolio.

One does not often think about job security, family matters, family health, and the amount of debt you owe as factors in an asset allocation decision, but they very important. Making an emotional decision to change your portfolio when other factors are stressing you typically does not lead to a better outcome. Ignoring outside risk factors when setting a portfolio asset allocation strategy can lead to too much "life" risk, and that can produce behavioral mistakes down the road.

In this second edition of *All About Asset Allocation*, I have enhanced the behavioral finance section. There is also a new chapter on when to change an allocation and how to do it. These new tools assist investors with implementing and maintaining their investment policy so it can roll with life's punches.

The fundamental concepts written in this book provide a blueprint for the design, implementation, and maintenance of a prudent, reliable, lifelong investment plan. In some cases, the plan goes beyond the grave. Read it, study it, create a plan, implement it, and maintain it. You will not be disappointed.

ADVICE FROM EXPERIENCE

There is an old saying that if you really want to get to know people, you should either marry them or manage their money. I have been married to the same wonderful woman for most of my adult life, and I have also had the fortunate experience of getting to know many people over the decades by personally managing their investment portfolios.

As a professional, it has been my job to understand people's personal, financial, and family situation so that I can best advise them on investment decisions. This means asking about personal and some nonfinancial issues that may affect their outlook in the future. It is only with this understanding that my company can help guide an investor toward a prudent asset allocation. This process is by no means static. It is an ongoing challenge.

What I have learned over the years is that every investor has unique issues, and then we all have issues that are very similar. We all have liabilities that need to be paid for in the future, and we want to ensure there is enough money to meet those needs. We are concerned about health care, taxes, educating our children and grandchildren, and then helping them later in life if needed. Most important, we do not want to outlive our own money and become a burden to our families. That is the biggest fear most people have about money.

What differs about how we view money is the amount we each need to cover future liabilities. In other words, we differ in lifestyle. Different careers and opportunities lead us to different standards of living. What may be comfortable for one person may not be good enough for another. Matching current assets and future income streams to those different liabilities is a challenge. This is where reasonable expectations, financial planning, and proper investment policy come in.

INVESTMENT POLICY

Investment policy is a statement about how you will implement and maintain your investment portfolio. It is typically a simple and concise document that it is easy *for you* to understand and follow. Some people write a policy for themselves, and other people go to a professional. The advisor may do a complete financial plan in an effort to find the investment policy that best fits your needs.

Everyone has different financial needs, different investment experiences, and different perceptions of risk. These differences make designing portfolios a multifaceted and challenging exercise. Accordingly, the information in this book cannot cover every scenario, and the asset allocation examples in this book should be viewed as examples, not recommendations. There is no one-size-fits-all solution, especially when people are approaching their preretirement age. It will be up to you to grasp the important concepts that drive a successful asset allocation and then develop a portfolio mix to meet your special needs and circumstances.

Over your lifetime, how you divide your investments among stocks, bonds, real estate, and other asset classes will explain almost all your portfolio risk and return *providing you have the discipline to maintain your plan.* This makes the asset allocation decision one of the most important decisions in your life and is worth spending considerable time understanding. At its root, asset allocation is a simple idea: diversify a portfolio across several unlike investments to reduce the risk of a large loss. Controlling risk through a prudent asset allocation plan and proper portfolio maintenance keeps you focused on the big picture during difficult periods in the market cycle, and this discipline is the key to your long-term investment success.

DIFFERENT ASSET ALLOCATION STRATEGIES

There are three different types of asset allocation strategies. One is a long-term strategy that is the focus of the book. It does not require making short-term predictions about the markets in order to be successful. The other two require short-term market prediction in order to be successful. I leave those to the television talking heads.

1. Strategic asset allocation (no predictions needed)
2. Tactical and dynamic asset allocation (requires accurate market predictions)
3. Market timing (requires accurate market predictions)

This book is all about long-term strategic asset allocation. This strategy is commonly known as "buy and hold"; however, I believe it is best described as "buy, hold, and rebalance." Strategic asset allocation focuses on selecting suitable asset classes and investments to be held for the long run. An asset allocation should not change based on the cyclical ups and downs of the economy or because some cynic publicly doubts the strategy and then personally benefits from investors who waver. Once this allocation is set, it does need occasional review and perhaps tweaking, especially when there are changes in a person's life.

Tactical asset allocation is not the topic of this book, and this is the only place I address it. Tactical asset allocation assumes active changes to an investment mix based on short-term market forecasts for returns. These predictions may be a function of fundamental variables such as earnings or interest-rate forecasts, economic variables such as the outlook for economic growth in different countries, or technical variables such as recent price trends and charting patterns.

Market timing is tactical asset allocation in the extreme. It is an all-in or all-out decision on asset classes. For example, a market timer may start the year 100 percent in stocks, change to 50 percent stocks and 50 percent in bonds sometime during year, and end with 100 percent in cash. Market timing is for people who believe they can consistently forecast major movements in the market and thus beat the market by trading.

Tactical asset allocation and market timing sound like wonderful ideas, and they sure make a good sales pitch. However, just about every unbiased academic study ever conducted shows that this type of asset allocation advice is no better than a flipping a coin. The advocates spin a good tale about how they can weave in and out of the markets, but they don't consistently make money doing it.

The only reliable asset allocation strategy is the one discussed in this book. A well-balanced multi-asset-class portfolio that is maintained over time has the highest probability of success.

All About Asset Allocation focuses on selecting the right asset-class mix for your needs, choosing low-cost investments that represent those asset classes, implementing the strategy, and maintaining it. The facts and figures are presented in as straightforward a manner as possible. Some of the data are technical, so I have tried to illustrate these concepts with figures and explain their meaning in easy-to-understand terms. When you have finished reading all the chapters and you understand the important concepts in each chapter, you will possess the knowledge and the tools you will need to put together a sensible portfolio allocation that will serve you well for many years ahead.

A REVIEW OF THE CHAPTERS

All About Asset Allocation is divided into three parts. All three are equally important. Accordingly, the best way to read this book is to start on the first page and read all the way through to the last.

Part One explains the need for investment policy and the basic theory behind an asset allocation strategy. Chapter 1 explains why creating a viable investment plan is critical to success, and how asset allocation works in the plan. Chapter 2 is all about investment risk. Risk is defined in many different ways by many different people, ranging from losing money to the volatility of portfolio returns. Chapter 3 covers the technical aspects of asset allocation based on a two-asset-class portfolio. It covers basic formulas and historical market relationships. Chapter 4 expands into multi-asset-class investing. Adding more asset classes to a portfolio can reduce risk and increase long-term return.

Part Two is the discovery of investment opportunities. Chapter 5 discusses the methodology used to segregate asset-class types and styles. Chapter 6 looks at the U.S. equity market and its various components. Chapter 7 looks at international markets and how diversifying overseas helps U.S. investors. Chapter 8 is an examination of the U.S. fixed-income market and its various components. Chapter 9 covers real estate investing, including home ownership. Chapter 10 is an explanation of alternative asset classes including commodities, hedge funds, precious metals, and collectibles. All chapters provide a sample list of appropriate mutual funds and ETFs. By the time you have finished reading Part Two, you will have a comprehensive list of potential investments to consider.

Part Three is about managing your investment portfolio. Chapter 11 focuses on methods used to forecast various market risks and returns, along with a list of this author's estimates. Chapter 12 covers a life-cycle concept of investing and provides several examples of potential portfolios. Chapter 13 is an interesting chapter on behavioral finance. The right asset allocation is the one that matches both your needs and your personality. Chapter 14 is new to this edition. It covers when it is appropriate to change your asset allocation and how to do it. Chapter 15 finishes up with a discussion of fees, taxes, index funds, and the pros and cons of hiring professional management.

The appendixes offer a wealth of extended information on asset allocation books and helpful investment Web sites.

PART ONE

Asset Allocation Basics

Planning for Investment Success

KEY CONCEPTS

- Investment planning is critical to long-term success.
- Asset allocation is the key element of investment planning.
- Discipline and commitment to a strategy are needed.
- There are no shortcuts to achieving financial security.

A successful lifelong investment experience hinges on three critical steps: the development of a prudent investment plan, the full implementation of that plan, and the discipline to maintain the plan in good times and bad. If you create a good plan and follow it, your probability of financial freedom increases exponentially.

An investment plan provides the road map to fair and equitable investment results over the long term. Your asset allocation decision is the most important step in investment planning. This is the amount of money you commit to each of various asset classes, such as stocks, bonds, real estate, and cash. It is your asset allocation that largely determines the growth path of your money and level of portfolio risk in the long run. Exactly how you invest in each of these asset classes is of lesser importance than owning the asset classes themselves, although some ways are better and less expensive than others.

What is you current investment policy? Consider the follow-ing two portfolio management strategies. Which one best describes you today?

- *Plan A.* Buy investments that I expect will perform well over the next few years. If an investment performs poorly or the prospects change, switch to another investment or go to cash and wait for a better opportunity.
- *Plan B.* Buy and hold different types of investments in a diversified portfolio regardless of their near-term prospects. If an investment performs poorly, buy more of that investment to put my portfolio back in balance.

If you are like most investors, Plan A looks familiar. People tend to put their money into investments that they believe will lead to profitable results in the near term and sell those that do not per-form. The goal of Plan A is to "do well," which is not a quantifiable financial goal. What does "do well" mean? Plan A provides no guidelines for what to buy or when to buy it, or when to sell because of poor performance or changing prospects. Academic research shows that people who trade their accounts based on near-term performance tend to sell investments that eventually perform better than the new investment they buy.

I have talked with thousands of individual investors about their portfolios over the years. It is interesting to ask people what their investment plan has been and if their returns have met their expectations. Most people will say that they have some type of invest plan, and they will say that their performance is generally in line with the markets, but both these statements are wishful think-ing. An analysis of their portfolio often shows little evidence that any plan actually exists or has ever existed and that their invest-ment performance tends to be several percentage points below what they guessed it might have been. The sad truth is that a major-ity of investors choose their stocks, bonds, and mutual funds ran-domly with little consideration for how they all fit together or the amount they pay in fees, commissions, and other expenses.

CHARACTERISTICS OF A PLAN

Successful investing is a three-step process: (1) plan creation, (2) implementation, and (3) maintenance. It is an important step forward for people to recognize that they need a good investment plan and good investments in the plan to meet their long-term financial objectives. Once people come to that realization, they need a method for creating their plan, which is where this book comes in. Second, then they need to implement the plan, because a good plan not implemented is no plan at all. Finally and most important is a process for maintaining the plan, because discipline drives long-term results.

A good plan has long legs and should last several years without major modifications. Annual reviews and adjustments are appropriate, with major changes occurring when something has changed in your life. Adjustments to plans should never be made in reaction to poor market conditions or be based on a comment some talking head made on television. You would not quit your job and change occupations because you are going through a slump nor should you change your investment plan because your portfolio is suffering in a bear market. These off periods are natural and expected, and you must learn to live with them.

Put your investment plan in writing, because a written plan is not soon forgotten. Your *investment policy statement (IPS)* should include your financial needs, investment goals, asset allocation, description of investment choices, and why you believe this plan should get you to your goals over time. I guarantee that you will not be making many snap investment decisions if you have the discipline to read your IPS before you make any change.

All the planning in the world will not help if a plan is not implemented and religiously maintained. Most investment plans never become fully implemented because of a host of excuses including procrastination, distractions, laziness, lack of commitment, and the never-ending search for a perfect plan. I estimate that less than 50 percent of investment plans written are actually fully put into place. But that is not the whole story. Regular maintenance is the key to success following plan implementation. Markets are dynamic, and so is your portfolio. Periodic maintenance is needed to ensure that a portfolio is kept in line with the plan.

It is likely that less than 10 percent of all investment plans are fully implemented and maintained long enough and with enough discipline to make them work efficiently. Perhaps you may think I am being pessimistic, but that is what I have witnessed in my many years in the investment business. Many great investment plans fall by the wayside each year. There are a lot of good intentions out there, but there is much more procrastination.

THERE ARE NO SHORTCUTS

Money and life are intertwined in our culture. Our financial well-being is always on our minds. Will we have enough money? Will our children have enough for college? Is my income secure? What will happen to Social Security? Will I be able to afford health care? Are taxes going up? Will I be able to sell my house at the price I want when that time comes? Will I have to borrow money? What is my credit score? Most working people struggle to cover their living expenses let alone save enough for future obligations including retirement. They question when or whether they will be able to retire, and if they do retire, whether they will have a lifestyle that makes them comfortable. In the final years of life, decisions must be made about who gets our unspent money, how they get the money, and who is going to execute our estate. Money management is a never-ending battle from the time we get our first paycheck until we end our stay on this great planet.

Money matters are stressful, and investment decisions are part of that stress. When we save a little money, we don't want to lose it by investing poorly. Yet we do want a respectable rate of return. The earlier in life a person learns to invest money, the better off that person will be both financially and emotionally.

Unfortunately, proper investing principles are not taught to the general public. There are no required courses on investing in high schools or trade schools or as part of a required curriculum at colleges, law schools, or medical schools. In addition employers do not require employees to educate themselves about investing their 401(k) or other retirement accounts. The government does not get between investors and their money unless there is fraud or misrepresentation involved. The public is all alone on financial education, and, unfortunately, that typically results in an expensive trial-and-error process.

Learning about investing through trial and error takes years of disappointments before you are able to discern good information from bad. It is very common for people to slip far behind the market averages during this learning period, and most people never make up the losses. When people realize that they have made investment mistakes and have fallen behind, they tend to compensate by becoming either overly conservative or overly aggressive. Both are bad. Once-burnt, twice-shy investors may not reach their financial goal if they do not formulate a plan that is aggressive enough to get there. Other people may become more aggressive in an attempt to get their money back quickly. The newspapers regularly print stories of people who decided to swing for the fences only to end up losing much more or being swindled by an unscrupulous advisor.

When young people make investing mistakes, they are not too damaging because these people typically have little in the pot and they have years of work and savings ahead. However, when an older person makes the same mistake, it can be devastating. The papers are full of sad stories about retirees' life savings being wiped out because they put all their eggs in one basket and lost, or perhaps they were taken by the likes of a Bernie Madoff.

Enron Corporation was a highly publicized corporate bankruptcy that resulted from accounting fraud that ruined the financial lives of many people nearing retirement age. You could not pick up a newspaper or popular magazine without seeing an article about a former Enron employee who lost nearly all his or her savings as a result of the company's collapse. Some former Enron workers considered selling their homes just to pay bills. Others were so devastated by the event that they did not know what would become of them. The stories typically included photographs of the victims depicted in a state of despair.

Did the people in this country learn from Enron? No. Over the next decade, thousands of bankruptcies and near bankruptcies claimed the retirement savings of hundreds of thousands of rank and file employees who believed in those companies by purchasing their bonds. Some of those companies are household names, including General Motors, Lehman Brothers, AIG, Bear Stearns, and Chrysler. Will these bankruptcies of too-big-to-fail companies teach others to diversify their investments and lower their portfolio risk using asset allocation? Not likely.

WHY PROFESSIONAL ADVICE DOES NOT ALWAYS HELP

How do you learn about investing and at the same time avoid costly mistakes? One way is to hire a professional investment consultant, if you are lucky enough to find a good one. Hiring an advisor is a hit-or-miss proposition. The range of experience and education in the investment advisor industry is very broad. There are many professionals who are committed to their profession and would be very helpful in setting up an investment plan. And then there are those, regrettably, who would do more harm than good.

The investment business pays an abnormally high salary. Earnings for the typical advisor are on par with a well-paid physician or attorney. However, unlike physicians and attorneys who are required to have years of education before seeing patients and clients, investment consultants hired by a large brokerage house can start managing clients' money within a few months of deciding to get into the industry, and they can earn significant income in a couple of years if they are good salespeople.

The requirements for becoming a registered representative at a brokerage firm or an independent fee-only advisor are surprisingly low. You don't need a degree in finance or have any college. All you need to do is be able to read and write English, be felony free, and pass a simple exam. It takes about as much time and effort to become registered as a broker or advisor as it does for a 16-year-old to get a driver's license, with one exception—the 16-year-old must show competence when driving before getting to the license. Since the barrier of entry into the investment field is so low, it should not be surprising when the *Wall Street Journal* publishes a long list of brokers and advisors each week who have been disciplined by the regulatory authorities for gross negligence, misappropriation of client funds, and outright fraud.

I do not want to be too critical of the brokers and advisors in the investment industry because there are many outstanding people out there. The problem you have is separating the good from the bad. There is no easy shortcut to doing this. Even those with the best credentials have fallen. And it takes only one bad decision by an investment advisor to wipe out your entire life's savings. Bernie Madoff's former clients know that too well.

THE ASSETS IN ASSET ALLOCATION

At its core, asset allocation is about dividing your wealth into different places to reduce the risk of a large loss. One hundred years ago, that may have meant your burying some cash in Mason jars around the barn in addition to hiding money in your mattress and the cookie jar. If your house went up in flames, at least the buried Mason jar money would survive.

I am not advocating putting money in a mattress or in Mason jars as an asset allocation strategy. This book focuses on placing money in publicly available investments such as mutual funds and exchange-traded funds (ETFs), and how that fits in with other assets such as your home, other real estate, businesses, hard assets such as coins and art, restricted corporate stock and stock options, and any claim you have on employer pensions, Social Security, and an annuity income.

Figure 1-1 is an investment pyramid that divides investment into five parts. The pyramid is used to classify assets and illustrate differences in liquidity and discretion that you may or may not have with those assets.

FIGURE 1-1

The Investment Pyramid

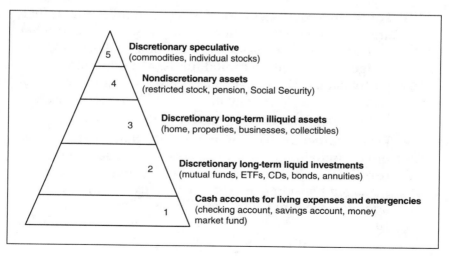

5 — Discretionary speculative (commodities, individual stocks)

4 — Nondiscretionary assets (restricted stock, pension, Social Security)

3 — Discretionary long-term illiquid assets (home, properties, businesses, collectibles)

2 — Discretionary long-term liquid investments (mutual funds, ETFs, CDs, bonds, annuities)

1 — Cash accounts for living expenses and emergencies (checking account, savings account, money market fund)

Here are brief descriptions of the five levels:

1. Level one is the base of the pyramid. It is characterized by highly liquid cash and cash types of investments that are used for living expenses and emergencies. This money is typically in checking accounts, savings accounts, and money market funds. This cash is not part of your long-term investment allocation, and you should not be overly concerned that your rate of return is low. The amount to keep in cash varies with your circumstances. I recommend 3 to 4 months in cash if you are single, 6 to 12 months in cash if you have a family, and 24 months when you retire.

2. Level two covers liquid, long-term investments. These are discretionary investments, meaning that you choose how to invest this money. The choices for investments typically include mutual funds, exchange-traded funds, certificates of deposit, and bonds. The accounts that hold these investments typically include self-directed retirement accounts, employee savings accounts, personal savings accounts, and fixed and variable annuities that are still accumulating (i.e., have not been annuitized). These assets can typically be converted into cash within one week.

3. Level three covers less liquid long-term investments that are also discretionary. They include your home and other real properties, businesses, art and other collectibles, hedge funds, venture capital funds, and other limited partnerships. These investments are less liquid than level two securities. They may be converted to cash over time, but it could take weeks, months, or even years.

4. Level four tends to cover investments that you have little or no discretion over. These assets can include employer-restricted corporate stock and stock options, employer-managed pension plans, Social Security benefits, and annuities that are paying out. These assets have strict rules governing what the money can be invested in, who can take the money, and when.

5. Level five is somewhat out of sequence. It covers speculative capital. These are the trading accounts that some people use to "play" the market. Investments at this level can be characterized as price-trend bets that have a short holding period. A trade may last for a few days or a couple of years. Investments can include, but are not limited to, common stock, niche mutual funds and ETFs, gold and precious metals, commodity futures, and commodity funds. These investments are hit-or-miss price guessing propositions. Place your bet, and hope for the best.

All five levels are important to your asset allocation. Some levels you have complete control over, and some you have no control over. You have complete control over the discretionary investments in your personal accounts and some retirement accounts. You have no control over Social Security benefits, employer-defined benefit pension plan investments, and company-restricted stock.

This begs the question: Will those nondiscretionary assets be there during your retirement? Or do you believe that the benefits from Social Security and employer pensions will be cut or perhaps eliminated in the future? Only a portion of these benefits will transfer to a spouse upon your death, and basically none of it goes to your family with the exception of a small amount of Social Security benefits for your children while they are young. If you purchase an annuity with your retirement money, income will go to you and perhaps your spouse, but not to your heirs unless you take a lower payout. All these issues play an important part in your ultimate investment plan, and you will have to consider them in your asset allocation.

STICK WITH CORE MUTUAL FUNDS AND ETFS

Asset allocation as framed in this book is mainly about prudently dividing your discretionary liquid investments among broadly diversified stock and bond mutual funds and exchange-traded funds. This strategy will reduce portfolio risk over time, and this leads to higher investment returns.

Some people may believe that they can jump-start their accounts by selecting superior securities or mutual funds within each asset class. This is attempted through self-management or by paying a professional advisor to pick investments. Neither works.

Trying to consistently pick investments that are going to beat their benchmarks is like trying to win a marathon wearing muddy boots. There is a lot of drag, and your odds of winning are very low. The high costs associated with attempting to beat the market will almost guarantee sluggish results.

In addition to high costs dragging down returns, a vast majority of investors, including professional money managers, do not have the needed information or skill to pick winning securities. By law, all investors must get the same breaking economic and company financial news at the same time. This means that no one has an advantage. Watching CNN, Bloomberg Television, and other financial news networks will yield no useful information that will enable you to earn excess returns over the market. There is a classic saying on Wall Street, "What everyone already knows is not worth knowing."

If you happen to become privy to relevant news that others do not have, you cannot use this information to earn extra returns in the market. That is insider trading. Just ask Martha Stewart. She went to jail for trading on inside information she received from the CEO of ImClone Systems, Inc. You could go to prison even if you receive no monetary benefit from passing someone else inside information. One famous case involved a Wall Street investment banker who past inside information to a prostitute in exchange for sexual favors. They both went to jail.

Even if you or your investment advisor do figure our something that others have not yet realized, you don't know if it's important information or if it's noise. Those people who can tell the difference are few and far between. Charlie Munger, the legendary investor and vice chairman of Berkshire Hathaway, explained to attendees at the 2004 annual shareholders meeting that Warren Buffett (CEO of Berkshire Hathaway) has been successful because he had a natural gift to sift through thousands of pieces of information and pick out the one or two items that had real market-moving relevance. He then said that the typical investor, including most professionals, spend too much time on irrelevant issues and miss the important things.

There are many people who claim that the markets are inefficient and that they can gain excess profits. Well, that's what they say. However, it is not true for a vast majority of investors. For the mere mortals among us, the markets might as well be efficient because we are not Warren Buffett, and neither are the advisors we visit. Consequently, we are not going to tap into the excess returns that may be available from time to time in an inefficient market.

HOT FUNDS AND COLD RETURNS

It often appears easy to forecast future market trends, because many market gurus claim that they have. But this is more marketing than fact. The gurus talk only about their winners. There is no independent study that confirms skill among the television personalities.

In truth, fads are difficult to forecast and more difficult to make money investing in. By the time you recognize something as a fad, the price of the stocks are already sky-high. Back in the early 1980s, only a handful of people predicted that home computers would become a household appliance. The name "Microsoft" could easily have been confused with that of a brand of bathroom tissue. Who would have guessed that Microsoft Corporation would be one of the most successful companies in the twentieth century?

When Microsoft was filing an initial public offering, *Popular Science* magazine was predicting that personal aero-cars would replace the family automobile by the twenty-first century. These carlike flying machines would take off and land in your driveway and eliminate all traffic jams. Today, there are no aero-cars in driveways, but almost every household has at least one home computer, phone, game, or other electronic device running Microsoft software.

Fad investing can be addictive—and costly. Many of the same people who suffered in the tech stock bubble and bust from 1996 to 2000 also suffered in the real estate boom and bust from 2003 to 2008. There are other fad traps that occurred recently. Alternative energy themes were the rage in 2008 when the price of oil hit $150 per barrel. Those stock prices collapsed by year-end when oil prices were back under $50. China stocks are all the rage. Unfortunately, a great economic growth story often becomes a stock investor's disaster. Gold is the hot investment as I write this second edition in early 2010. An ounce of gold reached $1,200 recently, and some people believe it will double to $2,400. We shall see.

An alternative to picking the right fad at the right time is to hire a smart and informed mutual fund manager to do it for you. Unfortunately, uncovering the next star mutual fund manager is just as difficult as predicting the next fad. Most people select mutual funds based on past performance. They use ratings put out by companies such as Morningstar, Inc., in Chicago. Cash flow studies show that a vast majority of new mutual fund contributions flow into funds that have recently received a 5-Star Morningstar rating for performance. The belief among investors is that these funds will outperform in the future. That is not likely.

Buying the Stars is not a reliable way to pick a winning fund. Five-Star ratings typically do not persist, especially when a rush of new money comes in and creates an insurmountable challenge to the fund manager to invest it. This typically means changing investment strategy, which is not what earned them the 5-Star rating.

Many best-performing managers this year will be next year's mediocre managers, or worse. "In the active fund business, nothing fails like success," according to John Bogle, the father of index fund investing. Performance chasing is such a huge issue that the Securities and Exchange Commission mandates that every mutual fund advertisement clearly state that *past performance is not an indication of future results.*

AVOIDING BAD ADVICE

You will undoubtedly come across financial advisors, newsletter writers, Web site bloggers, and other sources that infer that they have investment skill. This is not possible. Every advisor who claims to have skill cannot be above average. In aggregate, these advisors *are* the market, and after advisor fees, fund expenses, and trading costs, advisors' clients must perform below the market. It can be no other way.

During 1998 congressional testimony concerning the economic crisis caused by the collapse of Long Term Capital Management, Federal Reserve Chairman Alan Greenspan cautioned against buying into any new concept designed to outperform the markets. The following statement was given before the Committee on Banking and Financial Services of the U.S. House of Representatives:

This decade is strewn with examples of bright people who thought they had built a better mousetrap that could consistently extract an abnormal return from financial markets. Some succeed for a time. But while there may occasionally be misconfigurations among market prices that allow abnormal returns, they do not persist.

Indeed, efforts to take advantage of such misalignments force prices into better alignment and are soon emulated by competitors, further narrowing, or eliminating, any gaps. No matter how skillful the trading scheme, over the long haul, abnormal returns are sustained only through abnormal exposure to risk.[1]

Greenspan's last line is worth repeating, "No matter how skillful the trading scheme, over the long haul, abnormal returns are sustained only through abnormal exposure to risk." Superior investment performance requires increased exposure to risk. This means that advisors, bloggers, hedge fund managers, and bank trust officers can't make up their costs and beat the market without exposing a portfolio to considerable risk.

Even Warren Buffett took great risk early in his career by making large bets on a few investments that worked out. If he did not place big bets on a few companies in the 1960s and 1970s, he would not be wealthy today. Is this the way to do it? There are hundreds of thousands of would-be Warren Buffetts who were not so fortunate. Perhaps many of those people did have skill, but they got unlucky and their money ran out before their investments worked out. We will never know who they are.

If you admit that you do not have Warren Buffett's skill, then your investment strategy should be different. Don't try to win big with big bets on a few investments. Instead select an appropriate asset allocation and use low-cost index funds and ETFs to represent the markets you are investing in. Warren Buffett has publicly stated many times that index funds are the best way for most individuals to own commons stocks. Believe him.

A GREAT BUT BORING SOLUTION

Creating a workable asset allocation based on your needs and implementing your plan with low-cost index funds and ETFs provide an easy-to-understand, easy-to-maintain, reliable long-term investment strategy. This approach is also extremely boring and slow. There are no home run investments to brag about and no exciting trading stories to tell. Plus, you will have to listen to friends, family, and associates boast about how this or that investment made money for them and why your strategy is not relevant in today's market environment.

Investment performance is not about what happened last week, last month, or last year. It is about what happens over a lifetime. You will have the best performance and the last word with an asset allocation strategy. Chances are that people will be coming to you for investment advice over the long term. The funny part about those future conversations will be when other people admit that they had no idea what they were doing, and you just smile.

Money is not a game. Investing for the rest of your life and the lives of your loved ones is serious business. The asset allocation strategy outlined in this book may not be a glamorous solution, but it does works. Learn the basics, create a viable investment policy, implement your plan, diligently follow the plan, and grind out investment gains as they come. With this no-nonsense, businesslike portfolio approach, you have the highest probability of reaching your financial long-term goals. Sometimes boring is good.

TIME CHANGES INVESTMENT PRIORITIES

Your investment policy and portfolio asset allocation will be unique. It will be based on your situation, your needs today and in the future, and your ability to stay the course during adverse market conditions. As your needs change, your allocation will also need adjustment. Monitoring and adjusting is an important part of the process.

The Limitations of Questionnaires

One shortcut to an asset allocation decision is a "risk questionnaire" that brokers and advisors like to use. Wall Street has tried very hard to commoditize the asset allocation process so that it can push through a lot of people in little time. Risk questionnaires are the by-product of this push. How you answer the questions will land your portfolio in a preselected box of investments.

Risk questionnaires may yield some useful information if the questions are worded well, but overall they are not the answer to the asset allocation question. The questions typically address only one specific area: the maximum risk a person might be able to handle. Even this question cannot possibly be determined by a computer model alone. The questionnaire approach probably works better on young investors who have a lot more in common with one other than people in their fifties and sixties. These more established investors need a lot more attention in order to create a plan that reflects their unique situation.

Finding a person's maximum tolerance for risk takes a lot more than a questionnaire. It requires soul-searching. We tend to be brave in a bull market, and this means that it is not the ideal time to search for our risk tolerance. Soul-searching should be done in a bear market when we are not sure what is going to happen next.

Our Changing Needs

As your financial needs change, your attitude toward investing changes, and accordingly, the asset allocation of your portfolio will need to be adjusted to accommodate changes in your life. The following paragraphs touch on some of those issues and adjustments that occur during life. In this second edition you will find several passages that cover these topics in more detail.

Let's start with young investors and their investment strategy. Young investors should have at the core a savings plan. Learning to save is more important than learning to invest at this stage in life. A young person will likely try different investment strategies and lose money on most of them. But this is the time to experiment. Young investors have the luxury of time on their side. Mistakes are not large, because these investors have little money in the game and plenty of time to make up losses. A $5,000 loss on a $10,000 investment at age 25 is much easier to overcome than a $500,000 loss on a $1,000,000 investment at age 65.

As time passes, youthful dreams are gradually replaced by midlife realities. Careers are progressing, families are forming and growing, and daily life becomes predictable and routine. By midlife, people tend to have a good idea of their career potential and what their long-term earnings stream will be like. For the first time, people can envision how they might live in retirement and how they might refine their savings and investment plan to reach that goal.

Investors in their late fifties and early sixties are typically in their peak earning years and are starting to actively prepare for some form of retirement. Children are finished with school or close to it, and they hopefully have found jobs and started careers. During this time, people refocus their energy on those aspects of their personal lives that have been neglected while they were raising a family and plan to do what makes them happy; for many folks this means working less or not at all. By this time people should have accumulated enough retirement assets to be able to forecast a realistic retirement date, and their asset allocation should be reviewed and perhaps revised so that they can glide smoothly into the next stage of life.

Life is not forever. Portfolios tend to change as people enter their senior years. Investment decisions at this point may look beyond the grave. When people realize that they have enough money for the remainder of their life, they may consider investing a portion of the excess according to the needs and ages of their heirs. Ironically, this could mean that a portfolio becomes more aggressive than the one held currently.

Asset allocation is at the center of portfolio management in every phase of life. Younger investors will develop asset allocations from a perspective that's different from that of older investors because they are different, but that does not mean that young investors will have a more aggressive allocation than older people. It depends on each person's unique situation. Asset allocation is personal. There is an appropriate allocation for your needs at every stage in life. Your mission is to find it.

HOW ASSET ALLOCATION WORKS

Asset classes are broad categories of investments, such as stocks, bonds, real estate, commodities, and money market funds. Each asset class can be further divided into categories. For example, stocks can be categorized into U.S. stocks and foreign stocks. Bonds can be categorized into taxable bonds and tax-free bonds. Real estate investments can be divided into owner-occupied residential real estate, rental residential real estate, and commercial properties.

The subcategories can be further divided into investment styles and sectors. Examples of styles include growth and value stocks, large and small stocks, and investment-grade bonds and non-investment-grade bonds. Sectors can be of different types. Stocks can be divided by industry sectors, such as industrial stocks, technology stocks, bank stocks, and so on; or they can be geographically divided, such as Pacific Rim and European stocks. Bonds can be divided by issuer, such as mortgages, corporate bonds, and Treasury bonds. A well-diversified portfolio may hold several asset classes, categories, styles, and sectors.

Successful investors study all asset classes and their various components in order to understand the differences among them. They estimate the long-term expectations of risk and return, and they study how the returns on one asset class may move in relation to other classes. Then they weigh the advantages and disadvantages of including each investment in their portfolio.

The tax efficiency may also be a consideration if the investment is going in a taxable account. Investors should be aware of which asset class, styles, and sectors are better placed in a tax-advantaged account such as a retirement account and which ones are suitable for taxable accounts.

Asset allocation is the cornerstone of a prudent investment plan and is the single most important decision that an investor will make in regard to a portfolio. Once the fundamentals of asset allocation are understood and all the various styles and sectors of each asset class have been examined, it is then time to select the best investments to represent those asset classes. Once investment selection is completed, the investment policy is ready to be put into action.

THE ACADEMICS WEIGH IN

There are critics who question the validity of a long-term asset allocation strategy. They say that investors should be more in tune with what is happening in the markets today and make asset allocation adjustments as necessary. The academics do not agree.

In the January/February 2000 issue of the *Financial Analysts Journal*, Roger Ibbotson, a Yale finance professor and chairman of Ibbotson Associates, and Paul Kaplan, vice president and chief economist at Ibbotson Associates, published a landmark study titled, "Does Asset Allocation Policy Explain 40, 90 or 100 Percent of Performance?"[2] The study was conducted to answer the hotly debated question of whether it was the asset allocation of a portfolio or a manager's skill in picking stocks and bonds that drove portfolio performance. The study overwhelmingly concluded that more than 90 percent of a portfolio's long-term variation in return was explained by its asset allocation. Only a small portion of the variation in return was explained by the manager's ability to time the markets or individual security selections.

The Ibbotson/Kaplan report builds on two studies by Gary Brinson, L. Randolph Hood, and Gilbert Beebower, who looked at the same question 15 years earlier. In 1986, the three analyzed the returns of 91 large U.S. pension plans between 1974 and 1983.[3] At the time, they concluded that asset allocation explained a significant portion of portfolio performance. Brinson, Beebower, and Brian Singer published a follow-up study in 1991 and essentially confirmed the results of their first paper: more than 90 percent of a portfolio's long-term return characteristics and risk level are determined by the asset allocation.[4] Both those studies were also published in the *Financial Analysts Journal*.

There is overwhelming evidence that a large percentage of a portfolio's performance is determined by the long-term percentage of money that an investor places in stocks, bonds, real estate, money market funds, and other asset classes. *All About Asset Allocation* is a written to help you decide the important 90 percent: what portion of your portfolio should be allocated to various asset classes, styles, and sectors.

Academics have done a good job of quantifying the benefits of asset allocation. There are literally hundreds of papers on the subject, each one complete with an abundance of formulas, equations, acronyms, and industry jargon. I use some of these terms and formulas in an understandable way throughout the book. The concepts are explained as they are introduced. A glossary is provided at the end of the book if you come upon an term you are unsure of.

INVESTMENT SELECTION

Creating an appropriate portfolio is a two-step process. First, people should select an asset allocation mix that is best for their needs. Second, they should select individual investments that best represent those asset classes.

The selection of investments to represent asset classes takes a lot of time because there are thousands of investments to choose from. I try to make the investment selection easy in this book. For further reference, I've also written other books, including *All About Index Funds*, 2nd edition, and *The ETF Book*, 2nd edition.

In general, you are looking for investments that have broad asset class representation and low fees. Index mutual funds and ETFs are a perfect fit for this purpose. They give you broad diversification within an asset class at a reasonable cost. However, you need to be very selective in the funds you buy. There are vast differences in cost and strategy even among index funds and ETFs. One fund may be managed identically to another except that the fees are significantly higher. Another fund may say it tracks a stock market index, but that index is not a traditional market benchmark, and it does not move with the markets.

Another consideration when selecting a fund is how the fund is managed. You can select a passive fund in which the manager attempts to match the performance of a benchmark index that follows a market, or an actively managed fund in which the manager is trying to beat a particular market. I am not an advocate of using actively managed funds. On average, actively managed funds are much more expensive than passive funds, and rarely do active managers have enough skill to overcome the fees and commissions charged.

It is also important to note that the data from market indexes are the backbone for study and design of asset allocation strategies. This makes index funds and ETFs that follow these benchmarks an excellent choice for a portfolio. Their low cost, broad diversification, low tracking error with the markets, and high tax efficiency make these index funds and ETFs ideally suited to an asset allocation strategy. There are a large and growing number of index funds and ETFs on the market today that track many different asset classes, styles, and sectors. Several of these funds are highlighted at the end of each chapter in Part Two.

DON'T OVERANALYZE

The information presented in this book will get you thinking deeply about how to optimize an asset allocation for your needs. That is exactly the intent of this book. You should spend some time thinking about how the strategy works before you design a portfolio and implement a plan. However, at some point you must finish your work and implement your decisions.

There can be a tendency to overanalyze market data in an attempt to find the ideal asset allocation. That is not a good idea. The ideal asset allocation can be known only in retrospect. You cannot know what it is today. Consequently, the quest to find the perfect plan becomes a never-ending undertaking. At some point you will hit analysis paralysis and nothing gets done. The Prussian General Karl von Clausewitz once said, "The greatest enemy of a good plan is the dream of a perfect plan."

You can never know everything about every asset class, style, and sector. Even if you were to become very knowledgeable about asset classes and how they work together, you still could not know for certain how the portfolio will act in the future. You can only develop a portfolio that has a high probability of success, implement the portfolio as is, and maintain it. No portfolio guarantees success, but a plan never implemented is sure to fail.

Take the time to establish a prudent investment plan for your needs, implement that plan, and begin to maintain it. Putting a good plan into action today is much better than searching for a perfect plan that cannot be known in advance.

CHAPTER SUMMARY

Successful investing requires the design, implementation, and maintenance of a long-term investment strategy that is based on your unique needs. Asset allocation is a central part of that plan. It determines most of your portfolio's risk and return over time. The strategy shifts the focus of investing from trying to pick winning investments to being diversified in many unlike investments at all times.

No one knows what will happen in the financial markets next week, next month, or next year. Yet we need to invest for the future. Asset allocation solves a problem that all investors face, namely, how to manage investments without knowing the future. Asset allocation eliminates the need to predict the near-term future direction of the financial markets and eliminates the risk of being in the wrong market at the wrong time. It also eliminates the risk of others giving you bad advice.

We have only a finite amount of time in life to build a portfolio that will sustain us during retirement, and it does not take many mistakes before this goal is put in jeopardy. You do not want to be the next person we read about in the newspapers who has lost his retirement savings by taking inappropriate risk or following the advice of the wrong advisor. Develop a good asset allocation plan, implement the plan, maintain the plan, and make adjustments as your needs change. Asset allocation is not an exciting investment strategy, but when it comes to making money, boring can be very profitable.

NOTES

[1] "Private-Sector Refinancing of the Large Hedge Fund, Long-Term Capital Management," testimony of Chairman Alan Greenspan before the Committee on Banking and Financial Services, U.S. House of Representatives, October 1, 1998.

[2] Roger G. Ibbotson and Paul D. Kaplan, "Does Asset Allocation Policy Explain 40, 90 or 100 Percent of Performance?" *Financial Analysts Journal*, January/February 2000, pp. 26–33.

[3] Gary P. Brinson, L. Randolph Hood, and Gilbert L. Beebower, "Determinants of Portfolio Performance," *Financial Analysts Journal*, July/August 1986.

[4] Gary P. Brinson, Brian D. Singer, and Gilbert L. Beebower, "Determinants of Portfolio Performance II: An Update," *Financial Analysts Journal*, May/June 1991.

CHAPTER 2

Understanding Investment Risk

KEY CONCEPTS

- Investment returns are directly related to investment risk.
- There are no risk-free investments after taxes and inflation.
- Practitioners view risk as investment volatility.
- Individuals view risk as losing money.

One of the oldest axioms on Wall Street is that *there is no free lunch.* You do not get something for nothing. Investors who take no investment risk should expect no return after adjusting for inflation and taxes. Unfortunately, taking investment risk also means that you can and will lose money at times. There is simply no way around this. There is no free lunch. The risk and return relationship of business is one of the few laws of economics that has stood the test of time throughout history. If people tell you otherwise, they are either selling snake oil or they are naive.

There is a direct relationship between the amount of risk taken and the *expected* return on an investment. People expect to earn a profit from stock and bond investments because they are taking a risk. Stocks pay a dividend from earnings, bonds pay interest, and real estate pays rents; however, those income streams are not certain. The greater the uncertainty that this income will materialize, the higher the expected return on the investment must be.

Investments with less risk of income disruptions have lower expected returns.

The changing risk perception on an investment is adjusted by market price. All else being equal, when the risk goes up, prices go down, and when risk goes down, prices go up. If the future cash flows of an investment such as a bond are known, investors who buy at lower prices expect to make higher returns because the risk of not receiving that cash flow is higher at that time, and investors who buy at higher prices expect to make lower returns because the perceived risk is lower at that time. With bonds, the risks are inflation, interest-rate increases, taxes, and a potential default by the issuer.

Portfolio risk cannot be eliminated although it can be partially controlled with an asset allocation strategy. Combining different investment types, each with its own unique risk and return characteristics, into one portfolio creates a unique risk and return trade-off in the portfolio. This is similar to making bread from flour, yeast, and water. The combined product has different characteristic from its ingredients.

A well-designed portfolio lowers overall risk through diversification, and this eventually results in a return for the portfolio that's higher than the weighted average return of the individual investments in the portfolio. This risk reduction phenomenon does not happen every year, but it does happen over several years if you are a disciplined investor. Once you grasp the mechanics behind asset allocation and accumulate information on different types of investments, you will be ready to design a portfolio that has an expected return and an acceptable level of risk for your needs.

THE MYTHICAL RISK-FREE INVESTMENT

The lowest-risk investment in the U.S. financial markets is a U.S. Treasury bill (T-bill), a government-guaranteed investment that matures in one year or less. T-bills are sold at a discount from face value and don't pay interest before maturity. The interest is the difference between the purchase price of the bill and its face value paid at maturity.

The U.S. Treasury issues T-bills weekly, and the interest rate is set by an auction system. The current T-bill rate is a good proxy for the interest an investor will earn in a money market fund because T-bills are frequently purchased in money market funds.

T-bills are often called a "risk-free" investment in the financial world because of their short maturity and government guaranteed return. However, *risk-free* may be an inappropriate choice of words. T-bills do have a reliable positive return; however, that return is subject to the corrosive effects of taxes and inflation.

Figure 2-1 highlights the year-over-year T-bill return minus 25 percent income tax and the inflation rate. There have been many years when the rate of return on T-bills has not kept pace with the inflation rate after taxes. Investors in T-bills and money market funds are losing purchasing power in the years when the bar in Figure 2-1 is below 0 percent. During these years, money invested in T-bills buys fewer goods and services than it did one year earlier.

Taxes are a big drag on T-bill returns. The "risk-free" T-bill return can easily be negative after adjusting for inflation and the amount the government reclaims in federal income taxes. For example, the nominal T-bill return in 2007 was 4.7 percent. The after-tax return was 3.5 percent, assuming that an investor pays 25 percent income tax. However, inflation was 4.1 percent that year, meaning that investors who owned T-bills lost 0.6 percent

FIGURE 2-1

Annual Treasury Bill Returns after Taxes and Inflation

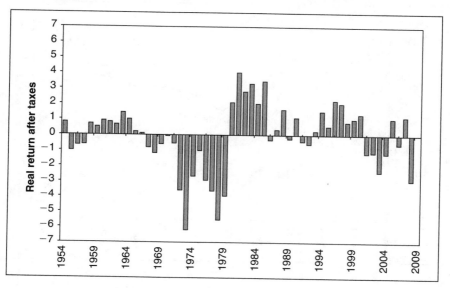

in purchasing power. The loss would have been greater for investors in higher-income tax brackets.

Figure 2-2 illustrates the compounded after-tax and after-inflation return of $100 that was continually reinvested in 30-day Treasury bills since 1955. The chart assumes that 25 percent federal income tax was paid each year on the return. The lowest point on Figure 2-2 was in 1980. The value of the $100 starting amount had dropped to $75.26. It took it 21 years to recover, and in 2001 it hit $100.39. Then the value began to drop again, falling to $93.40 by the end of 2009. If you think about this, for more than 30 years we have been paying our government to borrow money from us.

There are a couple of Treasury investments that are protected from the corrosive effect of inflation but not taxes. Treasury Inflation-Protected Securities (TIPS) and I-bonds are Treasury securities that protect principal and interest from rising inflation. The maturity value of these bonds increases in direct proportion to an

FIGURE 2-2

Cumulative 30-day T-bill Return after Taxes and Inflation, Assuming a 25 Percent Tax Rate, from December 31, 1954

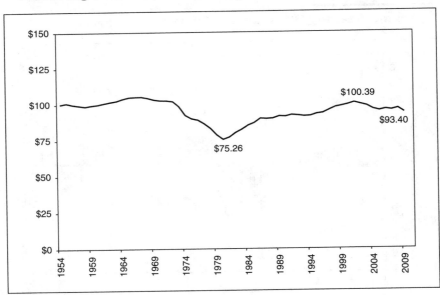

increase in the inflation rate. The interest paid during the period also increases with the inflation rate.

Some people argue that TIPS are a better representation of a risk-free rate than T-bills because inflation is factored out. But TIPS are not without their own risks. First, TIPS are publicly traded securities, and, as such, they fluctuate in value as interest rates rise and fall. The Barclays Capital U.S. Treasury Inflation Protected Securities Index fell by 2.4 percent in 2008 while the Consumer Price Index (CPI), a proxy for inflation, was up by 0.1 percent. Second, neither TIPS nor I-bonds escape taxation. Both the interest payments and the inflation adjustment gain are eventually taxed as ordinary interest income. More information on inflation-protected securities can be found in Chapter 8.

Risk-free investing is a myth. It does not exist. If there were a risk-free investment, it would have a federal government guarantee, stable pricing, and inflation protection, and the interest income would be free from all city, state, and federal income tax. That being said, if the government guarantees a bond, it must be AAA rated and stay AAA rated, which is a risk in itself. As of this writing, there is no such investment.

DEFINING INVESTMENT RISK

There are many definitions of investment risk, depending on who you are and what you are measuring. Risk can be price volatility, or the dollar amount loss on an investment, or a loss relative to inflation and taxes, or not meeting one's long-term financial objectives.

Academics often define risk as the volatility of price or return over a specified period. Volatility can be measured in different ways and over different periods. You can use price highs or lows or closing prices. You can measure volatility daily, weekly, monthly, or annually. High volatility means erratic investment returns, whereas low volatility means more consistent investment returns. Annual return volatility measurement tends to be the one most commonly used to compare asset class risk.

My view of price volatility is somewhat different from that of the academics. Price and return volatility do not define risk. Rather, they are a derivative of some other risk factor. With stocks, price volatility is based on wavering expectations of earnings and dividend growth. With bonds, it is the wavering expectations of future inflation and interest rates. With commodities, price volatility is caused by changes in the supply and demand curve.

Price volatility is not itself a part of an investment's income stream, and investors should not expect to make excess returns simply because an investment has price volatility. For example, the volatility of commodities is about the same volatility as stocks. However, commodities pay no interest, have no earnings, and pay no dividends. Consequently, the expected return of commodities is lower than those of stocks even though the price volatility is similar.

Pension fund trustees tend to view risk as the uncertainty that their employee pension obligations will be met in the future. Defined-benefit pension plans are managed so that the future payments to retirees are matched by the future expected value of the pension fund. An actuarial assumption of pension obligations is compared to a forecast plan value based on an estimated return on assets and future contributions. If the forecast plan value is equal to the obligation, the plan is fully funded and no excess contributions are needed from the employer. However, if the forecast value is less than the plan's obligations, there is an underfunded liability, and that represents a financial risk. An underfunded pension obligation means that the employer will have to commit more resources to the plan to maintain its solvency, and this could cause financial difficulty for the employer.

Mutual fund managers see risk as the underperformance of their fund compared to other fund managers with the same investment objective. If a large growth fund manager does not perform well in relation to other large growth fund managers, then the fund will lose assets as investors liquidate shares, not to mention that the manager will likely lose his or her job.

Unlike academics, pension fund trustees, and money managers, individual investors define risk in a more direct way. They define it as losing money. Nothing gets people's attention faster than when the value of their account begins to fall. It does not matter if a person made money for several years prior; it is the here and now that matters.

Consider the year 1987. It was the year the stock market crashed. What was the return of the market that year? The S&P 500 was up by about 36 percent through September 1987, and then it fell apart. On Friday, October 16, stocks unexpectedly fell by 9 percent.

The following Monday, known as Black Monday, prices came crashing down another 23 percent. Investors were shell-shocked. However, despite the October collapse, the market still stood in positive territory at the end of the month, and by year-end the S&P 500 was up a respectable 5.1 percent. No investor who had money in a diversified stock portfolio for the entire year in 1987 lost money, but that is not what people remember. We only remember how bad it felt to lose money on Black Monday.

Everyone wants to earn a fair return on his or her investments after inflation and taxes. This will require risk and probably losing money on occasion. All the broadly diversified portfolios introduced in this book have inherent risk and will go down in value periodically. It would be nice to know when these losses will occur so that we can sell beforehand, but that is simply not possible. No one can predict with any consistency when the markets will go up or down. If a person tells you she has found the secret to the markets, she is either naive or she is trying to steal your money. Either way, smile and walk.

There is no free lunch on Wall Street, and the asset allocation strategies in this book do not provide a free lunch either. Proper asset allocation can reduce the probability of a large loss and perhaps the frequency of losing periods, but it is not a panacea for the elimination of portfolio risk. You can and will have periods when your portfolio is down in value. The key to success with any asset allocation strategy is to have the right portfolio for your needs, keep costs low, and control risk so that you don't panic in the face of occasional losses.

THE BIG RISK IN EVERY INVESTOR'S LIFE

Pension fund managers have the most practical definition of risk, namely, not having enough money to pay future retirement liabilities. This is also a good definition for individual investors to adopt. Running out of money in retirement is everyone's nightmare. The thought conjures up images of living out your old age in miserable substandard housing and relying on government money for subsistence, or worse, relying on family charity.

Every pool of capital is accumulated for a reason. The assets will be used to pay for some future liability, such as income needs during retirement, a down payment on a home, college for a child, charitable causes, or a legacy for heirs.

Funding a future liability is the ultimate goal of an investment portfolio. Retirement is a good example of long-term cash-flow needs. If we save enough while working and earn a high enough return on our assets during our life, then our annual retirement income should match or exceed our annual cash retirement outflows.

There is a minimum dollar amount that each person needs to meet all his future needs. This amount can be thought of as our personal financial liability. The risk we all have is not accumulating enough assets to cover this liability. It makes sense to know what that amount is so that we can work toward it, or at least make a calculated guess.

The amount of money you will need is not the amount that makes you "feel" secure; it is the amount you actually do need to pay your bills and enjoy your life. All too often, people will overestimate the amount of money they believe will make them financially secure, and, consequently, they may take on too much investment risk. This could lead to an adverse outcome should the amount of risk be above a person's tolerance to take risk, because it could result in the wrong decisions during difficult market conditions.

Figuring out how much you need in order to be financially secure is not difficult. The amount is based on a combination of factors, including your age, health, spending habits, lifestyle decisions, taxes, pension income, Social Security benefits, investment income, and other items. It sounds like a lot of work, but you need to do the detailed analysis only once. Chapter 12 explains the calculations in more detail.

VOLATILITY AS RISK

Losing money is one definition of risk. Not matching future needs is another. Both these financial risks can be controlled once you have a clear understanding of where they originate. For that, a discussion of volatility is appropriate.

As mentioned earlier in this chapter, the up-and-down movement in the value of your investment is the definition of risk used by most academics and researchers. Volatility can be measured using any interval of time—minutes, days, weeks, months, or years. For decades, monthly volatility was most noticeable to individual investors. This is because we received monthly statements from our brokerage firms and see firsthand the actual gains and losses in the account.

For better or worse, people today are checking their accounts balances more. We all have instant access through the Internet, and we can even get updates over our personal digital assistants (PDAs) and cell phones. I do not believe this is a good thing because it makes people too short-sighted. But people are going to do it anyway. Heck, I do it. Unfortunately, the more often people look at their account value in a bear market, the more apt they are to do something that is not in their long-term best interest.

Volatility is measured in units of standard deviation; the larger the variation in value, the higher the standard deviation. Standard deviation (expressed as the Greek symbol σ) measures the average amount of data discrepancy around the data average. For example, assume that an investment has an average annual return of 5 percent and an annual standard deviation of 10 percent. This means that the average annual deviation from the 5 percent is 10 percent. Sometimes it is more and sometimes less, but on average it is 10 percent. In a "normal distribution" of annual returns over time, there is a 68 percent chance that an annual return will fall between −5 percent and +15 percent. Figure 2-3 illustrates this concept.

FIGURE 2-3

Normal Distribution

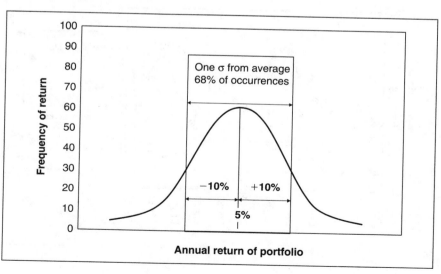

The standard deviation of asset-class returns is not static. There are times when the returns are more volatile than others. Figure 2-4 shows the rolling five-year standard deviation of returns for various asset classes. Small stocks have had the highest amount of variation over the years, followed by large stocks, corporate bonds, and Treasury bills.

A jump in volatility tends to be associated with falling returns for that asset class, and lower volatility is associated with higher returns. The fall in stock volatility during the 1980s and 1990s occurred during one of the longest bull markets in history. Stock volatility increased rapidly during the bear stock market of 2008 and early 2009, and the increase in corporate bond volatility was also noteworthy as bond prices fell.

The range of volatility in an asset class varies considerably, although it does tend to stay in a range for each asset class. For example, in Figure 2-4, the average standard deviation of small stocks averages 20 percent, plus or minus 8 percent over any decade. The average standard deviation of large stocks is about

FIGURE 2-4

Rolling 60-Month Volatility of Various Asset Classes

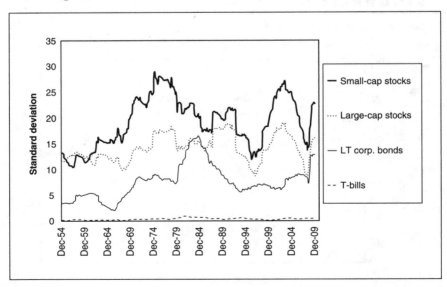

15 percent, plus or minus 5 percent over any decade. The average standard deviation of long-term corporate bonds is about 8 percent, plus or minus 3 percent, and T-bills had a standard deviation of about 0.2 percent on average, plus or minus about 0.2 percent.

What is noteworthy about Figure 2-4 is the consistency in the order of asset-class volatility. With stocks and bonds, the order of volatility in asset classes is very consistent. In almost every period, T-bills had the lowest volatility in every period, followed by corporate bonds, then large stocks, and finally small stocks.

As mentioned earlier, price volatility alone is not a reason to expect high returns. Just because something goes up and down in price doesn't make it a good long-term investment. Price changes can occur for many reasons, such as changes in the expectation of earnings and dividend growth for a company, the changing expectation of future inflation for a bond, and the expected supply and demand for commodities.

In the financial world, risk is the primary driver of return. The average standard deviation gives investors a rough idea of the relationship between the historic risk and expected return of one asset class relative to the historic risk and return of another. It should be no surprise that in comparing stocks, bonds, and T-bills, that stocks have had higher long-term return because of the higher risk. Table 2-1 illustrates this phenomenon.

Table 2-1 has three return columns. The simple average return column on the left is computed by summing the returns of all years and dividing by 60. The compounded return to the right is derived

TABLE 2-1

Asset-Class Data from 1950 to 2009

Asset Class	Simple Average Return	Standard Deviation (σ)	Compound Return	Volatility Return Loss
Treasury bills	4.8%	0.8%	4.7%	−0.1%
Long corporate bonds	6.6%	8.6%	6.2%	−0.4%
Large U.S. stocks (decile 1–2)	12.0%	18.1%	9.3%	−2.7%
Small U.S. stocks (decile 6–10)	15.3%	27.5%	11.2%	−4.1%

Source: CRSP Database, Federal Reserve

by linking the return in one year to that in the next in a continuous chain. The compounded return is also known as the annualized return. The last column on the right is the difference between the simple average return and the compounded return. This is the impact of price volatility on compounded returns.

The simple average return on small stocks is more than 4 percent higher than its compounded return. The reason is small stocks' higher price volatility. Greater variation in returns reduces long-term compounded returns exponentially. The simple average return on T-bills is about that same as the compounded return because T-bills had a very small standard deviation of returns.

Volatility creates lower returns and thus is itself a risk. If you can reduce the volatility in a portfolio, then the compounded return moves higher, closer to the simple average return of the weighted investments in the portfolio. This is how lower portfolio price volatility increases portfolio return over time. We'll go through some math to get to a better understanding of this important concept.

Refer to Table 2-2 for an illustration on how the variability of annual returns reduces the account value over time. Four portfolios are presented. Each portfolio starts with $10,000.

An analysis of the four portfolios in Table 2-2 confirms that all the accounts had a simple average annual return of 5.0 percent, yet each one had a different compounded return also known as the annualized return. Portfolio A's return had a 1.1 percent higher compounded return than Portfolio D because it had less annual volatility. The reason for the difference is *how* Portfolio A earned a 5.0 percent simple average relative to Portfolio D. Portfolio A had very consistent annual returns (+5 percent, +5 percent). Portfolio D had high variability in annual returns (+20 percent, −10 percent). Consequently, while the simple averages of Portfolio A and Portfolio D were the same (+5 percent), Portfolio A had the highest ending value, and Portfolio D compounded to the lowest.

The standard measure of volatility is the standard deviation. Think of standard deviation as the "average miss" from the portfolio's simple average return. A portfolio can have a simple average return of 5 percent even though it never actually earns 5 percent in any given year. The average annual miss from 5 percent is the portfolio's annual standard deviation.

TABLE 2-2

Four Portfolios with Different Standard Deviations

	Calendar Year Return	Portfolio Value
Portfolio A		
Year 1	+5%	$10,500
Year 2	+5%	$11,025
	Simple average = 5.0%	Compounded = 5.0%
Portfolio B		
Year 1	+10%	$11,000
Year 2	0%	$11,000
	Simple average = 5.0%	Compounded = 4.9%
Portfolio C		
Year 1	+15%	$11,500
Year 2	−5%	$10,925
	Simple average = 5.0%	Compounded = 4.5%
Portfolio D		
Year 1	+20%	$12,000
Year 2	−10%	$10,800
	Simple average = 5.0%	Compounded = 3.9%

Table 2-3 illustrates how to compute an average miss in a series of numbers. Please note that any observant math wizard will quickly realize that the data in Table 2-3 do not represent the exact standard deviations, but for illustrative purposes, they are close enough.

Back to Table 2-2. It is interesting to note that as the standard deviations of the portfolios increased evenly in 5 percent increments from 0 percent to 15 percent, the compounded return difference between the portfolios increased exponentially from one portfolio to the next. To illustrate, there was a 5 percent difference in standard deviation between Portfolios A and B and a 0.1 percent difference in compounded return, a 5 percent difference in standard deviation between Portfolios B and C and a 0.4 percent difference in compounded return, and a 5 percent difference in standard deviation between Portfolios C and D and a 0.6 percent difference in compounded return.

TABLE 2-3

Calculating Standard Deviation

Portfolio	Year 1 Return	Missed the Simple Average of 5%	Year 2 Return	Missed the Simple Average of 5%	Average Miss (~ σ)
A	+5%	0%	+5%	0%	0%
B	+10%	5%	0%	5%	5%
C	+15%	10%	−5%	10%	10%
D	+20%	15%	−10%	15%	15%

The lesson we learn from Tables 2-2 and 2-3 is that higher volatility of returns leads to lower compounded returns and vice versa. Accordingly, any strategy that lowers the return volatility of the portfolio without lowering the simple average return *will increase the compounded return*.

Another benefit from reducing long-term portfolio risk through a prudent asset allocation is that it helps an investor stay committed to a long-term investment strategy. People don't like to lose money. The chance of making an emotional sell decision goes up as the value of a portfolio goes down. Reducing the risk of a large loss in a portfolio increases the probability that investors will stay committed to their investment policy during difficult markets. Maintaining discipline in a bear or bull market is the key to a successful asset allocation strategy.

CHAPTER SUMMARY

There are no risk-free investments, and there are no risk-free asset allocation strategies. Every portfolio that attempts to earn an excess rate of return over taxes and inflation carries some risk of loss. Temporary loss of money in an account is not enjoyable; however, it can be controlled to a point. Developing and maintaining a long-term investment plan reduces overall portfolio risk, and that lowers the tendency for investors to overreact in a bear market. This fact alone increases the probability of investors reaching their financial goals.

There is a long-standing relationship between risk and return in any financial market. The markets with higher than expected return have the greatest uncertainty that this return will occur in the short term. This knowledge can be used to build a portfolio using different asset classes with different risk and return characteristics. The goal is to design a portfolio that has expected return and acceptable risk level so that you have a high probability of meeting your unique financial needs and future obligations.

Asset Allocation Explained

KEY CONCEPTS

- Diversification reduces the chance of a large loss.
- Rebalancing assets in a portfolio helps contain risk.
- Correlations between asset classes are not static.
- Low correlation among asset classes is preferred but difficult to indentify.

Diversification is the time-honored practice of spreading financial risk across different investments to reduce the probability of a large loss. A portfolio of 1,000 stocks is more diversified than a portfolio of 100 stocks. Asset allocation is a type of diversification that spreads the risk widely over different markets. It involves estimating the expected risk and return on various segments of the financial markets, observing how those markets interrelate over different time periods, and then logically and methodically constructing a portfolio of investments that represents those chosen asset classes in ways that have the highest probability of achieving a financial goal.

ASSET ALLOCATION: A SHORT HISTORY

In 1952, a 25-year-old graduate student from the University of Chicago named Harry Markowitz wrote a revolutionary research paper titled "Portfolio Selection." That 14-page paper would eventually change the way colleges and universities teach portfolio management. It would also change the methods used by investment professionals to manage portfolios.

Markowitz's paper explored the idea that financial risk is not only necessary but desirable in portfolio management in order to achieve a higher rate of return. He also noted that portfolio risk can be controlled through meaningful investment diversification. Markowitz pointed out that the risk of each individual investment is not as important as how all the investments work together to reduce overall portfolio risk. He used formulas borrowed from mathematicians to quantify the risk-and-return relationship achieved through diversification.

Figure 3-1 illustrates the diversification concept that the Markowitz and other researchers talk about. Each stock in Figure 3-1 has two types of risk: market-based risk known as systematic or beta, and unique risk inherent in each stock that is also called unsystematic risk. The greater the number of stocks in a portfolio that are spread across all industry sectors, the lower the unique risk each stock has on the portfolio return. This leaves only beta or market risk. Markowitz argued that a total market portfolio is the lowest-risk portfolio because it is the most diversified.

Markowitz's research paper was submitted to and published in the prestigious *Journal of Finance*. Initially, his paper titled "Portfolio Selection" was little noticed. It was considered too basic by many academic authorities. The information was so intuitive that none of Markowitz's professors at the University of Chicago dreamed that this small report would change the way portfolios were viewed and managed at every level in finance.

Markowitz expanded his published research during 1959 in a book titled *Portfolio Selection: Efficient Diversification of Investments*. The work earned Markowitz wide recognition in the financial economics field and eventually earned him The Bank of Sweden Prize in Economic Sciences in Memory of Alfred Nobel. Most people refer to this award as a Nobel Prize even though that is not technically correct. There is no Nobel Prize in economics. There is only The Bank of Sweden Prize in Economic Sciences. Nonetheless, the idea revolutionized portfolio management.

FIGURE 3-1

Diversification Reduces Stock-Specific Risk

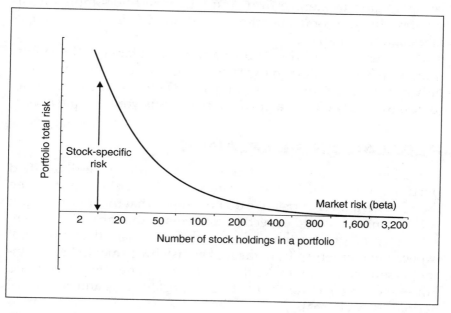

Markowitz's ideas on stock diversification eventually became known as efficient market theory (EMT). This is the general concept that markets are efficiently pricing securities based on known information, and therefore a market portfolio is the most efficient portfolio. EMT spawned modern portfolio theory (MPT), which in general is the study of the efficient allocation of asset classes within a portfolio.

It took several years for EMT and MPT to catch on in academia and longer in the commercial world. The math relied on advanced computing power to generate these efficient portfolios. Thus most people were not able to use the research effectively until the late 1970s. That was when computing power became more affordable, and in the 1980s MPT methods began to expand rapidly at bank trust departments and large private money management firms.

Today, Markowitz is known as the Father of MPT. His methodology is so prevalent that every individual investor has access to free basic asset allocation software on the Internet. It can be found on the Web pages of nearly every major mutual fund company and brokerage firm. You will even find simple investment portfolio recommendations based on MPT in popular magazines and newspapers.

The asset allocation information that blankets the public domain is a good start in explaining the strategy; however, it is only a start. As a serious investor, you'll want to know much more to design a truly effective portfolio that meets your unique needs.

REBALANCING EXPLAINED

In the long run, all the investments selected for a well-diversified portfolio are expected to generate a certain rate of return given their inherent level of risk. We do not know what that rate of return will be, but we should expect investments with higher risk to generate returns greater than those with lower risk. If you did not expect a higher return from the higher-risk investment, then a logical person would not make that investment and the price would fall (see Chapter 11 for more about expected risks and returns of various asset classes).

The problem with long-term investing is the short term. Nothing destroys a good long-term plan like extreme short-term volatility. That throws people off track, and they often do things that are emotional rather than rational.

The short-term performance of financial markets cannot be known in advance. They are not predictable, and at times they have much higher volatility than anyone expects. However, this does not mean that an asset class should be abandoned when it misbehaves. In fact, more of the asset class should be purchased.

You could build a perfect portfolio if you knew in advance which asset classes would perform well and which ones would perform poorly. Regrettably, those investors with enough experience in the markets know that it is not possible to predict when each investment will move up or down, or by how much. It is not prudent to attempt to switch and swap asset classes based on short-term market predictions. While this might work on occasion, do not confuse luck with skill. You will eventually make a big mistake that will cost you more than you ever gained. Instead, maintain a position in all investments all the time, and adjust the amount you have in each asset class as needed.

One practice that separates asset allocation from simple portfolio diversification is the *rebalancing* that occurs in asset allocation strategies on a regular basis. Rebalancing is the means by which you get the portfolio back to its original asset allocation target, thereby remaining prudently diversified. It is accomplished by selling a portion of the investment that is over its target allocation and buying more of the investment that is under its target allocation. For example, assume that your target allocation is 50 percent in stocks and 50 percent in bonds. Assume that after one year, the markets have moved the portfolio to 60 percent in stocks and 40 percent in bonds. Simply selling the extra 10 percent in stocks and buying 10 percent in bonds gets the portfolio back to its original asset allocation target of 50 percent stocks and 50 percent bonds. Rebalancing can also be done when new money is added to or withdrawn from an account and when dividends and interest are paid.

Rebalancing hinges on a theory called *regression to the mean*. That is, there is a natural tendency in the marketplace for all broad asset classes to return close to their historic risk profiles. This theory is highly controversial, and there are many naysayers. However, it is my observation that regression to the mean does appear to happen in the marketplace, and this helps the case for rebalancing.

Simply stated, regression to the mean assumes that all investments have a specific risk and return profile that they eventually follow. Stocks have higher risk than bonds, and as such, stocks are expected to generate higher returns than bonds eventually. When bond returns are higher than stock returns for an extended period, stock returns do tend make up the discrepancy and then some over the long term.

We do not know when these regressions will take place because the marketplace can become overly optimistic and overly pessimistic. In fact, some people say that the markets can become irrational. I do not want to make a judgment on market valuation. All rebalancing does is forces the sale of a small portion of the asset class that has gone up in value and forces a small extra purchase in the asset class that did not perform as well. This means selling some of the winners and buying more of the losers, whatever they are. Rebalancing may feel counterintuitive at first. However, the process basically follows the logic that it is better to sell high and buy low than the other way around.

Rebalancing is an essential component of all the asset allocation examples provided in this book. Assume that the portfolios in these chapters are rebalanced annually at the beginning of each year. This may not be the ideal rebalancing strategy, but then, there is no ideal rebalancing strategy. The rebalancing strategy that is best for you is the one you will implement without hesitation or procrastination. What works for you may not be what works for someone else. It does not make much difference, as long as it is done.

Table 3-1 offers a hypothetical example of how annual rebalancing reduces portfolio risk and increases annual return. The table assumes that two different investments are held over a two-year period. The first portfolio in Table 3-1 assumes that no rebalancing is done. This is the "let it ride" portfolio. The money placed in each investment at the beginning of Year 1 is allowed to "ride" untouched into the next year. The second portfolio assumes rebalancing after one year back to 50 percent in each investment. Part of the gain from the investment that went up is shifted into the investment that went down so that both investments have an equal amount at the beginning of Year 2.

TABLE 3-1

Annual Rebalancing Example

Investments	Return in Year 1	Return in Year 2	Compounded Return
Investment 1	+20%	−10%	3.9%
Investment 2	−10%	+20%	3.9%
Hypothetical Portfolios			
50% Investment 1 and			
50% Investment 2,			
no rebalancing (let it ride)	5.0%	2.9%	3.9%
50% Investment 1 and			
50% Investment 2,			
rebalanced annually	5.0%	**5.0%**	**5.0%**

Notice how differently the "let it ride" portfolio behaved compared to the rebalanced portfolio. Individually, both Investment 1 and Investment 2 earned a 3.9 percent compounded return over the two-year period. This means that the "let it ride" portfolio with 50 percent in each investment to start also has a compounded two-year return of 3.9 percent. However, a rebalanced portfolio that maintained 50 percent allocation in each investment starting in Year 2 eliminated the volatility of returns, and that increased the compounded return of the portfolio to 5.0 percent compounded annually.

The example is an exaggerated case. Rarely do investments cooperate the way I describe. But the theory is sound. Diversifying across many investments that are dissimilar and rebalancing those investments to their original target at the end of the year can reduce the annual volatility of the portfolio over time by enough to increase the compounded return. This "free lunch" from rebalancing is the essence of modern portfolio theory.

There are different methods of rebalancing. The two most popular ones are based on the calendar and percentage targets. When using a calendar method, investors choose to rebalance after a specific period of time, such as a year, a quarter, or a month. Other investors prefer to use asset class percentage targets. When a portfolio is off the target allocation by a certain percentage, it is rebalanced, regardless of when the last rebalancing took place.

A rebalancing strategy based on percentages may deliver slightly better performance than the calendar method; however, the difference is not much. The percentage strategy requires significantly more time to monitor and implement, and I do not believe it is worthwhile for individual investors to pursue this strategy. Therefore, annual rebalancing is the method used in this book. What is best for you is one you will actually maintain without procrastination. Annual rebalancing is simple and cost effective, and it takes only a little time each year to implement, which means that you are more likely to get it done.

CORRELATION EXPLAINED

Annual rebalancing helps capture a diversification benefit by selling some of an investment that did well and buying more of an investment that did not do as well. Of course, this assumes that the investments in a portfolio do not all act the same way at the same time. Therefore, the method of selecting investments that *normally* do not act the same way is as important as rebalancing itself. That said, I will also warn you that there are no two asset classes that relate the same way to each other all the time. These relationships are dynamic, and they can and do change without warning.

Selecting investments that do not go up and down at the same time (or most of the time) can be made easier with *correlation* analysis. This is a mathematical measure of the tendency of one investment to move in relation to another. The correlation coefficient is a mathematically derived number that measures this tendency toward comovement relative to the investments' average return. If two investments each move in the same direction at the same time above their average returns, they have a *positive correlation*. If they each move in opposite directions below their average returns, they have a *negative correlation*. If the movement of one investment relative to its average return is independent of the other, the two investments are *noncorrelated*.

The challenge facing investors is to find investments that have negative correlation, or noncorrelation, or at least low positive correlation with each other. If those investments can be identified and if the investments offer a positive rate of return after inflation, investors should place an appropriate percentage of their portfolio in each one and rebalance those investments annually.

I will state right now that there are no negatively correlated asset classes. At times an asset class will be negative correlated with the U.S. stock market; however, this negative correlation does not persist. Correlations are dynamic, not static. Even though there are people who will point to commodities and gold and say that these assets often have negative correlation with U.S. stocks, they do not produce any real return over the inflation rate.

Shorting the S&P 500 Stock Index also has negative correlation with stocks (shorting means selling the index without owning it). Shorting the S&P 500 is the opposite of buying the S&P 500, which cancels out the gains in the market. Again, there is no benefit to having an investment in your portfolio that does nothing for your long-term returns.

There is also no benefit from purchasing new investments that have a consistently high positive correlation with other investments already in your portfolio. This is a very common mistake that inexperienced investors make. During the late 1990s, many people thought that their portfolios were diversified because they owned several different growth stock mutual funds. When the technology and communications sectors of the economy collapsed between 2000 and 2002, all growth mutual funds fell concurrently because all those funds were heavily weighted in the same group of technology and communications stocks. That is when people learned that quantity diversification is not the same as quality diversification.

Figure 3-2 illustrates the movement in the returns of two mutual funds that have a consistently high correlation with each other. Figure 3-2 assumes a portfolio of 50 percent in Fund A and 50 percent in Fund B, rebalanced annually.

Since Fund A and Fund B are highly correlated, there would be no diversification benefit from owning both in a portfolio. Ideally, you would like to invest in two mutual funds that have a negative correlation. Figure 3-3 shows that Fund C and Fund D move in opposite directions, which means that the two funds have negative correlation. A portfolio of 50 percent in Fund C and

FIGURE 3-2

Perfect Positive Correlation Year-over-Year Returns

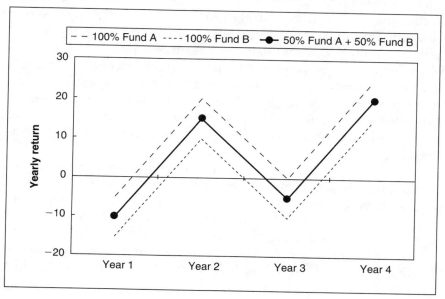

F I G U R E   3-3

Perfect Negative Correlation Year-over-Year Returns

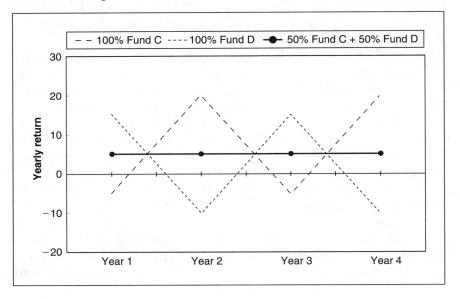

50 percent in Fund D, rebalanced annually, will result in a return that is less volatile than the return on either of the two investments individually. Negative correlation is theoretically ideal when selecting investments for a portfolio, but you are not going to find it in the real world. These pairs of investments just do not exist.

Correlation is measured using a range between +1 and −1. Two investments that have a correlation of +0.3 or greater are considered positively correlated. When two investments have a correlation of −0.3 or less, this is considered negative correlation. A correlation coefficient between −0.3 and +0.3 is considered non-correlated.

When two investments are noncorrelated, either the movement of one does not track the movement of the other or the tracking is inconsistent and shifts between positive and negative. Figure 3-4 represents two investments that are noncorrelated; sometimes they move together, and sometimes they do not. There is a diversification benefit from investing in noncorrelated assets. Typically, the best asset class pairs that you will be able to find have noncorrelation, or they may have positive correlation at times and negative correlation at other times.

Table 3-2 is a summary of the diversification benefits from correlation. The table assumes that all three portfolios have a simple average return of 5 percent per year, although they have different compounded returns because of the volatility of each portfolio. Portfolio 1 held two investments with negative correlation, and it produced the lowest risk and the highest return. In contrast,

FIGURE 3-4

Noncorrelation Year-over-Year Returns

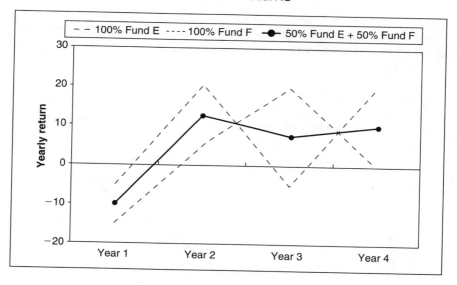

TABLE 3-2

Relationship between Correlation and Portfolio Return

Portfolio	Correlation of Assets	Simple Average Return	Compounded Return	Standard Deviation (σ)
1: 50% C + 50% D	−1.0	5.0%	5.0%	0%
2: 50% E + 50% F	0.0	5.0%	4.6%	10%
3: 50% A + 50% B	+1.0	5.0%	4.2%	14%

Portfolio 3 held two investments with positive correlation. That portfolio had more risk and achieved the lowest return.

Figure 3-5 illustrates the risk reduction benefit created by adding asset classes that have low or negative correlation with each other. Portfolio risk is reduced as correlation shifts from positive to negative, and the efficient frontier bows out further to the left, toward an area of lower portfolio volatility. This is the essence of risk reduction using asset allocation.

Developing a portfolio that holds assets that have negative correlation or noncorrelation with one another is very beneficial. The problem is finding those investments. They are rare. Just when you think you may have found a good noncorrelating investment, something changes and the investment becomes positively correlated. You will see many charts and tables throughout this book showing the correlations of investments shifting rapidly and without explanation.

FIGURE 3-5

Lower Correlation between Investments Reduces Risk

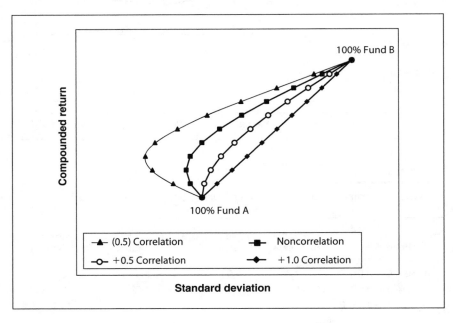

Since it is so difficult to find investments that are negatively correlated, in practice most portfolios are composed of investments that either are noncorrelated or have a low positive correlation with one another. Asset classes that have low positive correlation do have some diversification benefit, especially if you hold several types in a portfolio.

THE TWO-ASSET-CLASS MODEL

Finance professors begin teaching asset allocation techniques using two asset classes. The students learn about correlation, risk reduction, and the efficient frontier in a simple model of two investments that have low correlation with each other. After the students have mastered an understanding of the benefits of asset allocation using two investments, the professor expands the exercise into a multi-asset portfolio by adding a third, fourth, fifth, and sixth investment category. The remainder of this chapter follows the same path by explaining asset allocation using a two-asset-class portfolio consisting of U.S. stocks and U.S. Treasury bonds. Chapter 4 expands the discussion into a multi-asset-class model.

The two asset classes examined in this chapter are a U.S. large-stock index and an intermediate-term Treasury-note index. The S&P 500, an index of 500 leading U.S. corporations, is used as a proxy for U.S. large-stock returns. The Treasury note returns are based on two data series. Prior to 1973, the Treasury return is represented by the return on five-year Treasury bonds. Starting in 1973, the Treasury note returns represent the performance of the Barclays 1–10 Year Treasury Index, which is a diversified portfolio of short- to intermediate-term U.S. Treasury securities.

RISK-AND-RETURN FIGURES

In this chapter and for the remainder of the book, portfolio risk and return are illustrated using charts and tables. Figure 3-6 represents a classic risk-and-return frontier. The vertical axis in Figure 3-6 represents the compounded annualized return of a series of portfolios, and the horizontal axis is the risk as measured by the standard deviation of those annual returns.

FIGURE 3-6

Classic Risk-and-Return Efficient Frontier

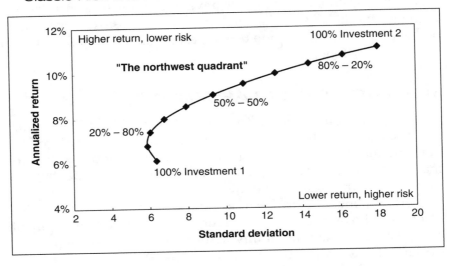

At one end of the chart is the risk and return for the first investment in a portfolio, and at the other end is the risk and return for the second investment. The points in between represent the risks and returns of portfolios using various asset allocations, spaced with 10 percent intervals. The points on a risk-and-return chart are linked together to form a line that represents all the different combinations of the two asset classes. Depending on which two asset classes are used, the line curves upward and to the left to varying degrees.

The vertical *y* axis is easy to understand because high returns are always better than low returns. However, an equally important factor in the chart is the risk measure on the horizontal *x* axis. The more volatile the annual returns of a portfolio, the further to the right on the horizontal *x* axis the points are. Points far to the right on the *x* axis depict very aggressive portfolios. Clearly, the preferable place on the chart is the area in the upper-left portion, depicting high returns with low risk. This area of the chart is often referred to as the *northwest quadrant*.

Turn your attention to Figure 3-7. A portfolio of 100 percent Investment A has the lowest return and the lowest risk. On the

FIGURE 3-7

Risk-and-Return Chart Showing Diversification Benefit of
Asset Allocation

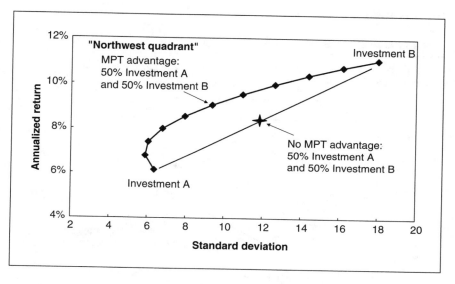

other hand, a portfolio of 100 percent Investment B has the highest
return and the highest risk. What would you expect the risk and
return to be of a portfolio that is 50 percent in Investment A and
50 percent in Investment B?

One might expect that a portfolio of 50 percent Investment A
and 50 percent Investment B would have a return-and-risk level
where the star is located, which is halfway between the two investments. However, the actual risk of 50 percent in Investment A and
50 percent in Investment B was much lower than expected, and the
return was higher. This was a result of annual rebalancing

Let's put some names to those two investments. Investment A
is actually the annualized return and standard deviation of the
intermediate-term Treasury notes from 1950 to 2009. Investment B
is the annualized return and standard deviation of the S&P 500
from 1950 to 2009. Each point on the line represents portfolios
using 10 percent increments of the two asset classes. This can be
seen in Figure 3-8.

Based on the return data calculated for Figure 3-7, there was an MPT advantage in the five-year Treasury notes and S&P 500 portfolio during the period measured. Table 3-3 quantifies what the advantage was.

FIGURE 3-8

Risk and Return by Decades, 1950–2009, Five-Year T-Notes and the S&P 500

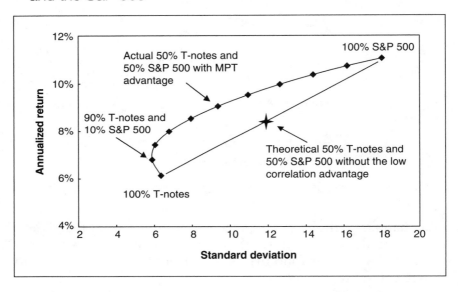

TABLE 3-3

Portfolio Returns, 1950–2009

Portfolio Characteristics	Annualized Return	Risk (Standard Deviation)
100% intermediate T-notes	6.1%	6.4%
100% S&P 500	11.4%	18.0%
Expected return and risk of 50% T-notes and 50% stock mix (no MPT)	8.6%	12.2%
Actual return and risk of 50% T-notes and 50% stock mix	9.0%	9.3%
MPT advantage (higher return, lower risk)	+0.4%	− 2.9%

Reducing portfolio risk increases portfolio return. The 50 percent intermediate Treasury notes and 50 percent S&P 500 Index portfolio had an increase in return of 0.5 percent per year created by a reduction in return volatility of 2.9 percent.

CORRELATIONS ARE NOT CONSISTENT

Finding asset classes that have low correlation with each other is not easy. Financial articles and books frequently give tables or matrixes showing single historic correlation numbers between different asset classes in the matrix. Then the authors suggest using these static correlation numbers to make investment selections for your portfolio. In a sense, the authors are implying that the single historic correlation number will remain constant going forward. That is wrong. Correlations are dynamic, not static. They change over time.

It is very difficult to predict the direction any correlation will go in the future. Past correlations are not a reliable indicator of future correlations. The numbers can change frequently and without warning. Some asset classes may become more correlated with each other, and others become less correlated.

Figure 3-9 is a visual representation of the shifting 36-month correlation between intermediate-term U.S. Treasury notes and the S&P 500 Index. If the correlation were fixed, the line would be straight across the chart. As you can clearly see, the line is hardly straight. There have been many periods of time when bond and stock returns moved in opposite directions from their averages (negative correlation) and several periods when they moved in the same direction with averages (positive correlation). There have also been many periods where there was no clear correlation between the two asset classes.

Over the past 20 years, the 60-month rolling correlation of returns between the five-year Treasury note and the S&P 500 has varied significantly. During the 1990s, the correlation was positive. Stock and bond returns moved in the same direction relative to their averages. Between 2000 and 2009, the correlation turned negative. The average correlation for the entire 20-year period was 0, suggesting that the two investments are not correlated.

Some investors may find it interesting that the correlation between stocks and bonds fluctuates as dramatically as Figure 3-9

FIGURE 3-9

Rolling 60-Month Correlation Intermediate-Term Treasury Notes and S&P

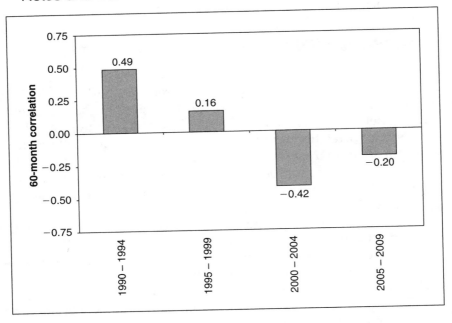

indicates. Prior to the correlation shift that started around 1998, there was a longstanding belief among investors that bond prices move in a similar fashion to stock prices. The thinking is that interest rates affect stock values. When interest rates fall, both bond prices and stock prices rise, and vice versa. That is simply not the case, and the recent decade ending in 2009 proved it.

The correlation between intermediate-term Treasury notes and the S&P 500 Index has shifted unpredictably over the last 50 years. Consequently, the diversification benefit from owning both intermediate-term Treasury notes and S&P 500 stocks has also been a moving target. Figure 3-10 is a series of independent risk-and-return charts for the two investments that cover each decade since 1950.

The efficient frontier for each decade starts on the left side with the risk and return of intermediate-term Treasury notes and ends at the right side with the risk and return of the S&P 500. In four out of six periods, the efficient frontier is upward sloping,

FIGURE 3-10

Diversification Benefit over the Decades, Intermediate-Term T-Notes and S&P 500

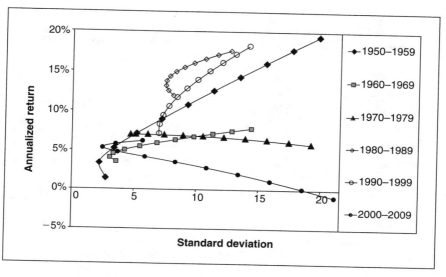

meaning that the return on the S&P 500 was greater than the return on intermediate-term Treasury notes. During the 1970–1979 and 2000–2009 periods, the return on the S&P 500 was less than the return on intermediate-term Treasury notes.

Table 3-4 crystallizes the connection between correlation and MPT gains in return from annual rebalancing. During the periods when the correlation between stocks and intermediate-term Treasury notes was highly negative, the portfolio risk reduction was also high as was the increase in portfolio return resulting from rebalancing. Two periods that exemplify this phenomenon are 1950–1959 and 2000–2009. In contrast, the period with the highest positive correlation was 1990–1999. This period also had the lowest risk reduction benefit and the lowest benefit from rebalancing, although those benefits still existed.

Figure 3-11 illustrates how one period can be vastly different from the next with the end results in each decade still being to your advantage. During 1990–1999, there was positive correlation between intermediate-term Treasury notes and the S&P 500. What resulted

TABLE 3-4

Benefits of 50% Stock and 50% Bond Diversification over the Decades

Period	Correlation during the Period	Reduction in Portfolio Risk	Increase in Return (MPT)
1950–1959	−0.53	−2.0%	+0.42%
1960–1969	−0.33	−2.1%	+0.26%
1970–1979	+0.28	−1.4%	+0.39%
1980–1989	+0.23	−2.1%	+0.17%
1990–1999	+0.44	−1.4%	+0.16%
2000–2009	−0.85	−5.1%	+0.84%

FIGURE 3-11

Diversification Benefits in Two Contrasting Decades

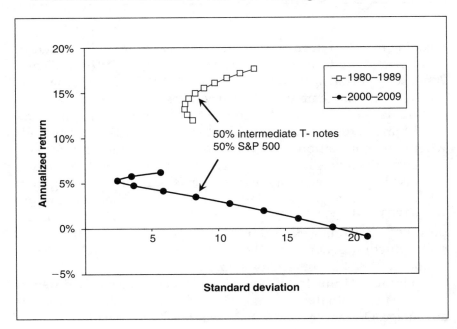

was a 50 percent stock and 50 percent bond portfolio that had about the same risk as a 100 percent bond portfolio with about 3 percent higher annual compounded return. There was a distinct negative correlation between the two investments during 2000–2009 that had portfolio risk only slightly higher than a 100 percent bond portfolio. The 50 percent bond and 50 percent stock portfolio had about a 3 percent lower return than 100 percent bonds, although it was still solidly positive during the worst decade for stocks in 60 years.

Figure 3-12 illustrates the difference in risk and return of each 50 percent stock and 50 percent bond portfolio for each decade since 1950. Notice first that the returns were positive every decade. Next notice that the return range was much broader than the risk variation. This brings up an interesting point that is discussed again in Chapter 12; over any 10-year period, it is easier to predict portfolio risk than it is to predict portfolio return. It takes about 30 years before a portfolio return prediction can work out in relation to portfolio risk. Asset allocation is for patient people.

FIGURE 3-12

50% Stock and 50% Bond Risk and Returns over the Decades

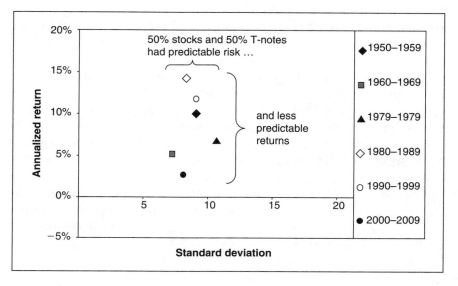

ASSET ALLOCATION IS NOT INFALLIBLE

You may find negatively correlated asset classes in your search for investments. But that is not the only reason to invest in that asset class. Every investment in your portfolio should be expected to earn a positive return over inflation in the long term. Consequently, an asset class that has negative correlation is of little use if the returns are at or below inflation, and you should discard it and move on. A negatively correlated investment may lower overall portfolio risk, but if it also lowers your portfolio returns, that is not a good thing in the long term. You cannot eat lower risk.

Here is the bottom line. It is basically impossible to find two negatively correlated asset classes that both earn positive returns over inflation. That being said, it may be possible to find a few asset classes that are noncorrelated with each other, and at least have enough varying correlation so that there is relatively low correlation on average during most 10-year periods.

A well-diversified portfolio includes several investments with varying correlations (see Part Two for details on investment selection). Some of those investments will be moving out of sync with the rest of the portfolio, while others are moving together. No one knows when any particular investment will become more correlated or less correlated with the others, which is why it is prudent to own several dissimilar investments. Having several types of investments with varying correlations will provide the overall MPT benefit you are looking for.

By studying asset-class correlations among investments that are expected to have a real rate for return over inflation and employing an asset allocation strategy using those investments, you will reduce the chance of a large portfolio loss and reduce portfolio risk over time. However, you will not eliminate these risks. You cannot eliminate all risk from your portfolio even if you have several investment categories in your portfolio.

There will be periods of time when even the most broadly diversified portfolios will lose money. When those periods occur, there is nothing an investor can do short of abandoning the entire investment plan, which is not a good idea. Trying to guess when down periods will occur and adjusting your portfolio accordingly will probably lose you more money and cause you more frustration than sticking with your plan and pushing through the storm.

Figure 3-13 provides an example of how 50 percent intermediate-term Treasury notes and 50 percent S&P 500 performed annually. The histogram covers all 60 years from 1950 to 2009. Most years the return was between negative 5 percent and positive 25 percent. The worst year was in 2008 with a negative 11.9 percent return, and the best year was in 1954 with a positive 27.7 percent return. There were 11 years out of 60 when the returns where negative. That is about 1 year in 5.

A single-year loss in a portfolio does not signal the failure of an asset allocation strategy. Rather, losses must be expected to

FIGURE 3-13

Annual Return Frequency Distribution 50% Intermediate-Term Treasury Notes and 50% S&P 500, 1950–2009

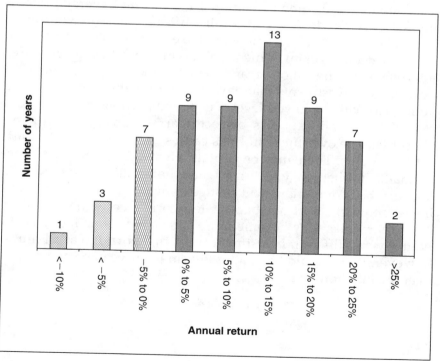

occur on occasion. However, for those who expect to make money every year, losing periods such as those that occurred in 1974, 2002, and 2008 can lead to the failure of an investment plan. By failure, I mean that the investor abandons his or her long-term strategy because he or she has lost money. You will lose money during your investing life and should expect to at times. It is better to prepare for it now so that you will not do permanent damage to your investment plan when losses occur again in the future.

If there is one thing that is certain in the financial markets, it is that there will come a time again in the future when even the best investment plan loses money. If you implement an asset allocation strategy and fully understand the risks and limitations, then you are well on your way to achieving the hidden diversification benefits that Harry Markowitz wrote about more than half a century ago.

CHAPTER SUMMARY

Portfolio diversification is the practice of buying several different investments to reduce the probability of a large loss in a portfolio. Asset allocation involves estimating the expected risk and return of various categories of investments, observing how those asset classes interrelate with one another, and then methodically constructing a portfolio of investments that have a high probability of achieving your goals with the lowest level of expected portfolio risk.

No asset allocation is perfect. Correlations between asset classes change over time, and this causes changes in the diversification benefits. There may be periods when a diversification effect is small, and there may be times when the benefit is large. No one knows when correlations will change or by how much. Sometimes investments in a portfolio become less correlated with each other, and other times they become more correlated. Thus it is wise to hold several different investment types in a portfolio at all times; however, they should have a long-term positive expected return over the inflation rate.

CHAPTER 4

Multi-Asset-Class Investing

KEY CONCEPTS

- Owning several asset classes is better than owning a few.
- Each new and unique asset class can reduce portfolio risk.
- Choose asset classes that have positive real returns and lower correlation.
- You can select a good asset allocation, but not a perfect one.

In Chapter 3, we look at the way two different asset classes can work together to form a lower-risk and higher-return portfolio. Multi-asset-class investing involves adding more asset classes to the portfolio to further reduce portfolio risk and increase the potential for higher return. It is not possible to know which types of investment will perform well at any given time; thus, it is important to retain all asset classes in a portfolio at all times and to rebalance these investments annually. Broad diversification and occasional rebalancing to control portfolio risk is the essence of multi-asset-class investing.

EXPANDING THE ENVELOPE

The Talmud has a saying:

> Let every man divide his money into three parts, and invest a
> third in land, a third in business, and a third let him keep in
> reserve.

> —Talmud, circa 1200 BC–500 AD

In today's terms, it means keep a third in stocks, a third in bonds, and a third in land. This will diversify a portfolio and guard it from total loss.

In this chapter, we expand the number of asset classes to analyze how these additions affect portfolio risk and return. In addition to the U.S. stocks and intermediate-term Treasury notes already discussed, three new investments are analyzed: Pacific Rim stocks, European stocks, and corporate bonds. A multi-asset-class portfolio helps you increase your portfolio return without increasing overall risk, or to target a return similar to a U.S. stock and U.S. bond only portfolio while taking less overall risk.

The addition of new investments should aid the portfolio over time—if the expected long-term return from each investment is higher than the inflation rate, and if the investments have unique risks that differ from the other investments already in your portfolio. Figure 4-1 demonstrates how adding unique asset classes shifts the characteristics of a portfolio with U.S. stocks and Treasury notes to a portfolio with lower risk and increased long-term return. These curves are known as "efficient frontiers." They represent the risk and return of two portfolios based on various percentages allocated to different asset classes.

Adding multiple asset classes pushes the efficient frontier toward the *northwest quadrant* of the chart. The northwest quadrant is an investment utopia. It is an optimal portfolio that investors attempt to construct, and it is the type of portfolio you should seek for yourself. The efficient frontier represents a portfolio with an efficient mix of assets that work well together over time.

Now for the bad news: utopia does not exist, at least not in the short term. The northwest quadrant is the goal. However, you will likely never reach the optimal point on the curve. Multi-asset-class investing will shift the risk-and-return characteristics of a portfolio *toward* the northwest quadrant over the long term; however, no

FIGURE 4-1

Moving Northwest with Multi-Asset-Class Portfolios

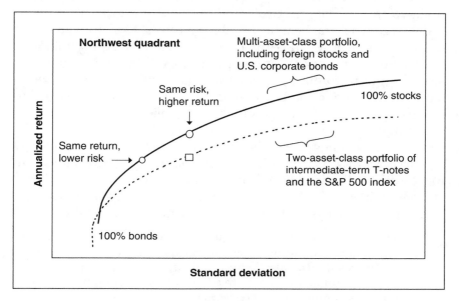

fixed asset class mix is always the most efficient one. You could spend your life trying to find the perfect portfolio. However, it can be known only in retrospect. There is no portfolio holding a fixed combination of investments that will consistently achieve high returns and low overall risk.

You could try to shift your asset allocation around periodically based on estimates of future returns, but that only creates more risk in a portfolio. Had you allocated out of stocks in early March 2009 because the gurus were predicting more losses, you would have missed the 60 percent gain in prices that occurred for the rest of the year.

The strategies in this book are counterintuitive to what may appear to be happening in the markets. When an investment goes down, that is when this book recommends buying, and when an investment goes up, that is when you sell. Regular rebalancing in a multi-asset-class portfolio means selling a percentage of an asset class that has outperformed and buying more of one that didn't. This may not be easy to do when everyone is talking about doing the opposite.

INTERNATIONAL STOCKS

Of the three new asset-class categories introduced in this chapter, the first two are international equity indexes. Foreign stocks have historically offered several benefits for U.S. investors. First, foreign stocks do not always move in correlation with the U.S. equity markets, which creates a diversification opportunity. Second, international stocks trade in foreign currencies. This offers investors a hedge against a decline in the U.S. dollar. Both are important reasons to have some foreign stock exposure in a portfolio.

Roger C. Gibson, CFA, CFP, is a well-known author on the subject of asset allocation. His first book, *Asset Allocation: Balancing Financial Risk* (McGraw-Hill), is a classic work on the subject. In March 1999, Gibson published an award-winning article in the *Journal of Finance* titled "The Rewards of Multiple-Asset-Class Investing." The article articulates the benefits of investing internationally:

> Diversification across two major forms of equity investing with dissimilar patterns of returns further reduces the equity risk. The result is a balanced portfolio, tilted toward equities, appropriate for an investor with a longer investment time horizon who is simultaneously concerned about risk and return. It is a remarkably elegant and powerful asset allocation strategy.

International equities include all publicly traded companies headquartered outside of the United States. The list includes large companies in developed nations, such as Sony Corporation of Japan, and small companies in emerging countries, such as Danubius Hotel of Budapest, Hungary. In all, there are more than 20,000 international companies that trade actively on foreign exchanges.

Several index providers cover the world's financial markets. They offer individual country indexes, regional indexes, and global indexes. For example, Morgan Stanley Capital International (MSCI) offers country indexes on dozens of markets. In addition, MSCI packages countries together into regions. The MSCI Pacific Rim Index includes Japan, Singapore, Australia, and New Zealand. The MSCI European Index includes the United Kingdom and several continental European countries, including Germany, France, Spain, Italy, Sweden, and Switzerland.

International indexes are available in both the local country currency and U.S. dollars, and that makes a big difference when you are measuring returns. Local currency indexes reflect the returns that people living in that country earn, and dollar indexes are what U.S. investors receive after converting the local currency to U.S. dollars. The news media in the United States generally publish only U.S. dollar returns, which is not the actual performance of the underlying stocks in local markets. There can be big differences in returns depending on the movement of the dollar in relation to the local currency.

Returns in U.S. dollars also vary considerable across geographical regions. Table 4-1 is a sampling of large-cap equity returns in

TABLE 4-1

U.S., European, and Pacific Rim Stocks

	S&P 500	European Index	Pacific Rim Index
1985	32.2	75.1	30.3
1986	18.5	42.7	74.1
1987	5.2	13.4	23.7
1988	16.8	15.4	33.0
1989	31.5	26.9	8.9
1990	−3.2	−1.0	−23.1
1991	30.6	14.7	22.9
1992	7.7	−3.6	−7.1
1993	10.0	29.5	53.1
1994	1.3	2.4	3.8
1995	37.4	22.6	7.1
1996	23.1	23.9	2.8
1997	33.4	21.8	−27.2
1998	28.6	24.5	−0.5
1999	21.0	19.2	52.5
2000	−9.1	−10.1	−21.6
2001	−11.9	−18.8	−19.4
2002	−22.1	−17.2	−7.9
2003	28.7	39.0	41.6
2004	10.9	21.7	22.8
2005	4.9	10.4	20.2
2006	15.8	34.6	19.7
2007	5.5	12.3	13.8
2008	−37.0	−47.3	−39.6
2009	26.5	35.8	24.2

U.S. dollars from the three global areas: the United States, Europe, and the Pacific Rim. The shaded cell represents the geographical region that had the highest-returning index for that year. The region of the world with the highest return varies over time. There is no pattern recognition or formula that can be used to predict the region that will outperform next.

Allocating assets across these three regions has been a good strategy. It created a better risk-adjusted return than having only U.S. equities. Figure 4-2 shows a risk-and-return diagram for U.S. stocks and international stocks using 10 percent increments, starting with no international stocks on the left side and ending with only international stocks on the right side. The international index I used is split evenly between the Pacific Rim and Europe, rebalanced annually. The international composite index dates back to 1973.

The interesting points in Figure 4-2 are at the two ends and at a 30 percent international position and 70 percent international position. The two ends show that U.S. stocks had lower risk and

FIGURE 4-2

S&P 500 and International Mix, 1973–2009

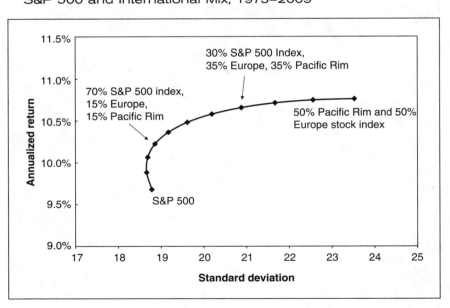

lower return than the international mix. The 30 percent position is where an investor gained about 0.5 percent in extra return over the U.S. stock market without adding any risk. After that point, each incremental gain in return is paid for with an increasing amount of risk. The 70 percent international position is an inflection point where returns gained basically end. From this point forward, adding more international stocks adds mostly risk.

Multi-asset-class investing works over the decades, but not every decade. There have been long periods when international stocks took away from a U.S.-only portfolio, and other times when there was no excess return advantage after adjusting for added risk. Figure 4-3 illustrates the risk-and-return chart over three independent decades starting in 1980.

International stocks have had higher volatility than U.S. stocks in all of the past three decades, although they did always

FIGURE 4-3

S&P 500 and International Stocks: Risk and Reward over Various Decades

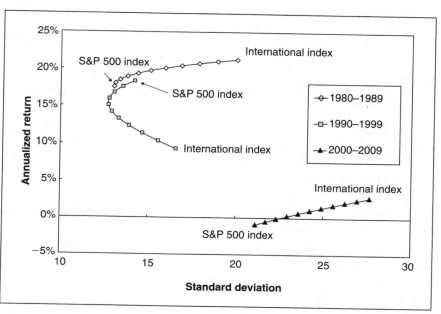

have higher returns. U.S. stocks outperformed international stocks by 8 percent annually during the 1990s. This led a few prominent icons in the investment industry to question the wisdom of owning international stocks. One of those was John Bogle, founder of the Vanguard Group of mutual funds.

I have the greatest respect for John Bogle, but I don't always agree with him, and this was one of those times. A single 10-year period is not a reason to be out of international stocks for a lifetime. By the end of 2009, after international stocks outperformed U.S. stocks by a wide margin, people saw the benefits of international exposure. Even John Bogle changed his view and now accepts an allocation of up to 20 percent in international stock index funds.

There have been and will be periods when international stocks reduce portfolio risk and increase return, and times when they do not. However, over a lifetime of investing, international equity is one way to add a diversification benefit over an all-U.S. stock allocation.

CORPORATE BONDS

Intermediate-term Treasury bonds have been the only fixed-income asset class discussed thus far. The second fixed-income class to be introduced is an index of U.S. intermediate-term investment-grade corporate bonds. This index includes bonds issued in the United States by predominantly U.S. corporations and a few bonds issued by large foreign corporations that are issued in the United States and denominated in U.S. dollars.

Table 4-2 is a sampling of period returns from the Barclays Capital Intermediate Term Treasury Index and the Barclays Capital U.S. Intermediate Credit Index. "Intermediate" generally means that the bonds in the index mature in 6 to 10 years. For all practical purposes the word *credit* means "corporate."

The reason the word *credit* is used rather than "corporate" in bond indexes is a matter of semantics. Corporations do issue all bonds in a credit index; however, a small portion of these bonds are asset-backed securities and commercial mortgages. Asset-backed bonds are backed by receivables such at credit card debt rather than by the corporation that issued the bond. An asset-backed security is its own entity that has its own credit rating. If an

TABLE 4-2

Treasury and Corporate Bond Indexes

Year	Barclays Intermediate T-Notes	Barclays Intermediate Credit Index	Credit Return Less T-Note Return
1985	17.8	18.5	0.7
1986	13.0	13.5	0.5
1987	3.6	3.9	0.3
1988	6.3	8.0	1.7
1989	12.7	12.9	0.3
1990	9.5	7.6	−1.8
1991	14.1	16.6	2.5
1992	6.9	8.2	1.2
1993	8.2	11.1	2.9
1994	−1.8	−2.6	−0.9
1995	14.4	19.2	4.8
1996	4.0	4.0	0.0
1997	7.7	8.4	0.7
1998	8.6	8.3	−0.3
1999	0.4	0.2	−0.2
2000	10.3	9.4	−0.8
2001	8.2	9.8	1.6
2002	9.3	10.1	0.8
2003	2.1	6.9	4.8
2004	2.0	4.1	2.1
2005	1.6	1.4	−0.1
2006	3.5	4.5	1.0
2007	8.8	5.6	−3.2
2008	11.4	−2.8	−14.1
2009	−1.4	15.9	17.3

asset-backed bond were to default, the company that packaged the assets into a bond would not be in default and would not be obligated to make the interest and principal payments on the security.

The shaded cells in Table 4-2 represent the highest-returning index for that year. Intuitively, one would expect corporate bonds to return more than Treasuries because the interest rate on corporate bonds is higher (see Chapter 6). Yet this is not always the case. Treasury bond returns were higher than the returns on corporate bonds in 9 out of 25 years from 1985 to 2009.

The "yield spread" is the difference in yield-to-maturity between two security indexes. The spread between Treasuries and corporate bonds widens or narrows as the risks in each market change. When corporate spreads narrow, corporate bonds perform well. When the spread increases, government bonds are outperforming.

There are a number of factors that explain why the yield spread increases and decreases. These factors tend to revolve around the boom-bust cycle of the economy. Spreads widen when investors see deteriorating economic conditions, and vice versa. More information on the behavior of credit spreads and bond investing in general is available in Chapter 8.

Notice in Figure 4-4 how negative correlation between Treasury bond and corporate bond returns reduced fixed-income risk during

FIGURE 4-4

Intermediate-Term T-Notes and Intermediate Corporate Bonds: Decade Risk and Reward

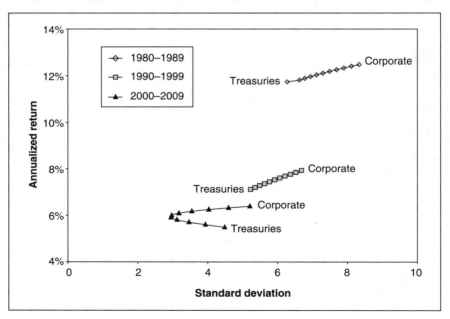

the past decade. Corporate bonds produced a higher return during most 10-year periods and no less return in the decades when they did not beat Treasuries.

The correlation between the Treasury index and the credit index averaged about +0.8 over the long term. This means that the two investments generally move together. However, there are times when the correlation has been distinctly negative, and returns differed considerably. The most recent occurrence of negative correlation appeared from 2007 to 2009. This period resulted in a strong diversification benefit.

A MULTI-ASSET-CLASS EXAMPLE

The following is an example of a multi-asset-class portfolio using the five asset classes covered in this chapter:

- U.S. large-cap equities (S&P 500 index)
- Large Pacific Rim equities
- Large European equities
- Intermediate U.S. Treasury notes
- Intermediate U.S. dollar–denominated corporate bonds

For purposes of illustration, the following global equity allocation and a U.S. fixed-income allocation are used:

- Global equity = 70 percent S&P 500 index, 15 percent Pacific index, 15 percent Europe index
- Bonds = 50 percent Barclays Intermediate-Term Treasury Index and 50 percent Barclays Intermediate-Term Credit Index

Figure 4-5 illustrates the difference in risk-and-return characteristics between a two-asset-class portfolio and a multi-asset-class portfolio. The two-asset-class portfolio holds U.S. stocks and Treasuries, and the multi-asset-class portfolio consists of the global equity mix and the fixed-income mix given earlier.

Table 4-3 quantifies the increase in percent return and decrease in risk from using a multi-asset-class approach during 1973 to 2009. Over that period of time, the return of the multi-asset-class portfolio at 50 percent stock and 50 percent bond portfolio

FIGURE 4-5

Multi-Asset-Class Portfolio versus Two-Asset-Class Portfolio, 1973–2009

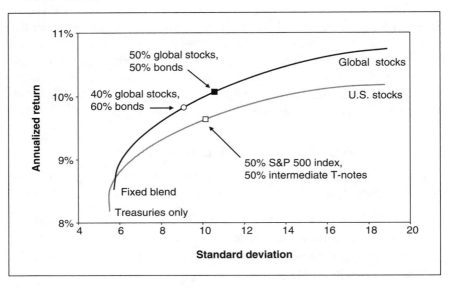

TABLE 4-3

Portfolio Returns, 1973–2009

S&P 500 + T-Notes	100% Treasuries	50% S&P 500, 50% T-Notes	100% S&P 500
Total return	7.7%	9.1%	9.7%
Standard deviation	5.5%	10.1%	18.8%
Multi-Asset class	**100% Bonds**	**50% Global Stock 50% Bonds**	**100% Equity**
Total return	8.0%	9.6%	10.2%
Standard deviation	5.7%	10.6%	18.9%

was increased by 0.4 percent annualized over using only Treasury bonds and U.S. stocks. A multi-asset portfolio of only 40 percent stocks provided higher returns and lower risk than a 50 percent U.S. stock and T-note portfolio. Adding three more asset classes to

U.S. stocks and T-notes pushed the efficient frontier line toward the desirable northwest quadrant.

You may be wondering, why bother with multi-asset-class investing for such a small percentage of increase in return or reduction in risk? First, the example includes only five asset classes, and you will probably use more. The diversification benefit should increase by adding more asset classes. Second, portfolio gains using asset allocation are measured in fractions of a percentage point. An extra return of 0.4 percent may not sound like much, but over a period of 10 years, a 0.4 percent increase in return on a $100,000 investment increases the portfolio by more than $4,000.

Wesley Branch Rickey (December 20, 1881–December 9, 1965) was an innovative major league baseball executive who is best known for helping break baseball's color barrier and creating the framework for the modern minor league system. Rickey once commented, "Baseball is a game of inches." In that same light, asset allocation is a game of *basis points*. A basis point is 0.01 percent return. If you add 10 basis points to your annual return (0.1 percent) without taking more risk, it makes a huge difference in the amount you have in retirement or whatever your goal is. So why not do it?

Figures 4.6 to 4.8 illustrate the risk-and-return characteristics of the five-asset-class portfolio versus the two-asset-class portfolio over three different decades. An asset allocation strategy that worked well during one period may not work as well during the next. The series of charts is provided to show that the benefits of asset allocation are often not measurable in the short term. That is why a lot of naysayers say, "It does not work." They lack patience, and they lack vision. They are looking for quick and easy solutions. Multi-asset-class investing requires a long-term commitment. Once you go down this road, it is for life. It is in a way like changing careers.

As illustrated in Figure 4-6, from 1980 to 1989, multi-asset-class investing in international stocks worked beautifully. The strategy generated an extra 0.8 percent in return using the multi-asset-class portfolio and presenting a negligible increase in risk.

The diversification benefit did not help a portfolio between 1990 and 1999, as illustrated in Figure 4-7. The returns were lower using the multi-asset-class portfolio during the period, and the risk was also lower. This is the reason some people started to question the benefit of international investing by the end of that decade.

F I G U R E   4-6

Multi-Asset-Class Portfolio versus S&P 500 and Intermediate-
Term T-Notes, 1980–1989

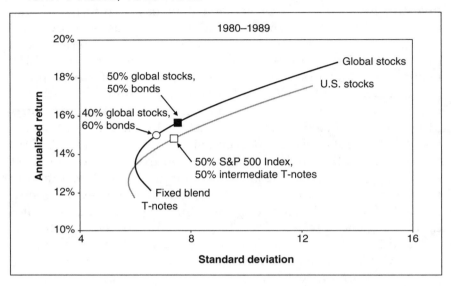

F I G U R E   4-7

Multi-Asset-Class Portfolio versus S&P 500 and Intermediate-
Term T-Notes, 1990–1999

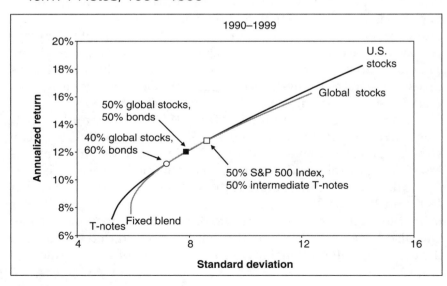

FIGURE 4-8

Multi-Asset-Class Portfolio versus S&P 500 and Intermediate-Term T-Notes, 2000–2009

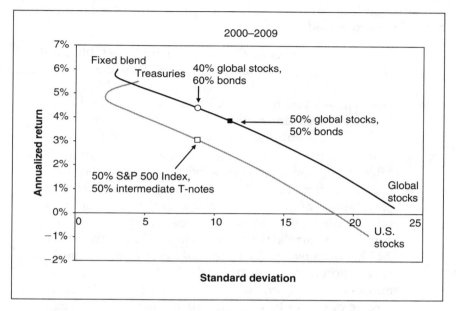

The first decade in the new millennium produced very different investment results from those in the previous decade. The return and risk of multi-asset-class investing was almost exactly the opposite, as illustrated in Figure 4-8. There was a considerable increase in return for investors in international stocks.

Modern portfolio theory reduces the number and size of unpleasant outcomes, but it does not eliminate them. Multi-asset-class investing is an important part of this process. It is important to develop a proper global portfolio that you are comfortable with under all market conditions because you will no doubt experience several disconcerting markets over your lifetime.

CONTINUING THE JOURNEY TO THE NORTHWEST

The quest for a multi-asset-class portfolio is just beginning. We added three new asset classes to U.S. stocks and T-notes: European stocks, Pacific Rim stocks, and U.S. corporate bonds. There are many others that can be added. Part Two of this book establishes parameters for discovering new asset classes that can push the efficient frontier further into the northwest quadrant.

As a prelude to Part Two, here are five points about discovering asset classes to consider:

1. It is nearly impossible to find low-cost investable asset classes that are consistently negatively correlated or even consistently noncorrelated with each other. Most of the asset classes you find and ultimately use will have positive correlation with each other at least some of the time. There is simply no getting around this fact.

2. The correlation between asset classes can and does change often. Investments that were once noncorrelated may become correlated in the future, and vice versa. Past correlations are a hint to future correlations, but not a reliable hint. Don't trust any research report or book that says, "The correlation between asset class 1 and asset class 2 is X," because by the time those words are printed, the correlation may have changed. The future risks, returns, and asset-class correlations cannot be known with any degree of certainty. Consequently, a perfect blend can never be known in advance.

3. During a time of extreme volatility when you want low correlation among asset classes, positive correlation can increase dramatically across all asset classes. Almost every asset class with any meaningful risk went down during the 2007–2009 credit crises. This list included commodities, which were heavily touted by some advisors as a safe haven during bear stock markets. They were wrong. Commodities returns were lower than stock returns in 2008.

4. U.S. and foreign stock markets are particularly vulnerable to higher correlations in bear markets. After the World Trade Center was attacked on September 11, 2001, all stock markets around the world fell by more than 5 percent. No amount of global stock diversification helped a portfolio during that horrific time.

5. A portfolio with more asset classes is better than a portfolio with fewer asset classes, within limitations. Any diversification benefit tends to diminish after about 12 different investments, and the maintenance cost required increases.

Asset allocation requires just as much common sense as it does quantitative number crunching. Accordingly, your study of this strategy should not stop here. There are a number of books, Web sites, and computer programs that can assist you. Roger Gibson's book, *Asset Allocation: Balancing Financial Risk* (McGraw-Hill), is a good start, along with *The Intelligent Asset Allocator* and *The Four Pillars of Investing* by William Bernstein (McGraw-Hill). I do not necessarily agree with all the asset classes selected by these authors, but I do agree with 90 percent of them.

The enemy of a good plan is the quest for a perfect plan because the quest for a perfect plan is an endless journey. The minutiae bog people down. They start to suffer from analysis paralysis, and nothing gets accomplished. Fight the urge to be perfect. Instead, design a good plan, implement that plan, and maintain that plan. You will be much further ahead by doing so.

The best portfolio you can design is one that fits your needs. If you are comfortable with the allocation, you will maintain it over a long period of time and during all market conditions. That is what really counts.

A FINAL WORD ABOUT MULTI-ASSET-CLASS INVESTING

There are several ways to select a multi-asset-class portfolio. One way is to answer a few questions on a questionnaire and feed those answers into a computer. The problem with this approach is that the computer is purely mathematical and relies too much on past risks, returns, and correlations. Basically, the computer simulation assumes that whatever happened in past is the most probable scenario for the future. This is an extremely unreliable way to make investment decisions. The world is constantly changing, and no computer simulation can accurately predict the changes that will occur or how these changes will affect a portfolio.

In addition, a computer does not know who you are and cannot assess your personality profile so that the allocation it recommends truly fits your needs. It does not know how secure your job is, or how healthy you are, or if you have special family needs. It does not know if your children have become financially independent or if your parents are still financially independent and will remain that way. No computer knows if Social Security is going to be around 25 years from now.

A computer model may be mathematically correct based on the very limited facts it is fed, but the answer it produces is not going to work if the allocation does not fit who you are, what your circumstances are, and what you are trying to accomplish. I believe in a more thoughtful, subjective approach to asset allocation.

Each investor has unique needs, experiences, and circumstances. The object is to build a portfolio that offers the potential return needed to reach financial goals while staying within a range of risk so that behavioral tendencies do not get in the way during difficult markets. Mathematical models can assist in considering how a portfolio could be put together, and then common sense needs to take over.

The approach advocated in this book is to consider a two-sided process. We look at both the rational left-side-of-the-brain solution along with the emotional right-side-of-the-brain solution. Information about this dual portfolio management process from the left side and right side can be found in Parts Two and Three.

CHAPTER SUMMARY

Multi-asset-class investing reduces portfolio risk and increases the potential for higher return. Owning several dissimilar asset classes is better than owning a few. Each new asset class reduces overall portfolio risk. By adding several different asset classes and sectors to a portfolio, you can create an efficient set of investments that work together to achieve your financial goals with less risk and higher expected return.

Finding asset classes that have low correlation with each other is a challenge. Correlations between asset classes can change significantly between time periods. Consequently, a methodology should be used to determine if an asset class is suitable for inclusion in your portfolio. That method is covered in Part Two of this book.

The enemy of a good asset allocation is the quest for a perfect one. Fight the urge to be perfect. It is not possible. Instead, design a good multi-asset-class portfolio, implement the plan, and maintain the plan. You will be glad you did.

PART TWO

Asset-Class Selection

A Framework for Investment Selection

KEY CONCEPTS

- All asset classes should have a real expected return over inflation.
- Asset class risks should be fundamentally different from each other.
- Varying rolling correlation levels test for unique risk among asset classes.
- Liquid and low-cost funds should be accessible.

Asset allocation is a simple concept that has several benefits. If you diversify your portfolio across several unlike investments that have real expected returns, you will reduce the risk of a large loss. Rebalance your portfolio back to a target allocation annually to control long-term risk and increase return. The challenge is finding those investments that have different characteristics and expected real returns.

Part Two is a review of most common asset classes that are available to you, and a few that are not so common or not so available. For many asset classes the cost and illiquidity of product negates any diversification benefit.

A FOUR-STEP PROCESS

At its core, an asset allocation strategy involves four steps:

1. Determine your investing portfolio's risk level based on your long-term financial needs and tolerance for risk. This is converted into an equity and fixed-income allocation.
2. Analyze asset classes and select those that are appropriate based on their unique risk, expected return, past correlation with other asset classes, and tax efficiency, if applicable.
3. Choose securities that best represent each asset class selected in Step 2. Low-cost index funds and select ETFs make good choices because they offer broad diversification and closely track asset-class returns.
4. Implement your asset allocation plan completely. Then rebalance your investments occasionally to control portfolio risk and enhance long-term return.

The rest of this book discusses these four steps in detail. Part Two discusses asset class and fund selection in detail. Part Three discusses portfolio management and, in particular, selecting an appropriate level of risk and return and maintaining the investment mix. I realize that this is backwards based on the four-step process. However, for our purposes, it works better to isolate various asset classes first and then discuss how to use them in different asset allocation strategies.

START WITH U.S. STOCKS AND BONDS

Your objective is to build a list of asset classes and investments for inclusion in your portfolio. Most U.S. investors start their asset allocation search with the broad U.S. stock market index and a broad U.S. investment-grade bond index as the cornerstones of an allocation. They then add more from there. This makes sense because U.S. stocks and U.S. bonds have real positive returns over time and varying correlation with each other (see Chapter 3). In addition, U.S. investors pay bills in U.S. dollars. Thus a fairly high percentage of your portfolio should be allocated to dollar-denominated assets rather than assets denominated in foreign currency.

Ideally, investors would like to add other investments that are negatively correlated with U.S. stocks and bonds. Negatively correlated investments would smooth out portfolio volatility caused by the U.S. stock and bond markets. Unfortunately, finding investments with consistent negative correlation with both U.S. stocks and U.S. bonds is a near impossibility. They just do not exist. If you think you have found a negatively correlated asset class, something will change and the correlation will unexpectedly shift to positive, usually at exactly the time when you do not want it to.

A correlation shift occurred with commodity fund investors in 2008. Just at a time when some investors became convinced that commodity funds would cushion their stock portfolio from a bear market, commodity funds became highly correlated with stocks and crashed further than stocks.

Another example was the correlation shift that occurred between the U.S. stock market and foreign stock markets after the September 11, 2001, terrorist attacks. The U.S. stock market closed for a week before opening significantly lower. But that did not stop all other major international markets from falling sharply. The correlations among global stock markets increase during a crisis, usually with every market going down.

Correlations between investments can change sharply and without warning in an unpredictable world. You may think your portfolio is hedged, but it is not. There is no known way to design a portfolio that is fully hedged against market downturns while fully participating in market upturns. There is no free lunch on Wall Street.

You will not find investments that have consistently negative correlation with the U.S. stock and bond markets and are also expected to generate real returns, but there are investments that have varying correlation with U.S. assets and do deliver real returns. These investments should be looked at closely. If you pack in enough varying correlation investments in your portfolio, something will be working in your favor most of the time.

GUIDELINES FOR ASSET SELECTION

The broad asset classes considered in Part Two include U.S. stocks and foreign stocks, U.S. bonds and foreign bonds, real estate, commodities, commodity futures, currencies, and collectibles. Categories within these asset classes include, but are not limited to, European, Pacific Rim, and emerging markets stocks; government bonds, mortgages, and corporate bonds; residential and commercial real estate; commodity funds that follow indexes; and gold, rare coins, and fine art. Some asset-class categories can be further divided into styles such as growth and value stocks, large and small stocks, investment-grade and non-investment-grade bonds, and other categories. We examine all these possibilities.

The purpose of this chapter is to give you a set of guidelines for isolating potential asset classes and the funds that represent them. These guidelines are applied to broad asset classes, their sub-categories, and styles within categories. You should have a list of investments for possible inclusion in a broadly diversified portfolio after reading through Part Two. This is not to say that all these investments will be included in your portfolio or that other investments that are not on the list should be excluded. It is simply a reference point to work from.

Potential asset classes for inclusion in your portfolio should have three important characteristics:

1. The asset class is fundamentally different from other asset classes in a portfolio.
2. Each asset class is expected to earn a return higher than the inflation rate over time.
3. The asset class must be accessible with a low-cost diversified fund or product.

Fundamentally Different

Asset allocation is risk diversification. In order to have risk diversification, each investment in a portfolio must be fundamentally different from other investments. This provides the portfolio with an assortment of unique risk characteristics.

The first criterion for selection is that an investment under consideration be quantifiably different from all other investments. Sometimes the difference between investments is obvious, and sometimes it requires significant analysis. It is easy to isolate fundamental differences between major asset classes. Stocks and bonds are uniquely different. They have different obligations from the issuer, have different income streams, and are even taxed differently.

Owning stocks means that you own a part of a company and are entitled to your fair share of the profits through dividends and share price appreciation. Consequently, equity investors have earnings risk. The value of the company stock falls if there are no earnings. Stock investors are also the last to receive anything in the event of corporate liquidation.

Bond investors lend money to a company or other entity that is obligated to make regular interest payments, plus pay back the loan on time. Interest payments must occur whether the company has profits or not. An issuer's obligation to bondholders is spelled out to investors in an agreement called a bond covenant. The biggest risk a bondholder faces is default risk, which is the risk that an issuer will not meet its financial obligations under the bond covenant. This makes the overall financial health of the issuer important to both stock and bond investors.

Differentiating between some categories is also straightforward within an asset class. A European equity index consists of companies with their headquarters in Europe. This makes it fundamentally different from a U.S. equity index, which consists of companies with their headquarters in the United States. By definition, European stocks and U.S. stocks are *mutually exclusive*. Membership in one index precludes membership in the other. For example, a company that has its worldwide headquarters in Europe cannot have its worldwide headquarters in the United States. It is either a European company or a U.S. company, not both.

Finding unique investments among category styles is more complicated. Styles are segments within categories rather than separate categories. For instance, there is not much fundamental difference between large U.S. stocks and small U.S. stocks. The accounting is the same, the exchange they trade on is the same, and the taxes are the same. Nonetheless, U.S. stocks can be divided so that a large-stock index is mutually exclusive from a small-stock index. Then the two indexes can be annualized to see if they exhibit significantly different risk-and-return characteristics.

An allocation between subcategories may be appropriate when they act differently during different periods in the economic cycle. For example, growth stocks tend to perform well in a recession and early recovery, while value stocks tend to do best well into a recovery and at economic peaks.

Value stock index funds and growth stock index funds tend to be mutually exclusive. There is no security overlap even though the stocks come from the same market. When security overlap occurs, it means that two investments generally hold the same securities and therefore are prone to be highly positively correlated with each other.

In the late 1990s, technology and telecommunications stocks were soaring in value. The best-performing mutual funds at the time were growth funds that were heavily invested in those sectors. Investors reacted to the surge by overweighting their portfolios in growth funds that were doing well. According to the Investment Company Institute (ICI), starting in late 1998, quarterly money flow into growth funds began to outpace the amount flowing into value funds. By the time growth stocks peaked in early 2000, investors were transferring billions of dollars out of value funds and into growth funds. Figure 5-1 illustrates this massive transfer of capital.

Mutual fund companies were quick to deliver new funds that whetted investors' appetites. Figure 5-2 illustrates the large number

FIGURE 5-1

Quarterly Money Flow into Growth Funds and Value Funds

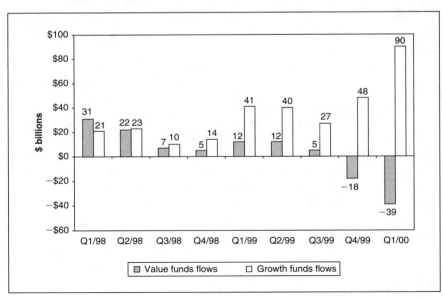

of new growth funds that opened during the late 1990s compared to the small number of conservative value funds that opened at the same time. When growth stocks fell sharply after 2000, portfolios that held several overlapping growth funds were devastated. Diversification does not simply mean owning several mutual funds with different names. The underlying assets in those funds need to be examined and compared using Morningstar style boxes or some other method discussed in the following chapters.

Some securities overlap can exist among mutual funds in your portfolio as long as you know it exists. For example, the S&P 500 is composed of predominantly large-company stocks, although there are also several midcap stocks and a few small stocks in the index. There would be some overlap of stocks if a person were to invest in both an S&P 500 Index fund and a small-cap index fund. For all practical considerations, the effect of a small-cap stocks on the return of the S&P 500 Index is negligible. As a result, you can add a small-cap index fund to an S&P 500 Index fund and obtain broader diversification without adding measurable securities overlap to the portfolio.

FIGURE 5-2

Number of New Growth and Value Funds, 1997–2000

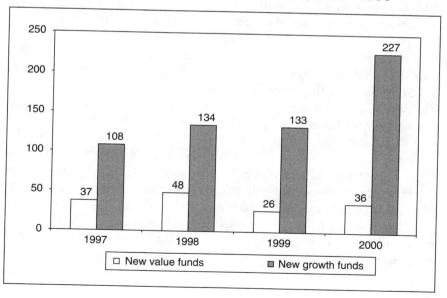

The Asset Class Has a Real Expected Return

Each asset class to be held in a portfolio for the long term should be expected to earn a return greater than the inflation rate. All investments have an inflation expectation built into the price. Bonds pay interest based on the expected inflation rate until maturity, plus a fair risk premium over inflation based on the riskiness of the bond. Stock prices have an inflation expectation built in and also grow above inflation as real earnings growth occurs and dividends are paid by the companies.

Securities that only keep pace with inflation are not suitable for a long-term investment. Buying these investments would mean diverting funds from investments that pay interest and dividends that provide real growth potential for an investment that pays no income or dividends and that has no growth potential beyond inflation. These assets may be fine for traders who wish to speculate on their near-term price movements, but this book is not about short-term price speculation. It is about allocating capital into investments that have the potential for real long-term gains.

Commodities and precious metals are good examples of asset classes that historically have no real return. These asset classes are often touted as having occasional negative correlation with stocks and bonds which consequently lowers portfolio risk as times. However, there is no real return benefit from the money allocated to these investments over the long term.

Investors often read the high price volatility of commodities as a sign that this asset class should deliver real long-term returns in harmony with the price risk. This is incorrect. The price volatility alone does not generate investment returns. It is cash-flow factor that produces returns. It is the earnings growth from corporate stock that leads to cash dividends, interest income from bonds, rents from real estate, and the known scarcity value of collectibles such as rare coins. These are the things that create a real return. A barrel of oil does not swell into two barrels of oil, and an ounce of gold does not multiply into two ounces of gold. No commodity pays one penny in interest or dividends. Although the prices of commodities go up and down like a roller coaster, commodities have no ability to create real wealth for a long-term investor.

The Asset Class Has Low Correlation or Varying Correlation

After finding assets that pass the fundamental analysis test and the real return test, a third criterion for including an asset-class category in your potential list of investments is low correlation or varying correlation. Unique risk can be verified using a rolling correlation analysis. It is a visual illustration that shows how much the unique risk one asset classes has in relation to another over different periods.

Ideally, you are looking for investments that have consistent negative correlation. However you will quickly find with rolling correlation analysis that those investments do not exist. The next best option is to find investments that have a low correlation most of the time or a negative correlation some of the time.

As you may recall from Chapter 3, correlation is measured using a numerical range between +1 and −1. When two investments move higher or lower than their average returns at the same time, they have *positive* correlation. When two investments move in opposite directions from their averages, they have a *negative* correlation. Two investments are considered noncorrelated or have 0 correlation when they do not move in any particular uniformity around their averages.

Correlations shift over time in unpredictable ways. The extent of the shift tends to depend on how different the underlying risks are in two investments types. Investments that are positively correlated in one period can become noncorrelated or negatively correlated in the next. Consequently, any single period correlation measurement between two investments is of limited use.

Unfortunately, most college finance books cite only a long-term average correlation number to explain the relationship between two asset classes. A simple long-term average is rather useless because it give readers the false impression that the correlation does not change. To make matters worse, the single correlation number is often used by financial advisors and fed into computer models to create "optimal" asset allocation for clients. This approach may tell advisors how their clients *should* have allocated their assets in the past, but it tells you nothing about the optimal allocation for the future because the correlations have already changed.

In this book, "rolling" correlations are used as a reference for study rather than a static long-term number. Rolling correlations allow you to see how often correlations between asset classes shift and by how much. You'll get a general idea of the times when an investment helps a portfolio allocation because it had low or negative correlation, and the times it was of less help because the correlations were high.

Figure 5-3 illustrates the changes in correlation between U.S. stocks and bonds that has occurred over rolling five-year periods. It's a fine example of how unpredictable the correlations between two asset classes can be.

U.S. stocks and Treasury notes were negatively correlated during most of the 1950s. The correlation shifted over the next 40 years from negative to noncorrelated to positive. The peak positive correlation occurred in the mid–1990s. Then correlation shifted to negative again in the late 1990s, hitting high negative correlation by 2004 and again in 2008.

FIGURE 5-3

S&P 500 and Intermediate-Term Treasury Note Three-Year Rolling Correlations

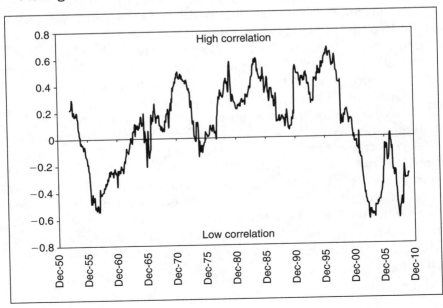

U.S. stocks and T-notes have provided good diversification in a portfolio over most periods despite the varying correlation. It is not necessary for two investments to have consistent negative correlation, or consistent noncorrelation, or even consistent low correlation for them to be useful in asset allocation. An investment will help reduce long-term portfolio risk and increase long-term return as long as it does not have consistently high positive correlation with another investment already in your portfolio.

The Asset Class Has Low-Cost Availability

An asset class that is being considered for inclusion on your investment list must be "investable." This means that there are low-cost marketable securities available that represent an asset class. Look for mutual funds that have low expense ratios and no redemption fees. An asset allocation strategy requires occasional rebalancing, and redemption fees would increase the cost to rebalance. I prefer index mutual funds and ETFs because they are low-fee and they track the indexes used to create the asset allocation. No-load actively managed mutual funds and inexpensive unit investment trusts (UITs) are acceptable substitutes in the absence of funds that track indexes.

The investment vehicle selected to represent an asset class or category in a portfolio should also provide enough diversification *within* the fund. Broad diversification within a fund ensures that the correlation between the investment vehicle and the asset-class category you studied is very high. For example, the correlation among most index funds that track a broad market of U.S. stocks is over +0.99. Accordingly, there are several index funds that are well suited to represent the total U.S. stock category.

Some asset-class categories are available only in expensive packaged products that are not well suited to individuals. These investments generally take the form of a limited partnership (LP). LPs typically have very high fees, illiquidity, tax inefficiency, loose regulation, and secretive holdings, and they are oversold by Wall Street brokers who say you are a very special investor. Stay away from tying up your money in high-cost illiquid investments unless you really know what you are doing. These products include hedge funds, private equity funds, venture capital funds, and fund-of-fund products. See Chapter 10 for more information on "Alternative Investments."

There are also asset-class categories that have no means of investment. For example, most people reading this book will not be trading museum-quality oil paintings by old masters. Consequently, it does not matter how they have performed except as a point of curiosity. Your time is better spent investigating asset classes that are investable.

THE GLOBAL FINANCIAL MARKETS

Asset allocation works best when the investments in a portfolio are fundamentally different from one another, have real expected rates of return, and have low or varying correlation with one another. As illustrated in Figure 5-4, the world is a very big place. There are many different asset classes, categories, and styles to consider. The United States still holds a preeminent place in the global capital markets, with about 45 percent of the world's tradable securities. The U.S. percentage is getting smaller every year.

FIGURE 5-4

Total Investable Assets in the Global Capital Markets, $50 Trillion as of 2009

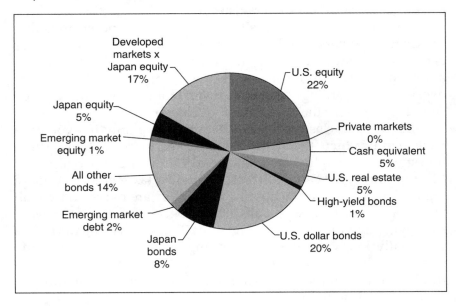

Emerging countries are becoming an increasingly important source of new securities. These include securities from China, India, Brazil, and Eastern European countries.

Several mutual fund companies have low-cost index funds and ETFs that cater to investors seeking global diversification at a low cost. Each year these providers create more investable securities covering asset classes and categories with the fundamental characteristics we are looking for. I am always on the lookout for new funds that provide access to new and unique risks in low-cost mutual fund and ETF products. There are not many offered with liquidity, diversification, and low cost. But once in a while something comes up.

The remaining five chapters in Part Two analyze the asset classes and categories highlighted in Figure 5-4, plus several others. Here is a summary of the asset classes, categories, and styles that are covered:

Chapter 6: U.S. Equity Investments
    Total U.S. stock market construction
    Size analysis (large and small)
    Style analysis (growth and value)

Chapter 7: International Equity Investments
    Developed markets
    Emerging markets
    Size and style indexes

Chapter 8: Fixed-Income Investments
    U.S. investment-grade fixed income
    U.S. non-investment-grade fixed income
    International fixed income

Chapter 9: Real Estate Investments
    Home ownership as an investment
    Rental property as an investment
    Real estate investment trusts (REITs)

Chapter 10: Alternative Investments
    Collectibles as investments
    Commodities and commodity exchange-traded funds (ETFs)
    Hedge funds, venture capital funds, and ETFs that follow
        these strategies

A list of potential mutual funds and ETFs is provided at the end of each chapter. Each of those investments represents the asset classes and categories discussed in that chapter. These funds are provided for information only and should be considered after further analysis, including reading the prospectus.

Which investments from the following chapters will actually make it into your portfolio is difficult to say. That is a function of many factors, including your time horizon, income need, risk tolerance, tax situation, and a variety of other factors. These considerations and others are discussed in Part Three of this book.

CHAPTER SUMMARY

At its core, asset allocation is a strategy of risk diversification. Different asset classes and categories have different risks that are not related to one another. Holding fundamentally different investments in a portfolio, each with an expected real return over inflation, reduces overall portfolio risk and increases return in the long run.

Finding investments with unique risk-and-return characteristics is a challenge. Different fundamentals mean that the asset classes represent mutually exclusive markets or different types of securities within markets that have distinguishable characteristics. The best diversifiers have different fundamental characteristics and have low or varying correlation with other investments.

A list of potential investments from each asset class is included at the end of the chapter covering that asset class. Those lists are designed to be a guide. Each investor is unique, and this means that each portfolio will be different.

U.S. Equity Investments

KEY CONCEPTS

- U.S. stocks have produced about 6 percent in real compounded returns.
- The U.S. stock market can be subdivided into many different categories.
- Diversifying among these categories can aid a portfolio over time.
- Mixing a broad index fund with small-cap value has produced the best results.

U.S. equities are a core position in almost every growth investor's portfolio. Approximately 150 million Americans own U.S. equities directly or indirectly through stock purchase, mutual funds, ETFs, variable annuities, employer retirement accounts, and other avenues.

This chapter focuses on the broad U.S. equity market and subsectors of the market. The index providers typically start with a large universe of U.S. equities as the base for their index products, and then they divide the universe into different categories based on company size (large, midcap, and small cap), valuation (growth or value), and industry groupings.

Interestingly, not all subsets of U.S. equities are highly correlated with one another. It is common for some categories of the U.S.

market to be performing well, while others are performing poorly. Thus, at times it is possible to gain a diversification advantage by overweighting a few of these categories. This chapter considers a few of those sectors.

A HISTORY OF U.S. EQUITY RETURNS

U.S. equities have delivered exceptionally good returns over the long term, and particularly over the last 60 years. As America prospered, established companies grew, and new companies and industries were established. U.S. corporations have enjoyed fairly steady earnings growth over the past century despite wars, recessions, and many bank failures. The earnings growth has lead to reliable dividend payments, an increase in market value, and real personal wealth creation for shareholders.

The broad U.S. market returned 10.9 percent annually from 1950 to 2009. That handily beat the 6.1 percent return on five-year Treasury notes and the 3.8 percent level of inflation. Table 6-1 shows the inflation-adjusted returns over different periods of time. Inflation-adjusted returns are also known as *real* returns because that is the amount of purchasing power investors gained or lost. The real return does not include taxes.

Real returns reinforce the fact that inflation is an invisible tax on all investments. The portion of return that is related to inflation cannot be counted as investment gain. When creating an asset allocation for your portfolio, you should always consider the expected real return of the investments you are considering.

TABLE 6-1

Inflation-Adjusted U.S. Stock and Bond Returns

	1950–2009	1968–1982	2000–2009	Historic Range over Inflation
U.S. stocks	7.2%	0.2%	−2.9%	5% to 7%
Five-year T-note	2.2%	0.3%	3.0%	1% to 2%

Source: Center for Research in Security Prices (CRSP); St. Louis Federal Reserve

It is not always easy to earn a real return in the U.S. stock market. There have been several periods of time between 1950 and 2009 when U.S. equities did not perform well. For 15 years, from 1968 to 1982, the inflation-adjusted return of U.S. equities was barely above the rate of inflation. From 2000 to 2009, U.S. stocks lost 2.9 percent annually with an adjustment for inflation. This was the worst performance for a real return since the 1930s Depression.

Stock investors should expect periods of time when equities do not make money after inflation. It is the nature of investment risk. This is also why time in the market is critical to stock investors. In the long run, equities have outpaced inflation by a wide margin, and they are expected to remain one of the best real return investments in the future. You have to stay invested during all market conditions to benefit from the gains.

U.S. EQUITY MARKET STRUCTURE

An initial public offering (IPO) occurs when a company sells stock to the public for the very first time. The new shares are distributed through a tightly controlled *primary* market. Investment bankers are hired to bring the company public, and part of that process is to promote the company to large institutional investors. Individual investors, like you and me, have very little chance to get in on the IPO market unless we have a special relationship with an investment banker or the large institutions are not interested in buying. This is not the fairest system for distributing IPO shares, but it is the way Wall Street works, and despite the envy we often hear from small investors who are often left out, it does work.

The newly issued company stock begins trading immediately on the *secondary* market. Here is where most stock transactions are done. Which stock exchange carries a new company depends on the company's board of directors as well as the financial history and the value of the company. Currently, over 26,000 U.S. company stocks have been issued in the United States; however, less than 20 percent meet the criteria to trade on a major exchange. Companies must meet certain size, price, and liquidity requirements to be eligible to trade on the New York Stock Exchange (NYSE) and the National Association of Securities Dealers Automatic Quote System (Nasdaq).

Companies that do not qualify for listing on an exchange are known as bulletin-board stocks. These small and often illiquid securities are traded in dealer-only market such as the OTC Bulletin Board and Pink Quotes.

The OTC Bulletin Board, or OTCBB, is an electronic quote system in the United States that displays real-time quotes, last-sale prices, and volume information for many over-the-counter (OTC) equity securities that are not listed on the Nasdaq stock exchange or a national securities exchange. All OTCBB securities must be reporting to the Securities and Exchange Commission (SEC) and current in their reporting obligations. The Financial Industry Regulatory Authority (FINRA) oversees the OTCBB although it is not part of the Nasdaq stock exchange.

Pick Quote is an electronic quotation system operated by Pink OTC Markets. In addition to OTCBB stocks, it covers inactive stocks, gray market stocks that rarely trade, penny stocks, and those with a narrow geographic interest. Many Pink Quote–only companies are not able or willing to provide financial information and required SEC disclosure documents. Years ago, securities dealers who were members of the National Quotation Bureau (NQB) would publish weekly bid and ask prices for these stocks on long sheets of pink paper, thus the name Pink Sheets. The list would be distributed to all brokerage firms.

Table 6-2 is a breakdown of where stocks trade in the United States. The table includes only individual U.S. common equities. It does not include listed bonds, preferred stocks, exchange-traded mutual funds, or foreign stocks listed on U.S. exchanges.

TABLE 6-2

Approximate Number of U.S. Companies on Each Exchange

Stocks Sorted by Exchange	Number of Companies	Percent of Total Market Value
NYSE (U.S. equities)	1,600+	80%
Nasdaq (U.S. equities)	3,400+	19%
Bulletin-board stocks	22,000+	<1%

Source: NYSE EuroNext, Nasdaq

THE BROAD STOCK MARKET

Wilshire Associates is a privately owned investment firm with headquarters in Santa Monica, California. Since its founding in 1972, the company has developed a wide variety of U.S. indexes, one of which is the Wilshire 5000 Composite Index. The Wilshire 5000, as it is commonly known, was the first U.S. equity index to capture the return of the entire market of U.S. stocks that trade on the NYSE and Nasdaq (the American Stock Exchange merged with the NYSE in 2008). Bulletin board stocks are not included in Wilshire indexes.

When originally introduced in 1974, the Wilshire 5000 Index held 5,000 stocks, thus the name. Today, the number of stocks in the index varies, depending on the number of stocks trading on the major U.S. stock markets. At times it is over 5,000, and at times less.

The major criteria for inclusion in the Wilshire 5000 Composite Index are as follows:

- Any U.S. equity issue: a common stock, real estate investment trust (see Chapter 9), or limited partnership. Nondomiciled U.S. stocks and American Depositary Receipts (ADR is a negotiable foreign certificate issued by a U.S. bank) are excluded.
- The security must trade in the United States on the NYSE or Nasdaq.
- The security must be the primary equity issue for the company.
- Bulletin-board issues are excluded.

The Wilshire 5000 Composite is the most complete broad market index. There are several others, including the Dow Jones Total Market Index, holding 4,200 stocks; the MSCI U.S. Broad Market Index, holding about 3,800 stocks; and the Russell 3000, holding 3,000 stocks. In addition, there are several broad market indexes that exclude microcap stocks. They are the Dow Jones U.S. Broad Stock Market Index, with approximately 2,400 companies; Morningstar Total Market, with about 1,600 stocks; and Standard & Poor's 1500 (a hand-selected index), which holds 1,500 companies.

Several low-cost index funds and ETFs are available that track the returns of these broad market indexes. A partial list of those funds is available at the end of this chapter.

SIZE AND STYLE OPPORTUNITIES

An investment in a total U.S. stock market fund is a solid foundation on which to base a stock allocation. From there, you can analyze various sectors of the U.S. stock market to possibly find an opportunity to add greater diversification through selectively overweighting one or more sectors. Investors should have a system for segmenting the market so that the sectors do not overlap.

All index providers classify the companies in their broad market indexes by style and size, and all providers have their own methodology. Most providers have three size categories: large, mid, and small; and at least two style categories: growth and value. A few have a third style category called core, neutral, or blend.

MORNINGSTAR CLASSIFICATION METHODS

There are several different classification methods published by index providers, and each has its own way of slicing the pie. Morningstar, Inc., in Chicago is a widely respected mutual fund and stock research company. The company has developed a comprehensive strategy for categorizing stocks that includes 97 percent of the U.S. equity market. The system is called the Morningstar Style Box. The nine-box grid divides stocks into three distinct size factors and three valuation factors. See Figure 6-1 for an illustration of the style box methodology. For a complete description of Morningstar's methodology, refer to the classification rulebook at www.Morningstar.com.

One limitation of Morningstar Style Box methodology is that it covers only about 1,600 stocks, thus overlooking more than 3,400 microcap issues that trade on U.S. exchanges. Accordingly, I took the liberty of adding an extra microcap stock portion to the bottom of the Morningstar Style Box in Figure 6-1 to illustrate 99 percent of the entire U.S. equity market, excluding only bulletin-board stocks.

FIGURE 6-1

FIGURE 6-1

Morningstar Style Box Methodology with Microcap Added

	Value	Blend	Growth
Large	LV	LB	LG
Mid	MV	MB	MG
Small	SV	SB	SG
Micro	Ultra small		

Morningstar Size Factor

The Morningstar size classification system categorizes companies according to their "free-float" market value. The free-float market value is defined as a company's total outstanding market value less private block ownership. In other words, the free-float market value of Microsoft stock does not include the value of the shares owned by Bill Gates. Free float is a common method of index construction that is widely becoming the standard for index providers.

The three Morningstar size classifications plus an extra micro-cap size cover 99 percent of the stock on the U.S. market. The four categories are:

- Large cap = largest 70 percent of investable market cap
- Midcap = next 20 percent of investable market cap (70th to 90th percentile)
- Small cap = next 7 percent of investable market cap (90th to 97th percentile)
- Microcap = remaining 2 percent of investable market cap (97th to 99th percentile)

Morningstar Style Factor

Morningstar divides its listings into three style categories depending on fundamental characteristics. These categories are value, blend, and growth. Morningstar categorizes companies using

TABLE 6-3

Variables and Weights Used by Morningstar in Style Analysis

Value Factors	Growth Factors
Price/projected earnings (50.0%)	Long-term projected earnings growth (50.0%)
Price/book (12.5%)	Historical earnings growth (12.5%)
Price/sales (12.5%)	Sales growth (12.5%)
Price/cash flow (12.5%)	Cash-flow growth (12.5%)
Dividend yield (12.5%)	Book value growth (12.5%)

a "multifactor" model that consists of five variables. Table 6-3 highlights those five factors. The most influential factors in the equation are the stock's price compared to its past earnings and price compared to projected earnings.

Morningstar first calculates a company's value score, then its growth score, and finally its overall style score by subtracting the value score from the growth score. If the result is strongly positive, the company is classified as "growth." If the result is strongly negative, the company is classified as "value." If the value score minus the growth score is not sufficiently different from 0, the stock is classified as "blend."

Breakpoints for value, growth, and blend are set so that over a three-year rolling period, each style represents one-third of the investable universe within each capitalization class. That keeps a nearly equal number of stocks in each style box. Morningstar reconstitutes each index twice annually (adding or removing stocks). It also rebalances the indexes quarterly (adjusting constituent weights).

The 5,000+ in the Wilshire Composite Index falls roughly into the boxes illustrated in Figure 6-2 based on Morningstar methodology. Each box contains the number of stocks in that particular box.

As of January 2010, the large-cap row holds 241 stocks, which represents only 5 percent of the Wilshire 5000 companies yet represents 70 percent of the free-float market value of the entire U.S. stock market. There were 578 midcap stocks that made up another 20 percent, and 784 small-cap stocks that accounted for 7 percent. The other 3,400+ microcap stocks are the remaining 3 percent.

FIGURE 6-2

Number of Stocks in the Morningstar Style Boxes

	Value	Blend	Growth
Large	74	78	89
Mid	184	214	180
Small	250	279	255
Micro	3,400+		

Source: Morningstar, December 31, 2009

ANALYZING FACTOR PERFORMANCE

Factors are broad portfolio characteristics that make one portfolio different from another. Two major factors that drive a portfolio's risk and return are its size factor and style factor. The size factor compares the average weighted market value of the stocks in one portfolio to the average weighted market value of stocks in another portfolio or an index. The style factor compares the weighting of value or growth stocks in one portfolio to another portfolio or an index.

Performance by Size

The weighted-average market value of the stocks in an index has a profound effect on that index's long-term performance. In the late 1970s, two academic researchers, Rolf Banz and Marc Reinganum, independently found that microcap stocks had a long-term return close to 5 percent per year higher than large-cap stocks.[1] This made sense because the stocks of tiny, less liquid companies had higher price volatility than larger company stocks and thus should be expected to generate a higher return over time.

Interestingly, using new financial models of risk and return developed by William Sharpe, researchers Banz and Reinganum found that microcap stocks had higher-than-expected returns even after accounting for the extra volatility. Something else was going on in the microcap marketplace that was not being picked up by the return volatility numbers. The extra return is likely payment for liquidity risk. Investors in microcaps should earn more because of the low volume of shares that trade. The price would often drop when an investor tried to sell any meaningful number of shares.

It was also interesting to Banz and Reinganum that sometimes the prices of microcap stocks moved in the opposite direction from large-cap stocks. That meant that the return on microcap stocks did not always correlate with the returns on the rest of the market. Accordingly, there may be a diversification benefit to owning microcap stocks in greater weight than the tiny position they hold in a total stock market index fund.

Table 6-4 offers excellent insight into the difference in return between the total stocks market and microcap stocks. The microcap index in Table 6-4 is derived by the Center for Research in Security Prices (CRSP). The CRSP Stock File indexes contain historical market

TABLE 6-4

Comparing Microcap Stocks to the Broad Market

Year	CRSP Total U.S. Stock Market	CRSP Microcap Index	CRSP Microcap Return Minus the Total Market
1995	36.8	33.3	−3.5
1996	21.8	19.1	−2.7
1997	31.8	24.1	−7.7
1998	24.1	−7.9	−32.0
1999	20.9	32.2	11.3
2000	−7.5	−13.4	−5.9
2001	−11.5	34.2	45.7
2002	−21.6	−14.1	7.5
2003	31.6	78.4	46.8
2004	12.5	16.8	4.3
2005	6.2	3.7	−2.5
2006	15.5	18.1	2.6
2007	5.8	−7.9	−13.8
2008	−36.7	−41.5	−4.8
2009	28.8	61.1	32.3

Sources: CRSP

summary data for all stocks traded on the NYSE and Nasdaq back to 1926.

Notice the large differences in return between the CRSP Microcap Index and the CRSP total U.S. market over several years. Those differences are surprising considering that both indexes hold thousands of publicly traded U.S. companies. Generally, academics believe that individual company risk is diversified away in a broadly diversified stock portfolio, leaving only market risk. For example, a randomly selected portfolio of 1,000 stocks diversified across several industries is expected to return almost the same performance as another portfolio of 1,000 stocks diversified in the same manner. This is not the case when a portfolio is made up of only microcap stocks. It acts differently from any random portfolio. Microcap indexes have a unique risk factor that cannot be diversified away by adding more microcap stocks.

Figure 6-3 reflects the 36-month rolling correlation between the CRSP total U.S. market, CRSP midcap stocks, and CRSP microcap

FIGURE 6-3

Total U.S. Market Index Correlations with the Microcap Index and Midcap Index 36-Month Rolling Correlations

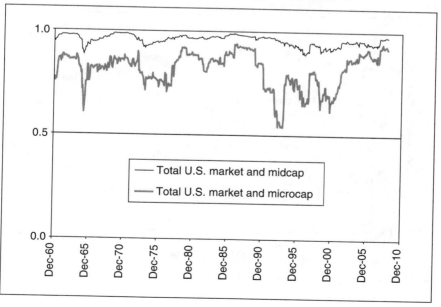

stocks. The CRSP Midcap Index is highly positively correlated with the broad market almost all the time. Consequently, a separate portfolio of midcap stocks is not an ideal diversifier for investors who own a total stock market index fund. Tiny microcap stocks offer better diversification because at times there has been low correlation between microcap stocks and the total stock market. The varying correlation from high to low signals diversification potential from the niche area of microcap stocks.

A portfolio that has an overweighting in microcap stocks acts differently from a total stock market portfolio. Figure 6-4 illustrates the theoretical diversification benefit that was achieved by adding 10 percent increments of CRSP microcap stocks to a total stock market index.

Had it been possible, over the 30-year period from 1980 to 2009, a portfolio of 80 percent in a total stock market index fund and 20 percent in a microcap index fund would have increased U.S.

FIGURE 6-4

Return Characteristics of Adding Microcap Stocks to a Total Market Fund, 1975–2009

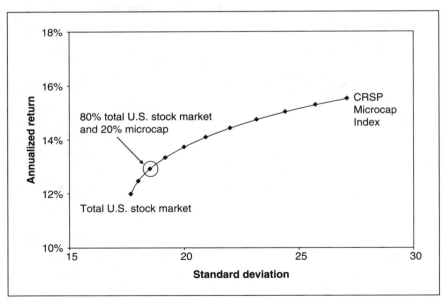

returns by 0.8 percent with a small increase in risk. However, the returns shown in Figure 6-4 are theoretical because there was no microcap index available in 1980. That's not the case today. You can now purchase a low-cost no-load total stock market index fund and a microcap index fund, although I admit that there are very slim selections in the microcap fund category.

The more than 3,500 microcap stocks that trade actively on U.S. exchanges count for only 3 percent of the value of the entire listed stock market. That is much less than the market capitalization of Microsoft or Exxon Mobil. Accordingly, the performance of any single microcap company on total market performance is about zero, and the performance of the entire microcap market on the performance of the overall U.S. market is close to zero. Overweighting microcap stocks in a portfolio as a separate U.S. stock category has had diversification benefits in the past and may add diversification benefits in the future.

Now the bad news: It is very difficult to find a true, low-cost, broadly diversified microcap fund. In fact, there really aren't any. This is a very difficult market to index. There are a few funds that have "microcap" in their title, but they are microcap-only funds. They invest in small-cap and midcap stocks.

Some actively managed microcap funds may be worth considering, but many are linked to a high sales commission or an exorbitant management fee. Still others are closed to new investors. Sometimes a closed fund will reopen for a short period of time, and you will need to have cash ready to invest when it does. This means monitoring certain funds for potential opening dates.

Make sure that the weighted market weight of the companies in which you have chosen microcap funds is no higher than $200 million and that the fund is widely diversified in at least 300 companies. Also ensure that the total expense is below 1 percent and that there is no commission for buying or selling shares. Good luck!

Performance by Style

The practice of categorizing stocks into style categories is as old as stock trading itself. Years ago, investors mainly used dividend yield to categorize growth and value stocks. Stocks paying high dividends were considered value plays, while stocks paying low dividends were growth plays. As more financial information became available, in part as a result of mandatory SEC reporting, investors became more sophisticated. Researchers created and compared ratios such as price/earnings ratios (P/E ratios) and the P/E to earnings growth. In addition, a company's market price/book value became a leading dividing line. It was widely believed that earnings and book value ratios gave clues to finding profitable investment opportunities. Stocks with low price/earnings and price/book ratios were considered better values than stocks with high ratios. In 1934, Benjamin Graham and David Dodd wrote guidelines that quantified these ratios in their timeless investment book *Security Analysis.* The book is still one of the most widely distributed investment classics of all time.[2]

Not much has changed since Benjamin Graham and David Dodd wrote the book on fundamental investing over 75 years ago. Today, investors still analyze the same fundamental factors and price ratios, and they still look for value using earnings and book value. Granted, there have been some changes in the way people analyze the data and the amount of information available to the public. However, the speed and accuracy of computers has made the analysis hundreds of times faster, even after an increase in the amount of data.

As security valuation progressed over the years, analysts and academic researchers began to agree on standard labels for categories of stocks based on styles. Companies that had a high market price relative to their fundamentals and outlook were labeled "growth" companies. Those with low market price relative to their fundamentals and outlook were labeled "value" companies. Some index providers use a third category for neutral stocks whose valuations fell between growth and value.

As style categorization became popular and computers made number crunching faster, it was natural for researchers to go back in history and reconstruct indexes based on style methodology. In the 1970s, researchers were able to compare historic style returns going back to the early 1900s with a high degree of accuracy. What this historic data showed was that value stocks outperformed growth stocks by several percentage points over the long term, and outperformed during most independent 10-year periods.

In addition, researchers have found that the value premium exists in foreign markets as well, suggesting that the same factors that drive U.S. value stock returns drive value stock returns in all countries. That observation begged the question, "Will the opportunities for returns be higher in global value stocks than in global growth stocks in the future?" There is great debate over this subject.

Growth advocates pounced on the relevance of the value premium. Some people called the value effect an anomaly that is not likely to occur in the future. Others questioned the accuracy of the studies. Still others said that the data is accurate in theory, but that when the theory is applied to real portfolios, trading costs and liquidity constraints erode away any value premium in the marketplace.

In June 1992, Eugene Fama and Ken French fired another volley in defense of the value effect when they published the most comprehensive paper on the subject in the *Journal of Financial Economics*. The paper was titled, "The Cross-Section of Expected Stock Returns."[3]

Fama and French (FF) put forth the notion that the performance of a broadly diversified U.S. stock portfolio relied on three primary risk axes to determine its return. Those three risk factors were the basic risk of the market itself (market risk or beta), the percentage of small-cap stocks in the portfolio by market weight (size), and the percentage of value orientation by market weight (the latter defined by the price/book ratio—BtM).

When FF measured how much exposure a widely diversified portfolio had to the three risk factors of beta, size, and BtM, they could determine with 95 percent accuracy how that portfolio performed in relation to the stock market *without knowing the actual return of the portfolio.* That meant that 95 percent of a portfolio's return is the result of the amount of risk taken in the three factors and that very little of a portfolio's return is the result of stock selection within the portfolio. The results were a blow to active portfolio managers who until this time had the public believing that it was their stock-picking prowess that had generated most of portfolios' investment return.

Here is an abbreviated explanation of the three FF factors that explain 95 percent of the return of a diversified U.S. stock portfolio:

1. *Market risk factor.* Commonly referred to as beta (β). All diversified stock portfolios move up or down to some extent with the overall total stock market. Beta is a measurement of the movement of a particular portfolio that is a result of movement in the broad market. On average, about 70 percent of the return of a broadly diversified portfolio is explained by β, making that factor the most influential in explaining portfolio returns.

2. *Size risk factor.* FF confirmed earlier studies' findings that small stocks have higher returns than the broad market and do not always move in correlation with the broad market. The size factor cannot be diversified away by adding more small stocks; therefore, they are their own unique risk factor. The greater the percentage of small stocks by market weight in a portfolio, the greater the size factor effects on a portfolio.

3. *Value risk factor.* FF quantified earlier studies showing that value stocks have had higher returns than the broad market and that value stocks do not always correlate with growth stocks. Like the size risk, the value factor cannot be diversified away by adding more value stocks; hence, value has its own unique risk factor.

FF has since created a set of indexes that measure size and style factors using their methodology. These indexes are available as a free download on Kenneth French's Web site at Dartmouth College.[4]

THE VALUE FACTOR CONTINUED

Tables 6-5 through 6-7 are comparisons of style returns using three index providers. FF provides the first set of returns, Frank Russell and Company provides the second, and Dimensional Fund Advisors (DFA) provides the third. The FF and DFA indexes go back to 1926, whereas the Russell indexes originate in 1979. The comparison given here uses 30 years of data from the inception of the Russell indexes.

TABLE 6-5

Comparing Large-Cap Funds, 1979–2009

	FF Large Growth	FF Large Index	FF Large Value	Russell 1000 Growth	Russell 1000	Russell 1000 Value
Annualized return	11.3	11.5	13.0	10.5	11.5	12.1
Standard deviation	16.6	15.6	16.1	17.8	15.6	14.9

Before discussing the results of the study, an explanation of the methodology is needed. There are large differences in stock selection methods in the FF/DFA value indexes and the Russell value indexes.

First, FF and DFA use only one fundamental ratio to separate growth from value. Specifically, FF use book-to-market as a proxy. Russell uses a multifactor model to separate growth and value. Second, the FF/DFA style indexes are mutually exclusive, meaning that if a stock is in one style, it is not in the other. Russell uses a graduated scale to make the transition from growth to value. If a stock in the Russell index has both value and growth characteristics, its market value could be divided into both segments. For example, a stock could have 60 percent of its market value attributed to growth and 40 percent to value. Third, FF neutral indexes are mutually exclusive from their value and growth indexes, whereas the Russell indexes do not have a neutral or core category.

Table 6-5 compares the difference in risk and returns between large growth stocks, large value stocks, and large core holdings of both the FF large-cap indexes and the Russell large-cap indexes.

Although there are large differences in the style methodology of the two index providers, over the past 30 years the outcomes are similar using both the FF large-cap style indexes and the Russell 1000 large-cap style indexes. When both methodologies were used, the performance of large-cap value stocks was found to be higher than the performance of growth stocks, and the risk as measured by standard deviation was less for value stocks than it was for growth stocks.

Table 6-6 is a similar comparison of the FF small-cap style indexes and Russell 2000 small-cap style indexes. The data reveal a significant difference between small-cap value and small-cap growth returns.

TABLE 6-6

Comparing Small-Cap Funds, 1979–2009

	FF Small Growth	FF Small	FF Small Value	Russell 2000 Growth	Russell 2000	Russell 2000 Value
Annualized return	7.9	12.8	17.2	8.8	11.3	13.3
Standard deviation	24.1	20.3	18.2	23.5	19.9	17.4

The excess return of small-cap value stocks over small-cap growth stocks was greater for each index over the 30-year period. In addition, the risk of small-cap value stocks as measured by their standard deviation was considerably less than that of small-cap growth stocks. The implication of the data is that the value premium is stronger in the small-cap sector of the market than in the large-cap sector.

Table 6-7 compares the value premium across the total stock market as measured by the Russell 3000 indexes and the DFA indexes, which are similar to FF indexes. The Russell 3000 is an index of the 3,000 largest U.S. stocks, adjusted for free float. It is divided into the Russell 3000 Growth Index and the Russell 3000 Value Index using Russell methodology. The DFA Marketwide indexes are composed of all stocks on the Nasdaq and NYSE weighted by market capitalization.

Figure 6-5 illustrates the rolling 36-month correlation between the Wilshire 5000 Composite and the DFA Marketwide Value Index

TABLE 6-7

Comparing Total Market Indexes, 1979–2009

	DFA Marketwide	DFA Marketwide Value	Russell 3000	Russell 3000 Value
Annualized return	11.7	14.0	11.4	12.2
Standard deviation	15.7	16.8	15.8	14.9

FIGURE 6-5

Total U.S. Market Index and DFA Marketwide Value 36-Month Rolling Correlations

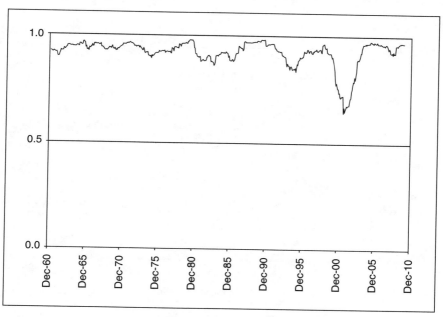

described earlier. Notice the sharp decrease in correlation between value stocks and the composite index during the late 1990s. That event resulted from the rapid run-up in the valuation of large-cap growth stocks, especially technology stocks, which tended to dominate the Wilshire 5000 Index at the time.

Figure 6-6 is an interesting 30-year risk-and-return chart that combines the Russell 3000 Index with the Russell 3000 Value Index and the Russell 3000 Growth Index over 30 years. At the top left of the chart is the Russell 3000 Value risk and return and at the bottom right is the Russell 3000 Growth risk and return. In the center is the Russell 3000. Starting with the Russell 3000, each subsequent point on the chart adds a 10 percent position up or down in the Russell Value and Growth indexes. The hypothetical portfolios were rebalanced annually.

Since 1979, the Russell 3000 Value Index has outperformed the Russell 3000 Growth Index by over 2 percent, and it did so with

FIGURE 6-6

Risk and Return Characteristics of Russell 3000 Indexes, 1979–2009

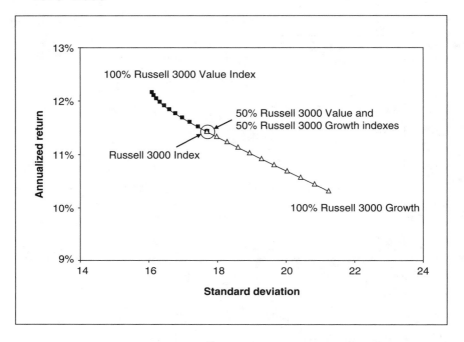

about 5 percent less risk! Based on this knowledge, why would anyone invest in growth stocks? Because growth stocks are perceived to have less total risk in their earnings growth, and less risk means less return.

Value investing has had merit because value stocks have outperformed growth stocks over most periods, and they did it with what appears to be less risk. However, the markets have a way of punishing those who think there is a free lunch. Fama and French would argue that there is more risk in value stocks, and that is why the returns were higher. The risk has simply not shown itself in the standard deviation of returns.

A second and important item of interest in Figure 6-6 is the point in the middle of the chart. A portfolio of 50 percent in the Russell 3000 Growth Index and 50 percent in the Russell 3000 Value

Index shows almost exactly the same risk and return as the Russell 3000 Index over the entire period. There was no benefit to holding a growth Fund and Value Fund in equal amounts. Yet, this strategy is one often recommended by investment advisors. A better strategy is to hold the total market and add elements such as small cap and value based on the total risk you are seeking.

SMALL-CAP VALUE AND RISK DIVERSIFICATION

We have observed that small stocks exhibit higher expected rates of return than larger stocks, albeit with a higher standard deviation of returns, and we have seen that value stocks have exhibited higher rates of return than growth stocks with less observable risk. This phenomenon is not unique to the U.S. market. Small and value premiums have occurred in markets all over the world.

There have been many explanations for the value effect in the market, although no one has pinpointed the exact reasons. Some say that the value premium was a result of the overly pessimistic earnings outlook for the value companies provided. Others say that undercoverage by stock analysts is a factor. Wall Street survives on investment banking fees, and it don't care much for unglamorous companies that are not issuing stock.

Whatever the reason for the value premium, it is assumed by most academics that value stocks have additional fundamental or economic risk. This risk is the reason value stocks have earned higher returns according to Eugene Fama and Ken French, whether this risk has been picked up in the standard deviation of returns or not.

We turn our attention to a small segment of the stock market that has both a size premium and a value premium. The category of small-cap value represents approximately 3 percent of the capitalization of the broad U.S. market. Table 6-8 documents small-cap value returns.

As expected, with both size and style factors affecting the return of this niche category, the year-over-year performance of small-cap value stocks deviates substantially from the performance of the large stock heavy total stock market.

TABLE 6-8

The Difference in Rreturn between the Total Market and Small Value Stocks

	CRSP Total U.S. Stock Market	FF Small Value	FF Small Value Less CRSP Total Market
1995	36.5	27.7	−8.8
1996	21.2	20.7	−0.5
1997	31.3	37.3	6.0
1998	23.4	−8.6	−32.1
1999	23.6	5.6	−18.0
2000	−10.9	−0.8	10.1
2001	−11.0	40.2	51.2
2002	−20.9	−12.4	8.5
2003	31.6	74.7	43.1
2004	12.5	26.6	14.1
2005	6.2	4.8	−1.3
2006	15.5	22.2	6.7
2007	5.8	−16.6	−22.4
2008	−36.7	−43.1	−6.4
2009	28.8	34.6	5.8

Figure 6-7 illustrates the historic rolling 36-month correlation between small value stocks and the broad market. The correlation averages about +0.8, with varying consistency. The periods of lower correlation points to unique risks among small value stocks, and this creates potential for a diversification benefit.

An interesting point in Figure 6-7 is the downward spike in correlation that occurred during the late 1990s and into the early 2000s. During that period, small-cap value stocks performed poorly in relation to the predominantly large-cap growth-oriented total U.S. market, and then the trend reversed and small value stocks catapulted above large-growth stocks after the millennium.

Investors who followed a broadly diversified asset allocation that included a total market fund and a small value index fund would have faired very well during the past decade. Of course, you needed to be there to win. As discussed in Chapter 5 and high- lighted in Figure 5-2, the late 1990s was a time when many investors

FIGURE 6-7

Total U.S. Market Index and FF Small-Cap Value Index, 36-Month Rolling Correlations

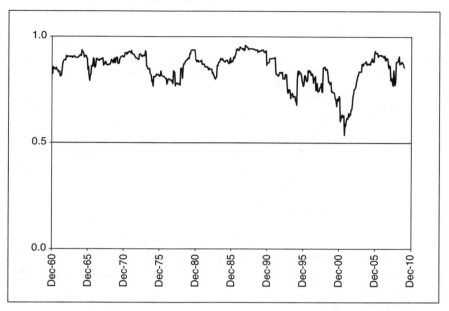

abandoned dusty value stocks in favor of glamour growth stocks, only to watch their money evaporate during the tech wreck.

Figure 6-8 illustrates the theoretical diversification benefit that was achieved by adding 10 percent increments of the FF Small-Cap Value Index to the total U.S. stock market. The point on Figure 6-8 that is most interesting is a portfolio representing 70 percent in the broad market and 30 percent in the small value index. Over a 30-year period, a mix of 70 percent in the total market and 30 percent in the small-cap value index would have increased U.S. equity returns by 2.0 percent with very little increase in observed portfolio risk.

Figure 6-9 sums up the chapter nicely by comparing the efficient frontiers between two portfolios. One portfolio uses microcap stocks as a diversification tool for the total U.S. stock market, and the other uses small-cap value stocks.

Historically, small-cap value stocks have added more return with less risk than microcap stocks, Nonetheless, I believe it is

FIGURE 6-8

Adding Small Value Stocks to a Total U.S. Market Fund; 1975–2009

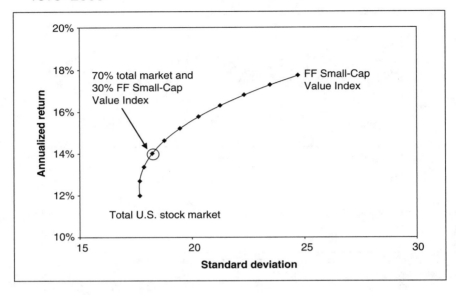

FIGURE 6-9

Comparing Portfolios that Add Small Value and Microcap, 1975–2009

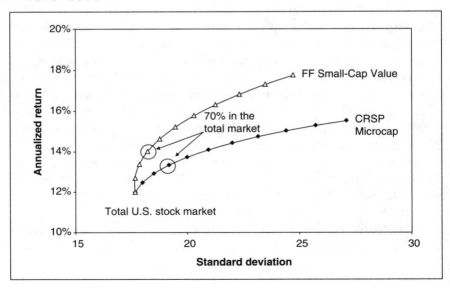

worth having both in a portfolio. Chances are that one or the other or both will benefit your portfolio over the long run.

This is not to say that the return premiums will be as high 30 years from now or will materialize at all. The news is out about the former excess returns from size and styling investing, and many investors have already incorporated FF research into their portfolio construction. This could cause a reduction in risk premiums. It is impossible to know.

As a reminder, the returns in Figure 6-9 are theoretical because there were no total market mutual funds or small-cap value index funds or microcap index funds available in 1975. Thus no investor could actually have held a portfolio of 70 percent in a broad market index and 30 percent in either index. That is not the case today. You can now purchase a wide assortment of total stock market index funds along with competing low-cost small-cap value index funds and a few microcap funds.

U.S. EQUITY INVESTMENT LIST

Table 6-9 gives a partial list of low-cost U.S. equity funds that are possible candidates for placing on your investment list. For more information on these and other low-cost no-load funds and ETFs,

TABLE 6-9

Select Low-Cost U.S. Equity Funds and ETFs

	Symbol	Benchmark
Total Stock Market Funds		
Vanguard Total U.S. Market Index	VTSMX	MSCI U.S. Broad Market Index
Schwab U.S. Broad Market ETF	SCHB	Dow Jones U.S. Broad Stock Market Index
iShares Russell 3000 Index ETF	IWV	Russell 3000 Index
Small Value Funds		
Vanguard Small-Cap Value Index	VISVX	MSCI U.S. Small Cap Value Index
iShares S&P SmallCap 600/BARRA Value	IJS	S&P 600/BARRA Value Index
iShares Morningstar Small Value	JKL	Morningstar Small Value Index
Microcap Funds		
Bridgeway Ultra-Small Co. Mkt.	BRSIX	CRSP Decile 8–10 (smallest stocks)

go to the Web site of the fund provider. A list is given in Appendix A. In addition, read *All About Index Funds*, 2nd edition, by Richard A. Ferri (McGraw-Hill, 2007) and *The ETF Book*, 2nd edition, by Richard Ferri (John Wiley, 2009).

CHAPTER SUMMARY

The cornerstone of any equity portfolio is a broadly diversified U.S. stock market index fund. There are several different total U.S. stock market indexes and index fund providers. The most complete U.S. stock market index is the Wilshire 5000 Composite Index. Other broad market indexes include MSCI, Russell, Morningstar, and Standard & Poor's. Most of these indexes are tracked by a low-cost index fund or ETF.

Microcap stocks represent only 3 percent of the total U.S. stock market and can add diversification to a broad market index fund. One problem with microcap stocks is finding a fund that gives you exposure to this niche market. Many microcap funds are closed to new investors, and the ones that are still open either tend to be expensive or do not stick to a pure microcap strategy.

A small-cap value fund is a one-fund-fits-all method to add size and style premium exposure. There are many small-cap value indexes available to choose from, and you'll want to study the differences in those indexes before selecting a fund to represent this niche sector of the market.

NOTES

[1] Rolf W. Banz, "The Relationship between Return and Market Value in Common Stocks," *Journal of Financial Economics*, vol. 9, 1981, pp. 3–18; Marc R. Reinganum, "Misspecification of Capital Asset Pricing: Empirical Anomalies Based on Earnings Yield and Market Values," *Journal of Financial Economics*, vol. 9, 1981, pp. 19–46.

[2] Benjamin F. Graham and David L. Dodd, *Security Analysis*, 4th rev. ed. (New York: McGraw-Hill, 1972) (originally published in 1934).

[3] Eugene F. Fama and Kenneth R. French, "The Cross-Section of Expected Stock Returns," *Journal of Financial Economics*, vol. 48, pp. 427–465, June 1992. The authors followed with a second paper, "Common Risk Factors in the Return of Stocks and Bonds," *Journal of Financial Economics*, February 1993, vol. 33, no. 1, pp. 3–57.

[4] Kenneth French Web site: http://mba.tuck.dartmouth.edu/pages/faculty/ken.french/index.html.

CHAPTER 7

International Equity Investments

KEY CONCEPTS

- International equity provides currency diversification.
- Developed markets include advanced countries.
- Emerging markets and frontier markets expand into new geographic areas.
- International equities exhibit size and style premiums.

The world is a very big place, and investment opportunities abound. There are many stock and bond markets around the globe offering U.S. investors substantial diversification benefits. Some opportunities can be found in developed markets, such as those in Japan, Australia, Germany, and the United Kingdom, and other opportunities are found in the emerging markets of less-developed countries, such as China, India, Turkey, and the countries of Eastern Europe. A well-diversified portfolio includes all investable regions of the world.

Investing internationally offers diversification benefits, although is not without added risk. Foreign stock prices tend to be more volatile than U.S. stock prices. The extra volatility is a product of many variables, including (1) foreign currency risk caused by a strengthening of the U.S. dollar, (2) political risk caused by government action or inaction, (3) trading and custody risk caused by exchange restrictions on nondomestic investors, (4) regulatory risk caused by a lack of oversight and a weak judicial system, and (5) information risk caused by a lack of disclosure by foreign companies.

Because of all the extra risks involved, diversification is the key to international equity investing. No one knows which country will outperform the global markets in the near term, or whether the U.S. dollar will strengthen or weaken. Accordingly, investors would be wise to consider owning a small slice of every country and rebalancing their global exposures annually.

CURRENCY RISK

Currency fluctuations play an important role in the risk and return of international investments. When U.S. investors buy foreign stocks and stock funds, they are also converting dollars into a foreign currency. Changes in the value of that currency relative to the dollar will affect the total loss or gain on the investment. Figure 7-1

FIGURE 7-1

U.S. Dollar versus Other Major Currencies

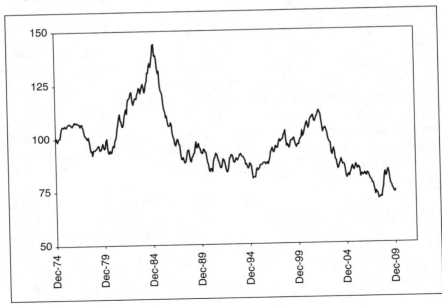

illustrates the value of the U.S. dollar in relation to other major world currencies.

As you can see, the U.S. dollar has been trending lower for many decades. That being said, past trends are not an indication of future trends. Where the dollar goes next is an unknown.

U.S. stocks and a composite of developed market international stocks have had almost the same return in their native currency. When the value of the dollar rose during a specific period, U.S. investors profited from more U.S. stocks than from international stocks. The opposite was true when the dollar fell. During the period from 1995 to 2001, the dollar was strong against other major currencies, and the U.S. stock market outperformed international stocks. U.S. stocks did not keep up with international stocks for the remainder of the decade as the dollar weakened.

GLOBAL MARKETS AND INTERNATIONAL INVESTING

International stocks are often referred to as "foreign" stocks and less frequently as "overseas" stocks. It is all the same. International companies have their corporate headquarters located outside the United States. Their primary accounting currency is the currency native to the country of their corporate headquarters.

The media often refer to large companies with a worldwide presence as multinational firms. However, technically there is no such thing. For accounting and tax purposes, a company is domiciled in only one country and reports earnings in its native currency.

All foreign companies list their shares on a local stock exchange, and many larger companies list their shares on exchanges outside their native land, to increase ownership. When foreign companies list shares on a U.S. stock exchange, they do it through American Depositary Receipts (ADRs). ADRs represent shares of foreign stock held on deposit in a U.S. bank. The bank converts the shares into U.S. dollar-denominated ADRs, which trade alongside U.S. securities on the NYSE and Nasdaq. As an aside, many large U.S.-based corporations also list their shares on foreign exchanges, such as those in London and Tokyo.

Global equity mutual funds invest in both U.S. and international companies. Selecting a global index fund is a good option if you have only a little money to invest and want to have some international exposure without having to buy both a U.S. stock index fund and an international stock index fund. However, with a global index fund you do not have control over the country or regional allocation of your investment. The amount owned in each country is based on the value of that country in relation to all others in the global index the fund is tracking. With an actively managed global fund, a manager will decide which countries and regions he or she wants to invest in. In both index funds and active funds, the country and regional weights will change over time.

Building your own U.S and international stock allocation is a better method than using a global fund because there are greater diversification opportunities. In addition, holding different regional funds in a portfolio and rebalancing them annually helps you control the amount of risk exposure to any particular region and currency.

CATEGORIZING GLOBAL MARKETS

Economists have traditionally divided the world into two distinct categories: developed markets and emerging markets. The difference between the two categories is based on both the size of the economy per capita and the level of development in the public stock and bond markets.

Developed markets are countries whose economy has advanced to the point where the per capita gross domestic product (GDP) exceeds approximately $10,000 per year and that have deep and mature securities markets. Examples of developed markets include Australia, Germany, Japan, and the United Kingdom. Developed markets can be grouped into three regions: North America, Europe, and the Pacific Rim. North America includes U.S. and Canadian companies. Europe includes the United Kingdom and continental Europe. The Pacific Rim covers several major markets, including Japan, Australia, Hong Kong, and South Korea, a recent addition.

Emerging countries that do not meet the GDP requirement and have less-developed financial markets are said to be emerging. Emerging markets can be divided into early-stage frontier markets and later-stage developed emerging markets, depending on the country's progress toward a more open and free market-based economy. Examples of frontier markets include Bulgaria, Argentina, Vietnam, Sri Lanka, and Kuwait. Later-stage emerging markets are further along in their development of free markets and include Mexico, Taiwan, Russia, China, and South Africa. As a matter of interest, most emerging market mutual funds concentrate their holdings on late-stage emerging markets because those countries have the largest percentage of market capitalization.

Figure 7-2 illustrates the value of world market allocation over time based on the percentage of global market value in each region. The chart is divided among four regions: North America developed markets, the Pacific Rim developed markets, European developed markets, and a rapidly expanding emerging market sector that now holds over 12 percent of the world's equity capitalization, according to MSCI.

FIGURE 7-2

Global Equity Markets by Percent of Value

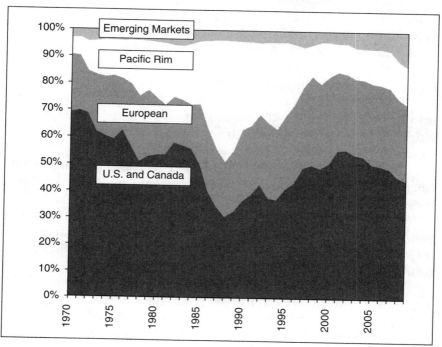

Countries that have fledgling stock markets that are not categorized as either developed markets or emerging markets generally fall under the category of frontier markets. The frontier markets make up less than 1 percent of global market capitalization. They include Argentina, Bahrain, Botswana, Bulgaria, Romania, Saudi Arabia, and Serbia, to name a few.

DEVELOPED-MARKET INDEXES

The most widely followed international index of developed-market countries is the Morgan Stanley Capital International Europe, Australasia, and the Far East Index, better known as the MSCI EAFE. The EAFE Index is composed of approximately 1,000 large-company stocks from 23 developed markets located in Europe and the Pacific Rim. The index is broadly diversified. It is designed to include at least 85 percent of the market value of each industry group within those 23 countries.

The best way to think of the EAFE Index is as a big international S&P 500 that covers all developed countries except the United States and Canada. The EAFE Index is a float-adjusted index and includes only tradable securities. Closely held blocks of stock and industry cross-holdings are not counted. Morgan Stanley does not attempt to control sector weights, country weights, or regional weights in the EAFE Index.

MSCI reports the EAFE Index performance in two ways: one is in local currency, and the other is in U.S. dollars. Table 7-1 provides insight into how much currency fluctuations affect return on a year-over-year basis.

MSCI has published the returns on EAFE and its components since 1970. Index methodology and return information is available for free on www.MSCI.com.

Table 7-2 compares the return on the EAFE Index net of dividends to the return on the total U.S. stock market. Net of dividends includes an adjustment for a foreign withholding tax that some countries place on dividends paid to outside investors.

The EAFE Index underperformed U.S. stocks between 1970 and 2001. In my view, the return on the EAFE Index was very good. The problem was that the return on the U.S. stock market was great. EAFE performance overtook the U.S. market in 2001 and

TABLE 7-1

Currency Effects on U.S. Investors in the EAFE Index

	EAFE Return in Local Currency	EAFE Return in U.S. Dollars	Currency Effect on U.S. Investors
1997	11.8%	2.1%	−9.7%
1998	10.6%	20.3%	9.7%
1999	31.7%	27.3%	− 4.4%
2000	−8.5%	−14.0%	− 5.5%
2001	−17.5%	−21.2%	− 3.7%
2002	−27.5%	−15.7%	11.8%
2003	17.4%	39.2%	21.8%
2004	10.2%	20.7%	10.5%
2005	26.1%	14.0%	− 11.9%
2006	13.8%	26.9%	13.1%
2007	1.2%	11.6%	10.5%
2008	−42.1%	−43.1%	− 1.0%
2009	24.7%	31.8%	7.1%

TABLE 7-2

Comparing Risk and Return from 1970 to 2009

	MSCI EAFE Net of Dividends ($)	Total U.S. Stock Market
Annualized return	9.5%	10.1%
Standard deviation	17.1%	15.9%

continued in this vein for the rest of the decade. Perhaps we are on the cusp of a reversal this decade, or perhaps not. It is not possible to predict which region of the world will outperform in the future. Accordingly, it is good policy to both U.S. stocks and international stocks in your portfolio at all times.

Some investors question the continued viability of holding international stocks because of the increase in correlation with U.S. stocks. Figure 7-3 illustrates this phenomenon. Since 1998, the correlation of the EAFE Index and the U.S. total market has increased

FIGURE 7-3

MSCI EAFE in U.S. Dollars and Total U.S. Market, Rolling
36-Month Correlation

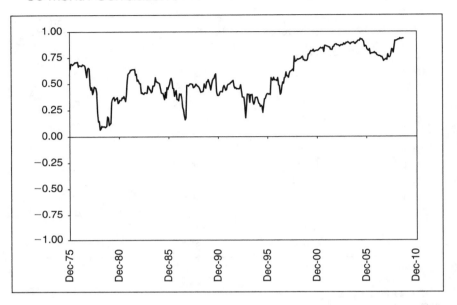

from about + 0.5 to about + 0.8. This should not be a concern. We
know that correlations can change abruptly, and the correlation
between the EAFE Index and U.S. markets may turn at any time.
There is still a diversification benefit even with high current correlations, as you will see next.

DECOMPOSING THE EAFE INDEX

To gain a better understanding of international investing, it helps
to drill down to the performance and correlations of the underlying regions that make up the EAFE Index. The EAFE can be
broken down into two separate geographical indexes: the MSCI
Europe Index and the MSCI Pacific Rim Index. Figure 7-4 gives you
a visual impression of how different the returns for different geographical regions can be. As you see, at times the returns of all
regions can be similar, such as in 2008, and at other times they can
differ substantially, such as in 2005.

FIGURE 7-4

Return Differences between U.S., European, and Pacific Rim Markets

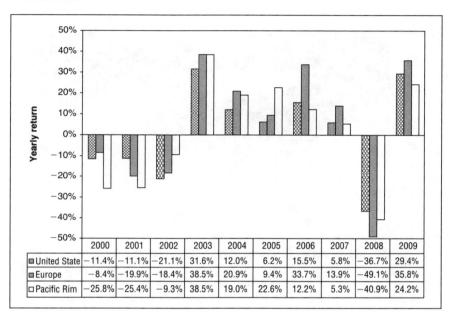

	2000	2001	2002	2003	2004	2005	2006	2007	2008	2009
▨ United State	−11.4%	−11.1%	−21.1%	31.6%	12.0%	6.2%	15.5%	5.8%	−36.7%	29.4%
▨ Europe	−8.4%	−19.9%	−18.4%	38.5%	20.9%	9.4%	33.7%	13.9%	−49.1%	35.8%
▢ Pacific Rim	−25.8%	−25.4%	−9.3%	38.5%	19.0%	22.6%	12.2%	5.3%	−40.9%	24.2%

Figure 7-5 illustrates the trends in exchange rates and local market valuations that have caused the weight of the EAFE to swing between Europe and the Pacific Rim over the years. In the early 1970s, Europe dominated the EAFE Index, with a 78 percent market share. By 1988, as a result of a huge run-up in Japanese stocks, the Pacific Rim dominated the EAFE Index, with 70 percent. In the 1990s, fortunes reversed again. A bear market in Japan and a bull market in Europe pushed Europe back over a 70 percent market share. Recently, the shift is away from Europe and back to the Pacific Rim.

Splitting up these regions and analyzing individual correlations gives us more insight into the overall market. Figure 7-6 illustrates the rolling 36-month correlation between the MSCI Europe Index and the U.S. equity market, and the MSCI Pacific Rim Index and the U.S. equity market. Recall that the correlation between the U.S. stock market and the EAFE Index has increased since 1998.

FIGURE 7-5

Percentage of EAFE Index in European and Pacific Rim
Developed Markets

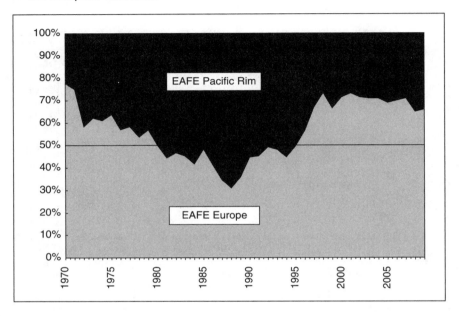

Figure 7-6 shows that the correlation between the United
States and Europe has been traditionally higher than the correlation between the United States and the Pacific Rim. The increase
in correlation between the United States and Europe that
occurred after 2000 coincided with the introduction of the euro, a
single currency that 11 European Union countries adopted in
1999. Perhaps the euro has led to a permanently higher correlation between the United States and Europe, and perhaps not.
Time will tell.

There was also a jump in correlation between U.S. stocks,
European stocks, and Pacific Rim stocks during the credit crisis
from 2007 through 2009. I don't expect the correlations to continue
at this high a level after the global recovery takes hold and each
economy goes its own way. Accordingly, I recommended that
investors continue to invest in all regions of the world and rebalance portfolios annually.

FIGURE 7-6

Rolling 36-Month Correlation between Total U.S. Market, Europe, and the Pacific Rim

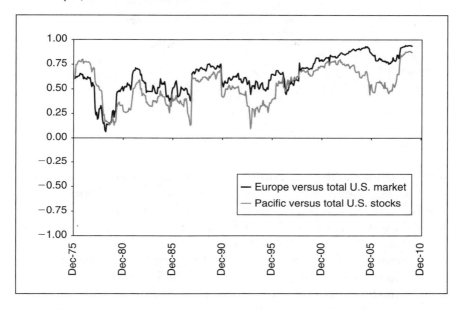

A BETTER INTERNATIONAL ALLOCATION

EAFE Index performance should equal the U.S. market over the long term, plus or minus currency adjustments. There's no reason to believe that one market or one industry within a market is going to produce higher returns for very long, since capital can flow freely to most developed nations. We live in a global economy. If there is an opportunity to profit from stocks in one developed market, then money will quickly flow across continents to bring that market up to its fair value. For example, all developed countries have large banks that make loans around the world. The banking industry in Europe is not going to outperform the banking industry in the United States for very long.

Since all regions are expected to perform the same over the long term, why bother to invest internationally? You invest internationally mainly to gain currency diversification and, to a lesser degree, to increase security diversification. Diversifying away from

TABLE 7-3

Slicing the EAFE into Regions, 1970–2009

	EAFE Index, Net of Dividends in U.S. $	50% MSCI Europe, 50% MSCI Pacific
Annualized return	9.5%	10.1%
Standard deviation	17.1%	17.7%
40–year high	69.4%	68.6%
40–year low	−43.4%	−44.9%

Source: Morgan Stanley

the U.S. dollar with your equity allocation is an inexpensive way to gain currency exposure. The benefit of currency diversification is maximized by your taking positions in different global regions that have different currencies, and rebalancing your portfolio annually to reestablish your target positions.

Figure 7-5 clearly illustrates the flip-flop in value between the Pacific Rim and European indexes over the last 40 years. Table 7-3 shows that over the last 40 years, the EAFE Index has returned about 9.5 percent net of dividends and 10.2 percent before the foreign withholding tax (the S&P 500 returned 9.9 percent). During the same period, a portfolio with 50 percent in the MSCI Europe Index and 50 percent in the MSCI Pacific Rim Index rebalanced annually resulted in a compounded return of 10.1 percent net of foreign withholding taxes. That was 0.6 percent higher annually than the EAFE Index without a meaningful increase in volatility.

Until recently, it was not possible to invest directly in the EAFE Index or regions of the EAFE independently. Thanks to the rapid growth of index mutual funds, it is now possible to put your money in a combination of investments that follow most of the indexes previously mentioned. See the list of low-cost developed-market index funds at the end of this chapter.

OH, CANADA!

The U.S. neighbor to the north should not be forgotten. Canadian stocks account for about 6 percent of the international equity market and about 3 percent of the global equity market. Adding a Canadian index fund to a well-diversified developed-market equity portfolio can increase currency diversification and hedge against a decline in the U.S. dollar.

Canada's economy consists of three main industries: finance, energy (oil and gas), and basic materials (mining and lumber). An investment in a Canadian index fund increases the portfolio's allocation to natural resources, and that can act as a hedge against rising commodities prices. See the investment list at the end of this chapter for one ETF that follows the MSCI Canada Index.

EMERGING MARKETS

Broadly defined, an emerging market is a less-developed country that is improving its free-market economy and its standard of living. These countries are becoming more competitive in the global marketplace and opening their markets to more international investment. Emerging countries also have organized securities exchanges that trade stocks and bonds of large enterprises domiciled in that country. Foreigners are allowed to own those securities either directly or indirectly through a fund.

An investible emerging market is defined by a number of factors, including gross domestic product per capita, local government regulations, perceived investment risk, foreign ownership limits, and capital controls. The MSCI Emerging Markets Index covers 22 investible countries. It is a market-weighted index that uses the float-adjusted value of each company to reflect restrictions on foreign investment. Some countries have much larger stock markets than others. Consequently, at times an emerging market index can be dominated by a few countries.

In an effort to reduce market dominance in the MSCI Emerging Markets Index, the Dimensional Fund Advisors (DFA) created an equal-weighted emerging index. This avoids a large allocation to one or two countries.

Table 7-4 compares the risk and return of the DFA equal-weighted index to the market-weighted MSCI Emerging Markets Index. Since the inception of the DFA Index in 1999, the equal-weight methodology produced returns 0.5 percent higher than the market-weighted MSCI Index.

Figure 7-7 illustrates the return differences between the U.S. stock index, the EAFE Index, and the MSCI Emerging Markets

TABLE 7-4

Emerging Market Performance, 1999–2009

	DFA Equal Weight Emerging Market Index	MSCI Emerging Markets Index
Annualized return	14.6%	14.1%
Standard deviation	24.0%	24.9%

Source: MSCI and Dimensional Fund Advisors

FIGURE 7-7

Annual Return Differences between U.S. Stocks, EAFE, and Emerging Markets

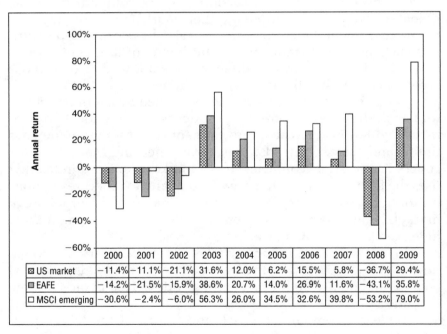

	2000	2001	2002	2003	2004	2005	2006	2007	2008	2009
US market	−11.4%	−11.1%	−21.1%	31.6%	12.0%	6.2%	15.5%	5.8%	−36.7%	29.4%
EAFE	−14.2%	−21.5%	−15.9%	38.6%	20.7%	14.0%	26.9%	11.6%	−43.1%	35.8%
MSCI emerging	−30.6%	−2.4%	−6.0%	56.3%	26.0%	34.5%	32.6%	39.8%	−53.2%	79.0%

Index. Notice how much more volatile the emerging market index is than either the U.S. market index or the MSCI EAFE Index for developed markets. Volatility is not a bad trait for an investment

FIGURE 7-8

Rolling 36-Month Correlation between the MSCI Emerging
Markets Index and the Total U.S. Stock Market

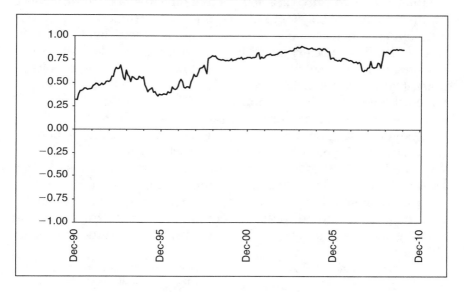

because investors are broadly diversified and rebalance their portfolios occasionally.

The rolling 36-month correlation analysis shown in Figure 7-8
illustrates that since its inception in 1988, the MSCI Emerging
Markets Index has increased its correlation with U.S. stocks, which
decreases the diversification benefit in the portfolio. Perhaps the
increase in correlation is a short-term phenomenon, and perhaps it
is permanent.

It would not be surprising if the correlation between the U.S.
stock market and emerging markets diverges over the next decade
as China, Russia, and India become more dominant global equity
indexes. The correlation between two markets can change very
quickly, and that past correlation is not a good prediction of future
correlation. Accordingly, a permanent allocation to emerging
market stocks is recommended for your potential investment list.
A table of emerging market index funds can be found at the end of
this chapter.

SIZE AND VALUE FACTORS IN INTERNATIONAL MARKETS

Chapter 6 explains three risk factors that have had a profound effect on the returns of U.S. stocks. According to researchers Gene Fama and Ken French, 95 percent of the return on a widely diversified U.S. stock portfolio can be explained by that portfolio's market risk (beta), percentage in small stocks (size risk), and percentage in high book-to-market stocks (value risk). Over the long term, U.S. small-cap stocks have achieved a return premium over large-cap stocks, and value stocks have achieved a return premium over growth stocks.

Several independent studies have confirmed that the behavior of widely diversified international stock portfolios is consistent with the three factors found in U.S. stock portfolio returns.[1] Using DFA indexes, Table 7-5 quantifies the historic premium paid to international small-cap stocks over international large-cap stocks and the premium paid to international value stocks over international growth stocks. An analysis of MSCI index data produced similar results.

Between 1999 and 2009 the international markets exhibited both a size premium and a value premium. Based on the DFA indexes, the international size premium annualized at about 3.9 percent over the period and the value premium was 4.7 percent. There was over a 2.0 percent annualized premium for value stocks and small-cap stocks based on MSCI EAFE indexes going back to 1975.

TABLE 7-5

International Size and Value Premiums, 1999–2009

Size Premium	DFA International Large-Company Index	DFA International Small-Company Index
Annualized return	4.8%	8.7%
Standard deviation	17.5%	18.5%
Value Premium	**DFA International Large-Company Value**	**DFA International Small-Company Value**
Annualized return	8.0%	12.7%
Standard deviation	21.4%	18.1%

The international size and value premiums have been documented in many countries during independent time periods. This leads researchers to believe that the two premiums are not an anomaly. Researchers are becoming more convinced that size and value premiums represent independent risks in the stock market that are not explained by beta, and, as a result, a premium for taking size and value risk is expected in the future.

SAMPLE INTERNATIONAL ALLOCATION

Part Three of this book includes several samples of portfolios that have international stocks in the asset allocation. Generally, the allocation to international stocks is about 30 percent of the equity portion of the portfolio. Within the allocation, a sample of international funds might be as follows:

- 30 percent in a Pacific Rim index fund
- 30 percent in a European index fund
- 20 percent in an international small-cap value fund
- 20 percent in an emerging markets index fund

This international portfolio is not a recommended portfolio— it is a sample of how a portfolio could be diversified internationally. There are many combinations of international funds that will provide adequate diversification with varying degrees of risk. Finding the one mix that is right for your unique situation is your mission. Whichever international mix you choose, maintaining that allocation through all market conditions is a key element of investment success.

INTERNATIONAL EQUITY INVESTMENT LIST

Table 7-6 gives a partial list of low-cost funds that are possible candidates for an international equity allocation. For more complete information on these and other low-cost no-load funds, read *All About Index Funds*, 2nd edition, by Richard A. Ferri (McGraw-Hill, 2007) and *The ETF Book*, 2nd edition, by Richard A. Ferri (Wiley, 2009).

TABLE 7-6

Select Low-Cost International Mutual Funds and ETFs

	Symbol	Benchmark
European Mutual Funds		
Vanguard European Index*	VEURX	MSCI European Index
iShares Europe 350 Index	IEV	S&P Europe 350 Index
iShares MSCI UK Index	EWU	MSCI United Kingdom Index
iShares MSCI EMU Index	EZU	MSCI EMU Index
Pacific Rim Mutual Funds		
Vanguard Pacific Index*	VPACX	MSCI Pacific Index
iShares MSCI Japan Index	EWJ	MSCI Japan Index
iShares MSCI Pacific ex-JPN	EPP	MSCI Pacific ex-Japan Index
Emerging Markets Funds		
Vanguard Emerging Markets*	VEIEX	Select Emerging Markets Index
iShares Emerging Markets	EEM	MSCI Emerging Markets Free
DFA Emerging Markets†	DFEMX	DFA Emerging Markets Index
International Value Funds		
Vanguard International Value	VTRIX	Actively managed fund
DFA International Value**	DFIVX	DFA International Value
International Small Funds		
Vanguard International Explorer	VINEX	Actively managed fund
DFA Small International†	DFISX	DFA Small International
DFA Small International Value**	DISVX	DFA Small International Value
Single-Country Funds		
iShares MSCI Canada	EWC	MSCI Canada Index
iShares FTSE/Xinhua China 25	FXI	FTSE/Xinhua China 25 Index

*Vanguard ETFs are also available.

†DFA funds are available only through select investment advisors.

CHAPTER SUMMARY

The international equity markets provide unique diversification opportunities for U.S. investors. The opportunities extend from established developed markets to emerging countries and from small-cap stocks to global giants. Unfortunately, excess return from international investing is not without risk. Foreign stocks are subject to currency risk, political risk, trading and custody risk, and regulatory risk, among others. An understanding of these risks is important during difficult market conditions.

The MSCI EAFE Index is a widely used benchmark for international investors. While the index is a convenient single measure by which to judge the level of all developed-market large-cap stocks, the shifting market weight of countries within the index does not make for a good investment. The problem is that there is no rebalancing in the index. Consequently, the weight of the index swings considerably among the geographic regions of the world.

Developed markets can be divided into two regions: Europe and the Pacific Rim. While buying an EAFE Index fund is a convenient way to invest in developed markets, the shifting allocation between Europe and the Pacific Rim is not the most desirable approach to asset allocation. Dividing developed markets into an equal portfolio of Europe and Pacific Rim and rebalancing annually is a better alternative than allowing your portfolio allocation to swing between the two regions.

Emerging markets have evolving economies, and that spells opportunity. However, those opportunities are not without added risk. Emerging markets are more volatile than developed markets, and there is the added risk of political uncertainty. As a result, a well-diversified emerging market fund is recommended.

Over the long term, international small-cap and value stocks have delivered higher returns than international large-cap and growth stocks. Adding a small-cap international fund and a value fund to your international portfolio may increase the return over time. Unfortunately, there is one disadvantage to this strategy: There is a genuine lack of available low-cost mutual funds that focus on small-cap international stocks.

NOTE

[1] For a summary of research on size and style premiums in international stocks, see Elroy Dimson, Paul Marsh, and Mike Staunton, *Triumph of the Optimists, 101 Years of Global Investment Returns* (Princeton, N.J.: Princeton University Press, 2002).

Fixed-Income Investments

KEY CONCEPTS

- There are several fixed-income categories to invest in.
- Different categories exhibit unique risks and returns.
- A diversified fixed-income portfolio enhances return.
- Low-cost bond mutual funds are an ideal way to invest.

There is no lack of diversification potential in the bond market. Fixed-income categories abound with unique investment opportunities. They include government bonds, investment-grade and high-yield corporate bonds, mortgage-backed bonds, asset-backed securities, and foreign debt. Using a broadly diversified fixed-income strategy can increase portfolio return without additional risk.

Fixed-income asset allocation is often overlooked in the investment advice industry. Books and articles on asset allocation tend to devote a significant amount of time to the benefits of equity asset diversification while largely ignoring fixed-income selection.

It is common for investment managers to place their clients' entire fixed-income allocation in government bonds only and ignore all other fixed-income categories. Those advisors tell clients that they "prefer to take their risk on the stock side." I tend to believe that they use only government bonds to make the advisor's job easy rather than to go through the extra work to create a properly diversified fixed-income allocation.

Investors should always use low-cost mutual funds in categories that would otherwise require significant analysis and expertise, such as high-yield corporate bonds and foreign bonds. The simplest way to gain instant fixed-income diversification is through a low-cost bond index fund or ETF. There are several low-cost funds available that follow popular investment-grade indexes, such as the Barclays Capital Aggregate Bond Market Index. A partial list of these funds is provided at the end of this chapter.

Tax considerations may be an important element in fixed-income asset allocation when bonds are held in a taxable account. Accordingly, tax-free municipal bonds may be appropriate when you are investing a personal account, joint account, or trust account. There is a discussion in this chapter about tax-free bond investing for investors who are in a high-tax situation.

The goal of this chapter is threefold: first, to help you appreciate the wide range of fixed-income categories that are available for investment; second, to demonstrate how fixed-income investments can work with other investments to reduce overall portfolio risk and increase long-term return; and third, to identify unique fixed-income categories that might be appropriate for your portfolio.

BOND MARKET STRUCTURE

The global bond market is as broad as it is deep. Investors have as much diversification potential on the fixed-income side of their portfolio as they do on the equity side. The range of bond opportunities stretches from governments to corporate to mortgages to foreign markets.

Index providers categorize bonds by different types and risk grades. The following is an example of how the bond market is generally segmented and categorized:

1. Federal, state, and local governments
   U.S. government backed
   Treasury-issued securities (bills, notes, bonds)
   Government agency issues
       insured by the Federal Deposit Insurance Corporation
       (FDIC) Certificates of deposit

State and local government municipal bonds
  General obligation backed by taxes
  Revenue bonds backed by income other than taxes
  Build America bonds (interest is subject to federal
    income tax)

2. Corporate fixed income
   Corporate bonds
     Investment-grade corporate (rated BBB to AAA)
     Non-investment-grade corporate (rated BB and lower)
     Industrial revenue bonds (municipal bonds subject to
       the alternative minimum tax)
   Convertible bonds
   Preferred stock and convertible preferred stock

3. Mortgages
   Government National Mortgage Association (GNMA)
   Federal Home Loan Mortgage Corporation (FHLMC)
   Federal National Mortgage Association (FNMA)

4. Asset-backed securities
   Pooled credit card receivables (Bank One, CitiGroup)
   Pooled auto loans (Ford, GM)
   Pooled home equity loans and other bank receivables

5. Foreign bonds
   Developed markets (sovereign and corporate)
   Emerging markets debt (sovereign, Brady, and corporate)

FIXED-INCOME RISK AND RETURN

The expected risk and return of various U.S. fixed-income investments can be categorized on a two-axis Morningstar Fixed-Income
Style Box, as illustrated in Figure 8-1. The fixed-income style box is
a nine-square box that gives you a visual snapshot of a fund's
credit quality and duration. The style box allows investors to
quickly gauge the risk exposure of their bond fund.

The horizontal axis of Figure 8-1 represents the maturity of a
bond, and the vertical axis represents its creditworthiness. The
two-axis model of bond maturity and creditworthiness explains

much of the risk and return associated with fixed-income investments. The more risk there is in a bond, the greater the expected
return. Figure 8-2 illustrates this relationship.

FIGURE 8-1

Fixed-Income Maturity and Credit Risk Grid

	Short term	Intermediate term	Long term
High risk	SH	IH	LH
Medium risk	SM	IM	LM
Low risk	SL	IL	LL

FIGURE 8-2

Fixed-Income Risk-and-Return Comparison

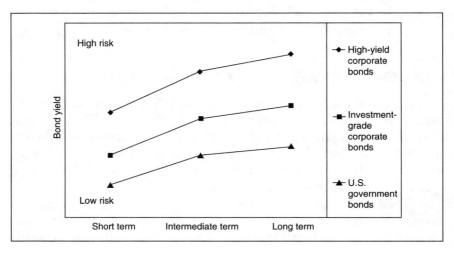

Interest-rate risk and credit risk determine how much a bond should pay in order to compensate investors for taking those risks. Higher potential returns are found in bonds with low credit quality and long-term maturities.

MATURITY STRUCTURE

Bonds are issued by governments and corporations using a variety of different maturities.

Figure 8-1 divides bond maturities into three ranges: short term, intermediate term, and long term. Short-term bonds have an average maturity of 3 years or less, intermediate-term bonds have an average maturity of 4 to 9 years, and long-term bonds have an average maturity of 10 years or more. Under normal economic conditions, you should expect to get a higher return from long-term bonds because that segment of the market has more interest-rate risk. If a bond loses value when interest rates move higher, it has interest-rate risk. Long-term bonds have more interest-rate risk than short-term bonds because they have a longer time before maturing. Since long-term bonds have more risk, investors should get paid a higher interest rate for bearing that risk.

Economic factors cause interest rates for different bond maturities to change at different times and by different amounts. Those interest-rate shifts create changes in the "spreads" between different maturities. On average, the spread between the 1-year and 10-year Treasuries is about 0.9 percent. The spread was more than 3.0 percent for much of 2009. Figure 8-3 shows the changing interest-rate spread between 1-year Treasury bills and 10-year Treasury notes since the early 1950s.

Most of the time, a 10-year Treasury note has had a higher yield than the 1-year T-bill. These are periods with a "normal" yield curve, so called because under normal conditions short-term T-bills are expected to yield less than intermediate-term Treasury notes. A "flat" yield curve occurs when the yield on T-bills and T-notes is the same. If T-bills have a higher yield than Treasury notes, this is known as an "inverted" yield curve.

There is a school of thought that believes that when the curve is inverted, the economy is slowing and the stock market will likely go down. There appears to be some support for this theory, although

Treasury Term Spread, 1-Year T-Bills, and 10-Year Treasury Notes

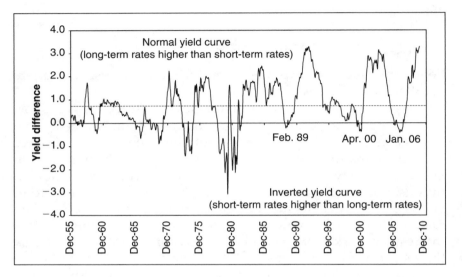

the timing is sketchy at best. Sometimes the curve becomes inverted a couple of years before stocks correct during a recession, and sometimes it inverts after the market has already started to pull back.

CREDIT RISK

Credit risk is illustrated on the vertical axis in Figure 8-1. Bonds that have more credit risk should pay a higher interest rate than bonds with low credit risk. Table 8-1 shows how three different credit-rating agencies categorize bonds by creditworthiness.

Investment-grade bonds have an S&P and Fitch rating of BBB or higher and a Moody's rating of Baa or higher. Direct and indirect obligations of a government agency, such as Treasury bonds and federal agency bonds, have the least credit risk and yield the least. The middle investment-grade credit level includes investment-grade U.S. corporations and municipalities with sound fundamental characteristics. These bonds receive an investment-grade

TABLE 8-1

Credit-Rating Agency Categories

	Moody's	Standard & Poor's	Fitch
Investment Grade			
Prime	Aaa	AAA	AAA
Excellent	Aa	AA	AA
Upper medium	A	A	A
Lower medium	Baa	BBB	BBB
Non-Investment Grade			
Speculative	Ba	BB	BB
Very speculative	B, Caa, Ca, C	B, CCC, CC, C	B, CCC, CC, C
Default		D	DDD, DD, D

rating from credit-rating agencies such as Standard & Poor's. They pay more interest than government bonds.

At the bottom of the risk ladder are high-yield corporate bonds and non-investment-grade municipal bonds. Companies and municipal bond issuers with below investment-grade debt ratings have questionable ability to repay their obligations. These bonds are also referred to as "junk" bonds because of their speculative nature. They are discussed in more detail later in the chapter.

Credit risk should be thought of as the amount that a bond will fall in value if the rating agencies cut the bond's rating. For example, if an AA-rated bond is cut to an A rating, the expected return to a new investor must go up to compensate for the lower credit quality, which means that the price of the bond will go down. Thus the amount that a bond will go down in value if the rating is cut is the bond's credit risk, which can also be thought of as its "downgrade" risk.

Figure 8-4 illustrates the historic yield spread between the highest-rated (Aaa) corporate bonds and lower-medium-rated (Baa) corporate bonds. The spread is calculated by subtracting the Aaa yield from the Baa yield. The credit spread appears to widen when the economy slumps into a recession and narrows when the economy begins to recover.

FIGURE 8-4

Credit Spread between Moody's Baa Yields and Aaa Yields

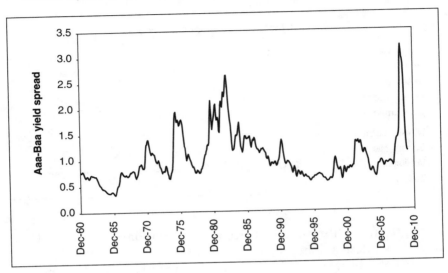

Some people believe that credit spreads widen and narrow for the same reasons that stocks go up and down. As a result, they say that using corporate bonds in a portfolio is nothing more than increasing the equity risk in a portfolio. While there are times when credit risk has a positive correlation with equity returns, the relationship is not consistent.

Figure 8-5 illustrates the rolling 12-month correlation between excess return on investment-grade bonds and excess return on equities (credit risk premium to equity risk premium). The credit risk premium is calculated by subtracting the monthly return on the Barclays Capital Intermediate-Term Treasury Index 1–10 Years from the return on the Barclays Capital Intermediate-Term Credit Index 1–10 Years. The equity risk premium is calculated by subtracting the return on Treasury bills from the return on the CRSP 1–10 Total Stock Market Index. Measuring the correlation between these two returns tells us if there is a relationship between them.

The average 12-month correlation between the credit risk premium and the equity risk premium suggests that *at times* the credit risk is related to the same factors affecting equity returns and that those times are particularly strong at the onset of an economic

FIGURE 8-5

12-Month Rolling Correlation between the Credit Risk
Premium and the Equity Risk Premium

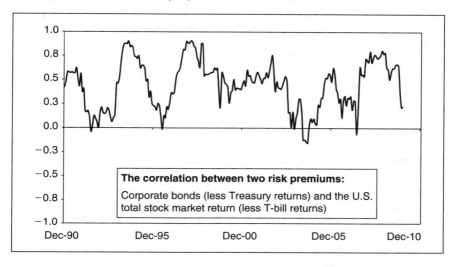

The correlation between two risk premiums:
Corporate bonds (less Treasury returns) and the U.S.
total stock market return (less T-bill returns)

downturn. At other times there is no correlation, and on rare occasions there is a slight negative correlation. The timing of the positive correlation between equities and corporate bonds is something to consider when you are deciding on the total risk in your overall portfolio.

INVESTING IN INVESTMENT-GRADE BONDS

Table 8-2 is an example of how the two risk factors of credit risk and maturity played out from 1973 to 2009. The higher interest-rate risk of intermediate-term Treasury bonds drove their return higher than the return on one-year Treasury bills. Also, the addition of credit risk increased the return of corporate bonds over Treasury bonds.

A well-diversified fixed-income portfolio includes a broad range of investment-grade bonds with different maturities, quality, and issuers. Most taxable investment-grade bonds issued in the United States are included in the Barclays Capital U.S. Aggregate Bond Market Index. As of January 2010, the Barclays Capital U.S. Aggregate Bond Index tracks more than 8,400 U.S. Treasury,

TABLE 8-2

Fixed-Income Investment Returns from 1973 to 2009

1973 to 2009	One-Year T-bill	Barclays Intermediate Treasury Index	Barclays Intermediate Credit Index
Annualized return	5.8%	7.7%	8.3%
Standard deviation	0.9%	4.3%	5.3%

TABLE 8-3

Composition of the Barclays Capital U.S. Aggregate Bond Index in 2009

Distribution by Issuer		Distribution by Quality	
Government Treasury/agency bonds	35%	AAA	78%
Government mortgage-backed bonds	38%	AA	4%
Corporate and asset-backed bonds	20%	A	10%
Commercial mortgages	3%	BBB	8%
Yankee bonds (foreign debt)	4%	BB or lower	0%
Distribution by maturity			
0–3 years	24.7%		
3–5 years	30.9%		
5–10 years	32.5%		
10–20 years	5.6%		
20–30 years	6.1%		

government agency, investment-grade corporate, and Yankee bonds (foreign bonds issued in the U.S. that trade in dollars). One exception is Treasury Inflation-Protected Securities (TIPS). TIPS are placed in a separate index because of their unique characteristics.

The bonds in the Barclays Capital U.S. Aggregate Bond Index have an average maturity of about 6.8 years. Over 70 percent of the holdings are in U.S. Treasuries, government agency bonds, and government-backed mortgages. The remaining bonds are investment-grade corporate bonds and Yankee bonds. All the bonds are investment grade. Table 8-3 is a breakdown of the index in 2009.

Several index funds are available that track the Barclays Capital U.S. Aggregate Bond Index. I recommend using one of these funds as the cornerstone of your fixed-income portfolio. A list of index funds can be found at the end of this chapter.

The Barclays Capital U.S. Aggregate Bond Index has many subindexes. One way the indexes are categorized is by maturity. The category with the shortest average maturity is the Barclays 1–3 Year Short-Term Government/Credit Index, which includes government and corporate bonds but no mortgages. The next category of maturities is the Barclays Intermediate-Term Government/Credit Index. The category with the longest maturity is the Barclays Long-Term Government/Credit Index.

You can adjust the interest-rate risk in your portfolio by using a combination of a total bond market index fund and one of the three subindexes based on maturity. For example, investors with a short-term investment horizon of five years or less should probably have a generous portion in a short-term bond index fund benchmarked to the Barclays 1–3 Year Short-Term Government/Credit Index. Investors who are retired and are withdrawing money annually may want to have at least one year's worth of withdrawals in the short-term fund.

ADDING OTHER FIXED-INCOME SECURITIES

A diversified fixed-income portfolio is not limited to the investment-grade bonds in the Barclays Capital U.S. Aggregate Bond Index. There are diversification benefits to be gained from other fixed-income securities. Those categories could include high-yield corporate bonds, TIPS, and foreign bonds, including emerging market debt. The following section looks as these sectors.

High-Yield Corporate Bonds

High-yield bonds are often referred to as non-investment-grade bonds, speculative-grade bonds, and junk bonds. Unlike investment-grade bonds, high-yield bonds have credit ratings that are in the lowest tier. They have S&P and Fitch ratings of BB or lower and Moody's ratings of Ba or lower.

Several entities issue high-yield bonds, including corporations, municipalities, and foreign governments. As a group, these securities are expected to earn a higher return than investment grade bonds.

High-yield bonds have a separate and distinct risk above and beyond credit risk because there is a real danger that the issuers will default on their obligations. Consequently, high-yield bonds have default risk in addition to credit risk. The added risk means that investors should get paid more over time.

Figure 8-6 compares the yearly returns on the Barclays Capital U.S. High Yield Corporate Bond Index to the returns on the Barclays Capital U.S. Aggregate Bond Index. Since the aggregate index includes most U.S. investment-grade bonds, the return difference between the two indexes is a result of changes in default risk.

Default risk increased from 2000 to 2002 as several large telecommunications companies defaulted on their bonds. In 2003 and 2004, defaults on high-yield bonds fell sharply, and, as a result, the risk of default on existing bonds also decreased. That

FIGURE 8-6

Comparing Annual Returns of High-Yield Bonds to the Aggregate Bond Index

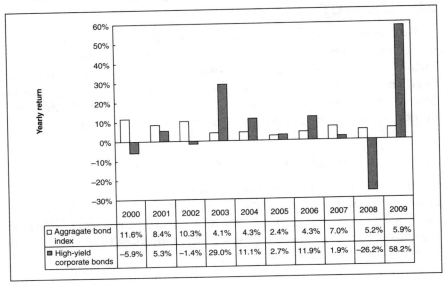

	2000	2001	2002	2003	2004	2005	2006	2007	2008	2009
☐ Aggragate bond index	11.6%	8.4%	10.3%	4.1%	4.3%	2.4%	4.3%	7.0%	5.2%	5.9%
■ High-yield corporate bonds	−5.9%	5.3%	−1.4%	29.0%	11.1%	2.7%	11.9%	1.9%	−26.2%	58.2%

continued to a low point in 2007. Then the credit markets fell apart again, and spreads on all corporate debt jumped significantly. The high-yield market again corrected back to normal spreads starting in late 2008. High-yield prices tend to recover earlier than the equity prices.

Some people believe that default risk is nothing more than a type of equity risk and therefore adding high-yield corporate bonds to a portfolio is the equivalent of adding more equity. That argument is not entirely correct. High-yield spreads tend to lead the stock market in forecasting future economic activity. Spreads started widening in October 2007 at the same time the stock market hit a new all time high. In November 2008, high-yield bonds started to recover several months earlier than the equity market turned higher. High-yield bonds were fully recovered in October 2009, while the stock market had only made up half the losses from the bear market. At the time, the S&P 500 crossed 1,050, which was well below the 1,552 October 2007 high.

High-yield bonds are volatile. Accordingly, an adjustment may need to be made in your overall stock and bond asset allocation if you are targeting a certain risk profile for the portfolio. For example, if you place 10 percent of your overall portfolio in a junk bond fund, you might consider reducing your equity allocation by a couple of percentage points to keep the overall portfolio risk at the same level as it was before adding high-yield bonds. Personally, I have never found the need to do this. You might decide otherwise.

One note of caution, I do not recommend buying individual high-yield bonds because of their high trading costs and a genuine lack of investment information. A better approach is to purchase a low-cost mutual fund that concentrates holdings in high-yield bonds. Mutual funds provide instant access to a broadly diversified portfolio of high-yield bonds that have been selected by an experienced manager. A couple of low-cost BB–B-rated high-yield U.S. corporate bond funds are listed at the end of this chapter.

Treasury Inflation-Protected Securities (TIPS)

Treasury Inflation-Protected Securities, or TIPS, were introduced in the late 1990s and are designed to protect against the damaging effects of inflation. Like traditional Treasury notes and bonds, TIPS pay semiannual interest and have a maturity date when the par value of the bond is returned. Unlike traditional Treasuries, the amount of the semiannual interest payments and the par value that is returned on TIPS are not fixed. Those items are linked to the rate of inflation during the issue period. If there was inflation during the time the bond was outstanding, the par value of the bond goes up with that rate of inflation. Since the par value of the bond goes up, the interest received is also higher. The inflation adjustment makes TIPS inflation risk-free, which is unique among all fixed-income investments.

Before investing in TIPS, there are a few things you need to know about the inflation adjustment. The fixed coupon rate is applied to the inflation-adjusted par price. If inflation occurs throughout the life of the security, the par value goes up consistently, and as a result every interest payment will be greater than the previous one. On the other hand, in the rather unusual event of deflation (lower prices), the par value of the bond goes down, and that means that your interest payments will decrease as well.

Before you get too excited about the inflation-adjustment feature of TIPS, you should understand that *all* bonds already have an inflation forecast built into their expected return. Assume that a traditional 10-year Treasury note is yielding 4 percent and that the 10-year TIPS is yielding 2 percent. The 2 percent difference in yield is the expected inflation rate over the next 10 years. The inflation number is already worked into the traditional Treasury yield, whereas it is not in the TIPS.

Investors can gauge what the consensus believes the inflation rate will be in the future by subtracting the yield on a traditional Treasury bond from the yield on TIPS of the same maturity. Figure 8-7 depicts the historical values of the expected inflation rate as the difference in yield between 10-year TIPS bond and a traditional 10-year maturity Treasury bond. By the end of 2009, the inflation expectation based on the 10-year TIPS/nominal spread was 2.23 percent. That was up from a historic 0.25 percent low in 2008.

Also illustrated in Figure 8-7 is the trailing 12-month inflation rate as measured by the Consumer Price Index (CPI). The change in the nominal TIPS spread appears to forecast inflation by about three months with some consistency.

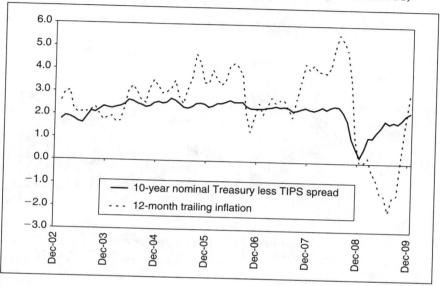

FIGURE 8-7

Treasury Yield Spread: Traditional Treasury Bond Yield to Treasury Inflation-Protected Securities (10-Year Maturities)

— 10-year nominal Treasury less TIPS spread
- - - 12-month trailing inflation

Since TIPS attempt to factor out long-term inflation risk, the "real" expected return on Treasury bonds is the market yield on TIPS. Real return is the amount that investors earn after inflation. One would expect the real return on 10-year TIPS to be constant over time because there is no credit risk in the bond. However, that is not what happens. When trailing inflation is high, the real return on TIPS tends to move higher, and when inflation is low, the real return on TIPS tends to drop.

The yield on TIPS is not entirely an inflation phenomenon. Taxes are another reason for the changing TIPS spread. Our federal government taxes the inflation it creates through fiscal and monetary policy, which is a tax on a tax. Since TIPS prices adjust upward with the inflation rate, income taxes must be paid on both the real income portion of the TIPs and the inflation-adjusted price portion. When inflation is high, investors need to make extra money on the income portion to pay the extra tax due on the inflation portion. Taxing inflation occurs with all investments, but it is more noticeable

FIGURE 8-8

Comparing Barclays Capital U.S. Aggregate Bond Index
Returns to the Barclays Capital TIPS Index

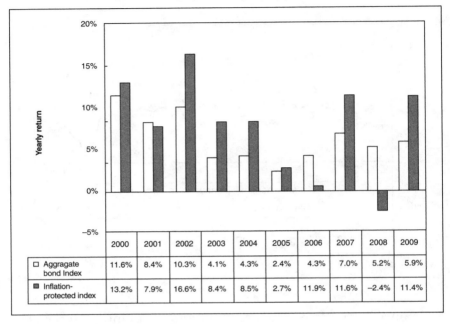

	2000	2001	2002	2003	2004	2005	2006	2007	2008	2009
☐ Aggragate bond Index	11.6%	8.4%	10.3%	4.1%	4.3%	2.4%	4.3%	7.0%	5.2%	5.9%
▣ Inflation-protected index	13.2%	7.9%	16.6%	8.4%	8.5%	2.7%	11.9%	11.6%	-2.4%	11.4%

with TIPS because the inflation portion is physically separated from
the real income portion.

The U.S. Treasury issued the first inflation-protected securities in 1997. The annual return of TIPS since 2000 is highlighted in
Figure 8-8. That figure gives you a good idea of the difference in
return that can occur between TIPS and the Barclays Capital
Aggregate Bond Index. TIPS are not a component of that index.

U.S. Treasury iBonds are also a type of inflation-protected
security that offers a way to save that protects the purchasing power
of an investment. Like TIPS, the interest and inflation gains from
iBonds are exempt from state and local income taxes. In addition,
there are a few features that make iBonds more attractive than TIPS.
First, they are sold at face value in small denominations of $50, $75,
$100, $200, $500, $1,000, and $5,000. Second, federal income tax on
iBonds earnings can be deferred until the bonds are cashed in or

they stop earning interest after 30 years. Third, earnings may be withdrawn tax-free for certain educational purposes. Of course, there are also disadvantages to iBonds. First, investors are limited to $5,000 per year per person. Second, iBonds cashed in before five years are subject to a three-month earnings penalty.

TIPS and iBonds are designed to protect investors from an unexpected jump in inflation. Since there are no inflation-adjusted bonds in the Barclays Capital U.S. Aggregate Bond Index, TIPS and iBonds can be added to the list of potential fixed-income investments to place in your portfolio.

FOREIGN MARKET DEBT

The global bond market is huge. At about $65 trillion, it has about the same market value as the global stock market. Half of the world's tradable fixed-income securities are denominated in U.S. dollars, and the other half are denominated in foreign currencies.

Countries are categorized into two broad types for investment purposes: developed markets and emerging markets. Developed markets are countries with advanced free-market economies and established financial markets. Emerging markets are less developed, with financial markets that may not be robust. There are index funds and ETFs available today that give you access to each type of foreign market debt at reasonable fees.

Figure 8-9 illustrates the difference in annual return that has occurred between the Barclays Capital Aggregate Bond Index and the Citigroup Global Government Bond Index (unhedged) that includes U.S. Treasuries. When a global index is unhedged, it means that local currency returns are included in the index performance. A hedged index would factor out currency risk and assume that all bonds are issued in U.S. dollars.

I am not a big foreign bond advocate. These funds do provide some extra currency diversification; however, the cost of that diversification is high. The fees associated with foreign bond funds are two to three times higher than the cost of a U.S.-only bond fund. Those higher fees negate much, if not all, of the currency diversification benefit. This cost keeps me out of international bond funds.

FIGURE 8-9

Barclays Capital Aggregate Bond Market Index and Citigroup Global Government Bond Index (unhedged)

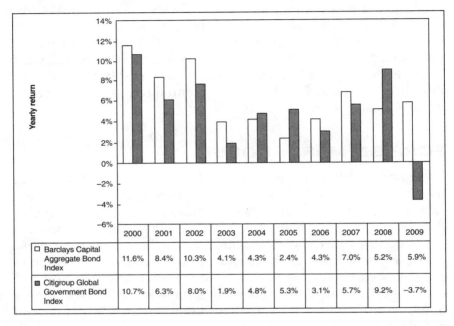

	2000	2001	2002	2003	2004	2005	2006	2007	2008	2009
☐ Barclays Capital Aggregate Bond Index	11.6%	8.4%	10.3%	4.1%	4.3%	2.4%	4.3%	7.0%	5.2%	5.9%
▨ Citigroup Global Government Bond Index	10.7%	6.3%	8.0%	1.9%	4.8%	5.3%	3.1%	5.7%	9.2%	−3.7%

Figure 8-10 represents the hypothetical return comparison of the Citigroup Global Government Bond Index 1–30 years adjusted for a 0.15 percent mutual fund fee to the Citigroup Global Government Bond Index fund adjusted for a 0.5 percent mutual fund fee. The total return of the global bond portfolio was unimpressive, especially considering that during this period the U.S. dollar was down 20 percent against other world currencies. In addition, the global index had more volatility. It is hard to make a case for adding international bonds to a U.S. bond portfolio given the unimpressive performance during a period of strong dollar decline.

Emerging market bonds are also worth a look, although their record is not long. The first emerging market bond mutual funds were established in 1993.

Emerging market bonds have credit ratings on par with U.S. corporate high-yield bonds. The high risk rating is a result of a less developed economic and banking structure and increased political

FIGURE 8-10

Hypothetical Return of U.S. Government Bond Fund to an Unhedged Global Government Bond Fund

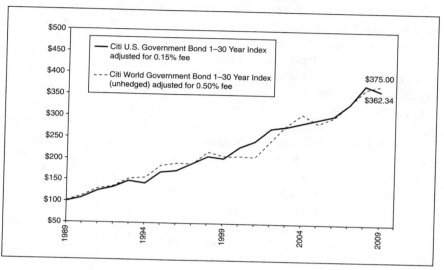

risk. The political environment of some emerging markets can change rapidly and unpredictably.

Like developed market debt, the stumbling block with emerging market debt is also the cost to gain exposure. Emerging market debt funds charge 1.0 percent per year in fees on average, according to the Morningstar Principia database. That is more than double the cost of any bond fund that I would invest in. There are a couple of international bond ETFs listed at the end of this chapter that have lower fees, but once again, I believe that the cost associated with foreign bond funds in general makes them unattractive.

TAX-EXEMPT MUNICIPAL BONDS

Thus far, we have discussed only taxable bonds. Depending on the type of portfolio you are creating and your income tax bracket, tax-exempt municipal bonds may play an important role in your asset allocation. In a taxable account, the after-tax return on municipal bonds will be higher for people in upper income brackets.

Typically, the interest income from a municipal bond issued in the state in which you live is free from all federal, state, and city income taxes (there are exceptions). For that reason, municipal bonds have lower interest payments than taxable government bonds or corporate bonds. However, after tax, the net return is higher.

To compare the yield on taxable bonds to that of tax-free bonds, simply multiply the taxable yield by your tax rate and subtract the result from that yield. If you buy an intermediate-term taxable bond that pays 4 percent interest and your tax on that income is 30 percent, the after-tax return will be 2.8 percent. If the yield on a comparable maturity municipal bond were higher than 2.8 percent, then it would be to your advantage to invest in the tax-free bond. As a rough rule of thumb, if your combined state and federal income tax rate is 30 percent or more, municipal bonds may be an appropriate choice for taxable accounts.

Investors in a high-income tax brackets should consider tax-free municipal bonds in place of investment-grade taxable bonds for their taxable accounts. You could buy individual bonds or a bond fund. A low-cost diversified tax-free bond fund is a good way to diversify the risk of any individual bond going into default. The more bonds a fund holds, the better. The disadvantage of a fund is that it may not be state-tax-exempt in the state you live in. Examples of very low-cost municipal bond mutual funds are listed at the end of the chapter.

PUTTING IT ALL TOGETHER

After completing your analysis of the fixed-income market, the next step is to select an asset allocation for your portfolio. Table 8-4 provides an example of a fixed-income asset allocation that my firm uses in portfolios that have taxable bonds.

Figure 8-11 illustrates the cumulative return of the portfolio in Table 8-4. Adding TIPS and high yield to a portfolio has increased the fixed income with only a marginal increase in risk.

It is impossible to know whether a multi-asset-class fixed-income portfolio will outperform Treasuries and investment-grade portfolios in the future. I believe it will, since investors should be rewarded for taking the added risks of high yield and disinflation. Accordingly, investors who take the time to learn about fixed-income asset allocation will be happy that they did.

TABLE 8-4

Fixed-Income Allocation Using Taxable Bonds

Fixed-Income Allocation	Fixed-Income Category
60%	Barclays Capital Aggregate Bond Index
20%	Treasury Inflation-Protected Bonds or iBonds
20%	High-Yield Corporate Bonds

FIGURE 8-11

Cumulative Returns of a Diversified Fixed-Income Portfolio and the Aggregate Index

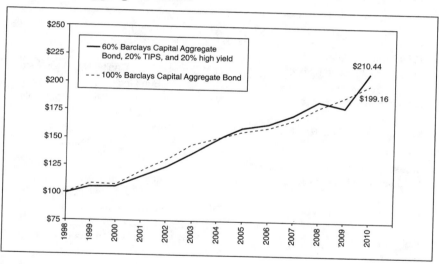

Please keep in mind that the portfolio in Table 8-4 is an example. Each investor should decide on his or her own how to allocation investments to meet his or her unique financial objectives and tax situation.

FIXED-INCOME INVESTMENT LIST

Table 8-5 gives a list of low-cost mutual funds that may be possible candidates for your fixed-income allocation. For more complete information on these and other low-cost no-load funds, read *All*

About Index Funds, 2nd edition, by Richard A. Ferri (New York: McGraw-Hill, 2007). In addition, go to www.Morningstar.com for a wide assortment of mutual fund tools and information.

ETFs that invest in corporate bonds and municipal bonds have certain considerations that investors need to be aware of. Because of illiquidity of most bonds during the credit crisis in 2008, some bond ETFs traded at a steep discount to their calculated net asset value price. Be sure that you are aware that discounts to calculated value can occur before you invest in a bond ETF that holds securities that could become illiquid in a poor market.

TABLE 8-5

Select Low-Cost Fixed-Income Mutual Funds

	Symbol	Benchmark
Total Bond Market Funds		
Vanguard Total Bond Market*	VBMFX	Barclays Capital U.S. Aggregate Bond Index
iShares Barclays Aggregate	AGG	Barclays Capital U.S. Aggregate Bond Index
Vanguard Short-Term Bond Index*	VBISX	Barclays 1–5 Government/Credit Index
Treasury Inflation-Protected Bonds		
Vanguard Inflation-Protected Securities	VIPSX	Barclays Treasury Inflation Notes Index
iShares Barclays TIPS Bond	TIP	Barclays Treasury Inflation Notes Index
Individual iBonds	Purchase through banks or the U.S. Treasury	
High-Yield Corporate Bonds		
Vanguard High-Yield Corporate Bonds	VWEHX	Actively managed B–BB grade
Foreign Bond Funds		
iShares S&P/Citigroup International Treasury Bond	IGOV	Japan is 25% of the fund
iShares JPMorgan USD Emerging Markets	EMB	BB rated bonds
Municipal Bond Funds		
Vanguard Inter-Term Tax-Exempt	VWITX	Actively managed, 6–12 years
Vanguard Limited-Term Tax-Exempt	VMLTX	Actively managed, 2–6 years

*Vanguard ETFs are also available.

CHAPTER SUMMARY

A well-diversified portfolio contains both fixed-income and equity investments. To obtain maximum benefit, the fixed-income portion of the portfolio should also be broadly diversified into several different fixed-income categories and rebalanced annually. Asset allocation of fixed-income investments leads to higher overall returns with little increase in portfolio risk.

There is no lack of diversification potential in the bond market. Fixed-income asset subclasses include government bonds, corporate bonds, home mortgage pools, asset-backed bonds such as those backed by credit card receivables, and foreign developed and emerging markets. A total bond market fund covers most investment-grade fixed-income securities.

The best way to build the fixed-income portion of a portfolio is through low-cost bond mutual funds, particularly bond index funds. Index funds closely track many of the fixed-income indexes used in data analysis in this chapter. Some fixed-income asset classes cannot be purchased with in index fund. For those asset classes, a low-cost actively managed mutual fund is appropriate. Investors in a high tax bracket should consider municipal bond mutual funds as a substitute for taxable investment-grade bonds.

Real Estate Investments

KEY CONCEPTS

- Real estate is a separate asset class from stocks and bonds.
- Real estate investment trusts (REITs) are a convenient way to invest in real estate.
- REITs have low correlation with common stocks and bonds at times.
- Home ownership provides both a place to live and potential gains.

One of the great insights of modern portfolio theory is that holding low-correlated asset classes in a portfolio and rebalancing periodically reduces total portfolio risk and increases long-term returns. Real estate is one of the few asset classes that has exhibited low correlation with stocks and bonds over extended periods of time. A well-diversified portfolio that holds real estate investments alongside stock and bonds has provided superior portfolio returns over one that does not include real estate. This was true even during the poor real estate market that occurred in the mid-2000s.

Investment real estate has two returns: an income component and a growth component. The Brandes Investment Institute and Prudential Financial, in collaboration with Professor Elroy Dimson of the London Business School, conducted a study of the long-term returns on U.S. real estate investments.[1] Dimson found that the long-term return on U.S. real estate has been on a par with the return on the U.S. stock market since the 1930s, as Table 9-1 shows. The study has not been updated through 2009, and real estate values have declined since 2004 by about 10 percent cumulatively. I took the liberty of making that adjustment in the long-term real estate return number in Table 9-1.

Further analysis of the Dimson data shows that the income return component from rents has been very consistent over the decades. Table 9-2 measures the average income return from real estate investments at about 7 percent, plus or minus 1 percent per decade. The 2000–2004 partial decade capital return in the report was revised to reflect the full 2004 year. I completed the set through 2009 based on data from other sources.

TABLE 9-1

Long-Term Returns on U.S. Real Estate

	Real Estate Total Return*	Total Stock Market	Inflation (CPI)
1930–2009	9.1%	9.2%	3.2%

*Brandes Institute report through 2004; author estimate through 2009.

TABLE 9-2

U.S. Real Estate Returns by Decade

Decade	Total Return	Annual Income Return	Capital Return
1930–1939	8.1%	8.4%	−0.3%
1940–1949	13.7%	6.3%	7.0%
1950–1959	6.2%	6.1%	0.2%
1960–1969	6.5%	6.2%	0.3%
1970–1979	10.1%	6.3%	3.6%
1980–1989	11.1%	6.5%	4.3%
1990–1999	5.5%	6.6%	−1.1%
2000–2009*	9.3%	7.5%	1.8%

*Brandes Institute report through 2004; author estimate through 2009.

Nearly all commercial lease contracts have a built-in inflation hedge. Landlords pass inflation increases to tenants based on a general level of prices increases. The ability of landlords to increase rent makes real estate investment particularly attractive as an inflation hedge in an investment portfolio.

In addition to rental properties, home ownership has been a long-term reliable investment as well as providing a place to live. Over the years, homeowners have enjoyed returns of over 3 percent per year, according to government housing data. This is on par with the rate of inflation.

Some areas of the country have seen housing prices appreciate at considerably higher rates in the 1990s and through most of the 2000s. This priced many new home buyers out of the market and caused others to take on too much debt. It also created overdone speculation from some short-term home flippers who were buying with little to no money down. The steep housing correction that occurred from 2007 to 2009 put an end to the speculation. Falling prices plus tax credits for new home buyers plus low mortgage rates orchestrated by the Federal Reserve Bank have stabilized home prices, in most markets.

If possible, investors should consider both home ownership and commercial real estate investment opportunities as an integral part of their long-term investment plan. There is only a finite amount of land available for building, and resources for construction are limited. At the same time the population of the United States continues to increase. Those two facts should keep prices steady in most markets, and they should push prices higher over the long term in the markets where good jobs are being created.

COMMERCIAL REAL ESTATE INVESTMENT OPPORTUNITIES

Investments in commercial real estate can be acquired in three ways: direct investment in properties, indirect investment through limited partnerships (LPs), and indirect investment through publicly traded real estate investment trusts (REITs). Each approach has its advantages and disadvantages.

Direct investment gives an investor full control over the property, including management of rents, costs, and selling decisions.

A direct investment typically leads to the highest return because it eliminates most intermediaries by relying on direct participation by the owner. The disadvantage of direct ownership is that it requires hands-on property management skills and knowledge of the real estate market. While a direct investor could hire a management company to handle the properties, this reduces the total return. In addition to management costs, prolonged vacancies and abusive or deadbeat tenants can also reduce returns. Finally, when an investor wants to sell, a poor resale market could make the sale of properties difficult or less profitable.

Investments in limited partnerships have the potential for attractive gains if you buy into the right one. Finding an honest and experienced general partner is the key. A competent and experienced general partner should handle everything, including the acquisition, management, and resale of the properties. The disadvantage of owning an LP is that the limited partners must remain passive. They are not allowed to participate in any stage of the business. Limited partners have no say in decisions about which properties will be bought, how they will be managed, or when the properties will be sold. In addition, limited partnership shares are generally illiquid. Limited partners often have a very difficult time selling their shares because it is hard to find another investor who is willing to offer a fair and reasonable price.

REITs are the simplest way to participate in the real estate market. Property REITs are like baskets of real estate properties that trade on a stock exchange. The public market for REITs provides instant liquidity. The disadvantage of REITs is the cost of management and administration. If the current income from the underlying real estate is around 8 percent, the income to REIT investors will be about 6 percent. In addition, REIT investors have no management say aside from voting annual proxies.

Over the past 20 years, the REIT market has grown significantly, and REIT mutual funds have become very popular. An investor can own a small slice of thousands of properties in various market segments across the country with the purchase of a REIT index mutual fund or ETF.

There are disadvantages to REITS also. REIT mutual funds have another layer of fund management on top of the management fees already inherent in the REIT management. A second disadvantage is that REIT prices do not typically reflect the true value of the underlying net asset value (NAV) of the real estate. REIT prices tend to be much more volatile than the price of the underlying real estate, and at times shares can trade at steep discounts and large premiums to NAV.

REITS AS AN ASSET CLASS

The investments recommended in this book are low-cost mutual funds. Accordingly, the only commercial real estate recommended in this book are equity REIT funds and ETFs. However, the lessons learned in this section can be applied to other forms of commercial real estate holdings.

In 1960, Congress wrote legislation allowing the formation of pooled real estate trusts that could trade on a major stock exchange. Real estate investment trusts were designed as a tax-efficient vehicle through which investors could own a diversified real estate portfolio. Companies that manage REITs are generally exempt from federal and state income taxes as long as the management company complies with certain Internal Revenue Service code requirements. These are the most important of those requirements:

1. Invest at least 75 percent of the total assets in real estate assets.
2. Derive at least 75 percent of the gross income from real property rents.
3. Pay dividends of at least 90 percent of the taxable income.

Though REITs were a novel concept in the 1960s, they did not catch on with investors. Institutions were not interested because the tax law prohibited five or fewer individuals from owning more than 50 percent of a REIT's shares. As a result, for the first 30 years, the market capitalization of the REIT industry grew to only $5.6 billion (including only equity REITs).

A tax law change in the early 1990s was the catalyst for an explosion in the REIT market. The change allowed pension trusts to take much larger positions in real estate investment without violating trust law. Because of the liquidity that REITs offered, institutions saw them as a perfect avenue for increasing their exposure to real estate.

According to the National Association of Real Estate Investment Trusts (NAREIT), between 1990 and 2009, the market grew from $5.5 billion in fewer than 60 small equity REITs to over 100 issues with over $250 billion of market capitalization. Although those sound like impressive numbers, equity REITs still represent a relatively small part of the overall commercial real estate market and less than 3 percent of the capitalization of the U.S. stock market.

The securitization of the real estate market still has a long way to go. The total value of the commercial real estate market is approximately $15 trillion, according to Federal Reserve data. But not all real estate is eligible for inclusion in REITs. Publicly traded corporations own a large amount of commercial real estate, which therefore is technically already included as part of their common stock price. After adjusting for corporate holdings, there is approximately $4 trillion in investible U.S. commercial real estate that is available, of which less than 7 percent is part of a publicly traded REIT.

Equity and Other Types of REITs

REITs are divided into three basic categories: equity, mortgage, and hybrid. Equity REITs are the only type that invests entirely in real estate properties. They are the purest form of real estate holding. Mortgage REITs do not own property directly. Instead, they finance properties through commercial loans. Mortgage REITs are basically a type of bond investment rather than a real estate investment. Hybrid REITs hold both properties and mortgages. As such, a hybrid REIT derives a portion of its return from the performance of properties and a portion from the performance of the mortgage portfolio.

The focus of this chapter on real estate is on isolating a unique asset class, that is, commercial properties. Consequently, the data in this book reflect the risk and return of only equity REITs. Data on mortgage REITs and hybrids are not included.

There are over 100 different equity REITs traded on the U.S. stock market. Those companies invest in a wide variety of properties, including shopping malls, office complexes, apartment buildings, and hotels. Investors who wish to own it all can purchase an index mutual fund of equity REITs that gives them an equity stake in tens of thousands of properties across the country.

The Performance of Equity REITs

The performance of equity REITs can be divided into two categories. The first is the performance of REIT share prices, and the second is the dividend payments and reinvestment return on the dividend. As long as REITs pay at least 90 percent of their taxable income out to shareholders in the form of a dividend, the company does not have to pay corporate tax on the earnings. For that reason, the majority of their performance comes from the dividend yield and reinvestment return on those dividends.

Figures 9-1 and 9-2 offer a graphic illustration of the importance of dividends to REIT investors. Figure 9-1 represents the growth of $1 invested in NAREIT equity price only. The chart does not include dividends or the reinvestment return on the dividends. Figure 9-2 illustrates the total return with dividends paid and reinvested compared to the total return of the U.S. stock market over the past two decades. The long-term returns are almost identical.

FIGURE 9-1

Equity NAREIT Index (Price Only) Generally Tracks Inflation
Starting Value of $1

FIGURE 9-2

Equity NAREIT Total Return Index versus the CRSP Total U.S. Stock Index Growth of $1

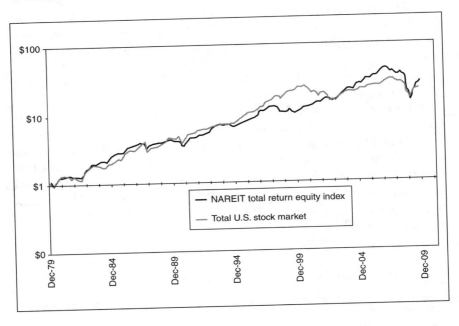

In general, the price only of equity REITs has increased with the return of inflation as measured by the CPI. That is understandable, given the fact that rents typically increase with the rate of inflation and that equity REITs are required to distribute 90 percent of their taxable income.

Once dividends and the reinvestment of dividends are added to the index, a different picture emerges. For all practical purposes, the risk and return of REITs and U.S. common stocks are close enough to say that they have the same long-term expected risks and returns.

Figure 9-3 illustrates the differences in year-over-year returns that have occurred between the total U.S. stock market, the Barclays Intermediate-Term Government/Credit Index, and the Wilshire REIT Index (an index of equity REITs). As you can see from the returns, there has been little consistency among the returns of the three asset classes.

FIGURE 9-3

Annual Returns on CRSP Total U.S. Stocks, Intermediate Bonds, and REITs

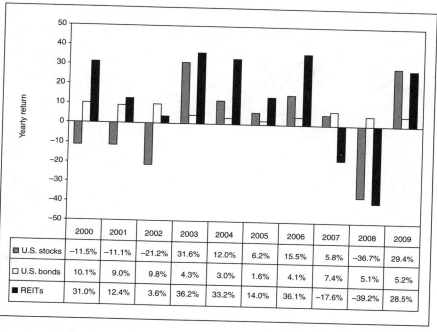

	2000	2001	2002	2003	2004	2005	2006	2007	2008	2009
▦ U.S. stocks	−11.5%	−11.1%	−21.2%	31.6%	12.0%	6.2%	15.5%	5.8%	−36.7%	29.4%
☐ U.S. bonds	10.1%	9.0%	9.8%	4.3%	3.0%	1.6%	4.1%	7.4%	5.1%	5.2%
■ REITs	31.0%	12.4%	3.6%	36.2%	33.2%	14.0%	36.1%	−17.6%	−39.2%	28.5%

CORRELATION ANALYSIS

Prior to the tax law changes concerning REITs in 1992, the risk-and-return characteristics of REITs were very similar to those of stocks. The high correlation between REITs and domestic stocks indicated that overall market movements affected real estate investment trusts.

By the early 1990s, the market's perception of these securities began to shift. The REIT market was evolving, and investor understanding of the sector was increasing. In turn, shifts in the market began to alter the behavior patterns of this asset class. Over the next 10 years, correlations between REITs and the rest of the stock market declined and actually became negative for a brief period in 2001. The correlation shifted again, and REITs become highly correlated with U.S. equities by the end of the decade. Figure 9-4 documents this phenomenon.

FIGURE 9-4

Rolling 36-Month Correlation between the NAREIT Equity Index and the CRSP Total U.S. Stock Index

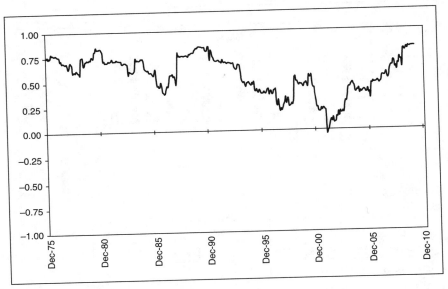

The varying correlation between REITs and the rest of the stock market has created a diversification opportunity for investors. Figure 9-5 represents the risk-and-return frontier that was created by adding REITs to a U.S. equity portfolio.

The risk and return on REITs and the U.S. market is close to the same. However, there has been a strong diversification benefit to owning REITs because of the varying correlation shown in Figure 9-4. Although the figure shows an efficient allocation of 40 percent in REITs and 60 percent in common stocks, I do not recommend putting more than 10 percent of your equity in REITs because REITs represent a narrow market sector, and there are a limited number of holdings available. Only about 100 REITs trade on U.S. exchanges.

The Wilshire REIT Index is similar to the NAREIT Index in that it represents all publicly traded equity REITs. The difference between the two indexes is that Wilshire began its index in 1987, and it did not include hospital or health-care facilities until 2002.

FIGURE 9-5

Risk-and-Return Chart for the CRSP Total Stock Market and Wilshire REIT Equity Index, 1980–2009

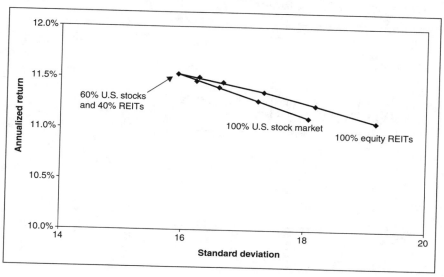

The benefit of using the Wilshire REIT Index is that it is investible, meaning that there are index mutual funds that track the Wilshire REIT Index.

Real estate prices and interest rates are related. As interest rates fall, real estate prices rise as demand increases. Therefore, many people assume that there must be a high correlation between the return on bonds and the return on REITs. However, this does not show up in the data. Figure 9-6 illustrates the rolling 36-month correlation between REIT returns and the returns from the Barclays Capital Intermediate-Term Index.

Figure 9-7 puts an investment in REITs into perspective. It illustrates the benefit of a multi-asset-class portfolio. The risk-and-return chart is based on a portfolio of intermediate-term bonds and an equity allocation of 20 percent REITs and 80 percent in the total stock market. At every point, an allocation to REITs lowered the risk of the portfolio, which in turn increased the long-term return.

Rolling 36-Month Correlation between the NAREIT Equity
Index and the Barclays Capital Intermediate
Government/Credit Index

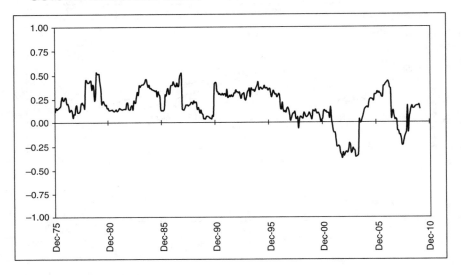

Comparison of Portfolios with and without REITs, 1980–2009

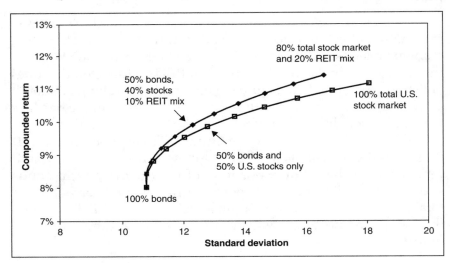

I reiterate that 20 percent in REITs may be too much. Only about 100 REITs are available on the U.S. exchanges. Real estate is still a narrow subsector of the U.S. market, representing less than 3 percent of market capitalization. Accordingly, my belief is that 10 percent of an equity portfolio allocation to a REIT index fund is enough.

Equity REITs are a low-correlation asset class that should be included on your list of potential investments. There are several low-cost REIT index funds that mirror the return on REIT indexes. See Table 9-3 at the end of this chapter for a partial list.

HOME OWNERSHIP

No chapter on real estate would be complete without a discussion of home ownership. In addition to providing living quarters, purchasing a home in a good location has proved to be a reliable long-term investment. Homeowners in the United States have enjoyed annual returns that have averaged slightly higher than the inflation rate over the decades. Despite a recent decline in the housing market, the interest on a mortgage remains a tax deduction, and some or all of the profit from selling your home is tax-free.

Figure 9-8 represents the average price of a single-family home since 1987, as published by the S&P Case/Shiller Composite–10 Housing Index. The data are collected from local tax offices and represent the sale price of properties that have closed. The index is designed to capture changes in the value of single-family homes in 10 large metropolitan areas in the United States. The index uses a repeated sales measure, meaning it measures average price changes in repeat sales of the same properties.

There are two measurements in Figure 9-8. One is the nominal price of homes, and the other is the inflation-adjusted price. For decades, that price of U.S. homes kept pace with the inflation rate adjusted for improvements, such as central heating and air-conditioning. Then in the mid–1990s, housing prices experienced a steady increase in real returns in some parts of the country. This became a speculative bubble in California, Arizona, Nevada, Florida, and a few other areas. The buying frenzy peaked in 2006, and prices soon cascaded down, bringing the rest of the economy

FIGURE 9-8

House Price Index versus the Consumer Price Index

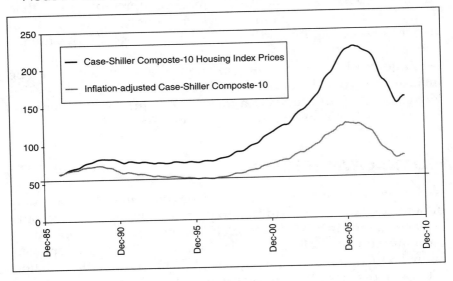

with them. Prices are approaching their long-term inflation-adjusted level as of this writing.

Figure 9-9 represents the year-over-year increase in housing, and there are several points of interest on the chart. The high-inflation years of the late 1970s and early 1980s drove housing prices up at double-digit rates. In the early 1990s, a recession and the Gulf War caused prices to flatten. Housing prices climbing steadily from 1995 until 2006, and then a housing collapse drove prices sharply lower in 2008 and well into 2009.

In retrospect, values during 2000 to 2005 are of particular interest. Housing prices continued upward during a difficult period in the U.S. economy, gaining between 4 and 7 percent per year. This advance occurred despite a collapse in the stock market, an economic recession, the tragic events of September 11, 2001, and two wars.

There were three main reasons for the increase in housing prices during the 2000–2003 period. First, people wanted to put their money into something they could see and touch after experiencing a collapse in the stock market. Second, mortgage

FIGURE 9-9

Housing Price Index, Year-over-Year National Price Change, 1974–2009

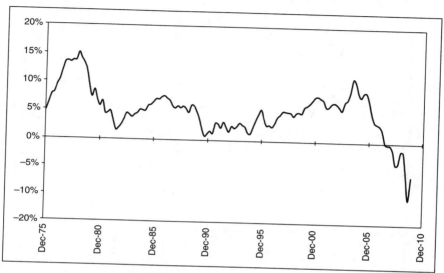

originators offered record low interest rates along with new mortgage products that required little money down. Third, the U.S. government provided buying incentives in the form of easy qualification rules and great tax benefits. Figure 9-10 reflects the 30-year mortgage rate as reported by the Federal Home Loan Mortgage Corporation.

When I wrote the first edition of this book in 2005, I stated that the gains in home prices may be close to peaking. At the time, my forecast was for a gradual decline in housing prices in some areas of the country. For once in my professional career I was right about the short-term direction of a market, although I was wrong in my forecast that the price decline would be gradual. Prices fell like a rock from 2007 to 2009, and foreclosures skyrocketed. That left many financial institutions with a lot of illiquid real estate they did not want and could not sell, and that in turn led to a global recession.

I believe that home prices are down to where they should have been all along without the bubble. I would not be afraid to buy a home at 2010 prices.

FIGURE 9-10

30-Year Mortgage Rates as Reported by the Federal Home Loan Mortgage Corporation

For practical reasons, home equity from the house you live in should be left outside the asset allocation of your investment portfolio. The primary purpose for buying the home is for you to have a place to live. Any appreciation of that property after taxes, interest expense, and inflation is purely incidental to its function as shelter. Trying to include your home as part of your asset allocation to real estate in an investment portfolio creates a number of problems because you can never be sure of the true market value, and you cannot rebalance your home equity against other assets.

REIT INVESTMENT LIST

Table 9-3 is a partial list of low-cost funds that are candidates for your REIT allocation. For more information on these and other low-cost no-load funds and the indexes they follow, read *All About Index Funds*, 2nd edition (New York: McGraw-Hill, 2007), and *The ETF Book*, 2nd edition (Hoboken, NJ: Wiley, 2009).

TABLE 9-3

Low-Cost REIT Mutual Funds

Equity REIT Index Funds	Symbol	Benchmark
Vanguard REIT Index Fund*	VGSIX	Morgan Stanley REIT Index
iShares Dow Jones U.S. REIT	IYR	Dow Jones U.S. REIT Index
SPDR Wilshire REIT	RWR	Wilshire REIT Index

*The Vanguard REIT ETF symbol is VNQ.

CHAPTER SUMMARY

Adding asset classes that have low or varying correlations to a portfolio reduces total portfolio risk and increases long-term return. Real estate is one of the few asset classes that has low correlation with bonds and varying correlation with stocks. A well-diversified portfolio that holds real estate investments alongside stock and bond investments has proved to be a more efficient portfolio than one that does not include real estate investment.

There are many ways to invest in the commercial real estate market; however, equity REITs are the most liquid and convenient way. Equity REITs are portfolios of apartments, hotels, malls, industrial buildings, and other rental property that trade on a stock exchange. Several low-cost REIT index funds that give you instant diversification across the entire REIT market are available.

In addition to investing in commercial real estate, make your home an investment. Traditionally, home prices have kept pace with the inflation rate and have outpaced inflation during a falling interest-rate environment. Pick your location carefully. Every town and city has areas that will appreciate more than others, and there are some areas of the country where home prices may not appreciate because there's no job growth.

NOTE

[1]Elroy Dimson, "A Perspective on Long-Term Real Estate Returns: United States," *Brandes Institute Journal*, April 2004, no. 1: 72–89.

CHAPTER 10

Alternative Investments

KEY CONCEPTS

- Alternative asset classes extend beyond traditional stocks and bonds.
- Many alternative asset classes are difficult to invest in.
- Illiquidity and high costs often overshadow any advantage.
- Some mutual funds and ETFs are now available at a moderate fee.

Modern portfolio theory is not limited to stocks, bonds, and real estate. Over the years, alternative asset classes have been playing a larger role in portfolio design. Alternative asset classes include investments in commodities, collectibles, and hedge funds.

Some say that the advantage of adding alternative assets to a portfolio is that they tend to exhibit low correlation with traditional stock and bond investments. For this reason, some people argue that alternative asset classes in a portfolio has the potential to lower overall portfolio risk and increase long-term return. I have doubts.

Stocks and bonds are for investing; commodities are for speculating. Commodities include physical assets and futures contracts that track the price of everything from wheat to gold to pork bellies. These are not growth assets. A ton of copper today will be a ton of copper 10 years from now and 100 years from now, and a ton of copper pays no dividends or interest.

Price volatility alone does not generate an inflation-adjusted return from an investment. It is cash flow that drives real returns higher. The earnings growth from corporate stock that leads to cash dividends, interest income from bonds, rents from real estate, and the known scarcity value of collectibles such as rare coins are the things that create real wealth. Commodity prices will go up and down with the volatility of stocks, but they will not deliver the return of stocks because they have no ability to create cash income.

The way people make money in commodities is to be on the right side of a price trend. Consequently, timing is everything. You could make money in commodities if you are one of the rare people in the world who has superior information about future supply-and-demand trends and then convert this knowledge into skillful trades, or if you get lucky and guess right on future prices.

No chapter on alternative investing would be complete without a discussion of hedge funds. These are private investment accounts for qualified investors. Hedge funds are mostly unregulated. Hedge funds are not an asset class. Hedge funds are pooled investment vehicles that are privately organized and administered by professional investment managers. What makes a hedge fund uniquely different is the manager's freedom to invest capital. A hedge fund may hold a large, concentrated stock position; employ a liberal use of leverage; use futures, options, swaps, and other derivatives; or sell investments short.

Investors became obsessed with the mystique of hedge funds from 2000 to 2008 as stock returns waned. This is especially true in the high-net-worth marketplace, where investors clamor for access to some hedge fund opportunities.

Hedge funds are very expensive. If the fund makes a gain, much of that gain goes to the hedge fund manager as a bonus in addition to his or her regular management fee. The funds are also illiquid, with many funds requiring months or even years before you are allowed to withdraw money. Finally, truly skilled hedge fund managers are not interested in managing your messy little pot of money, and you will not gain access to their fund unless you have many millions to put in. The hedge funds available to people of moderate wealth are not the same ones that multibillion-dollar investors have access to.

Be careful not to pay too much for access should you decide to use alternative assets. The costs of investing in commodities and hedge funds can quickly outweigh any diversification benefits. A good rule of thumb for all alternative investments is this: When in doubt, stay out.

COMMODITIES

Commodities are common products that are used every day, such as food, basic materials, and energy-related items. Food products include items such as sugar, corn, and oats; basic materials include items such as steel and aluminum; energy is traded in the form of crude oil, natural gas, and electricity. Another category is precious metals such as gold and silver. All together, these resources make up the global commodities market.

The global market for commodities is as wide as it is deep. Since commodities are dug up, manufactured, or grown in almost every nation in the world, there are hundreds of global commodities markets. There is trading going on someplace 24 hours a day, 7 days a week. If you want to buy an ounce of gold at 10:00 p.m., it can be arranged through any large commodities broker. If you want to sell oil at 3:00 a.m., that can also be arranged.

Pick up any *Wall Street Journal* and turn to the Money and Investing section to find a partial list of commodities that trade on U.S. exchanges. The *Wall Street Journal* gives both *spot* and *futures* prices. The spot price is what physical commodity is changing hands for today, while a futures price is a contract for delivery of a set amount of the physical commodity some time in the future.

Generally, commodities are divided into groups. Those groups are

- Energy: crude oil, heating oil, natural gas, electricity
- Industrials: copper, steel, cotton
- Precious metals: gold, platinum, silver, aluminum
- Livestock: live cattle, lean hogs
- Grains and oilseeds: corn, soybeans, wheat
- Softs: cocoa, coffee, orange juice, sugar

By definition, a commodity suggests abundance. There's a lot of it around, or it can be easily grown, dug up, or pumped out. Although there are occasional shortages that create a temporary jump in prices, the shortage tends to fix itself. If wheat prices rise because of greater demand, farmers will grow more wheat next season. If a shortage of steel causes prices to rise, producers will dig more ore. If oil is scarce, companies will pump more oil, explore for more reserves, and accelerate the pursuit for alternatives. In addition, as prices climb, new competitors come into the marketplace from all over the world.

If the price of a commodity stays high for an extended period of time, there is a move to find cheap substitutes. For example, if the price of gasoline remains high, auto companies increase research and development into electric-powered vehicles and alternative fuels such as hydrogen and natural gas. It may take several years for users and producers to figure out how to get around high energy prices, but eventually supply catches up with demand, and the price of energy drops.

If corn prices rise because of greater demand from ethanol manufactures, farmers will grow more corn next season and keep growing more corn until the supply exceeds demand and prices fall. Substitutes to corn cattle feed will increase, and a substitute to corn-based ethanol will be found. If a building boom causes a shortage of steel, prices will rise, producers will mine more ore, mini-mills will recycle more scrap, and new producers will come on line all over the world; and then the building boom will end and steel prices will plummet. Whenever a commodity is priced high enough to make a large enough profit, more of the commodity is created or harvested by current suppliers and new competitors bring more supply.

The supply-and-demand cycle is true even for precious metals such as gold. Although it is not always possible to locate more ore and dig it out, new techniques for extracting gold from the current production can increase supply. In addition, if prices are high enough, increased selling by governments and large institutions can dump a large supply on the market and quickly bring prices down. Finally, when the supply of gold is greater than the demand, the price falls back to its true economic value. This is likely the scenario occurring in 2010 as I write this book.

It may take several years for the new supply to meet demand. Start-up costs are high, and the discovery of new resources take time. Spikes in prices tend to not be good for long-term commodity producers because, more often than not, spikes in prices eventually lead to oversupply, which leads to rapid price declines and potential operating losses. Such is the boom-and-bust nature of the business.

Figure 10-1 illustrates the price of gold and oil adjusted for the rate of inflation since 1955. Both items are started at $1. There have been a few spikes in gold and oil prices over the years, but those spikes tend to fall back to the rate of inflation over time. Oil seems to fall back first, followed buy the price of gold.

Oil prices are always in flux because of constant changes in global supply-and-demand estimates. The price we pay for gasoline reflects these changes. In recent years, price uncertainty and hence volatility have been heightened as a result of increasing demand for oil from emerging markets such as China and India.

FIGURE 10-1

Gold and Oil Prices Adjusted for Inflation

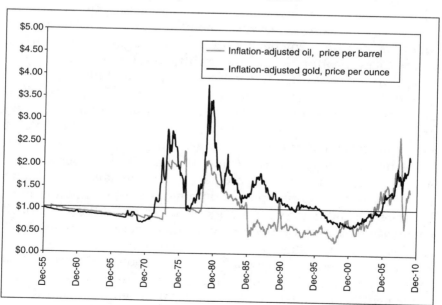

Nonetheless, the price of oil tends to have a boom-and-bust cycle. Figure 10-1 illustrates that the biggest run-up in price occurred in 1981 when oil hit an inflation-adjusted high.

There are data on gold prices going back thousands of years, and those data show that gold and inflation are basically one and the same. There have been large spikes in gold prices, followed by large price drops, but those movements tend to cancel each other out. Gold is a store of wealth that people hoard during bad economic times and sell when money is being made in other assets. Prices run up fast and then run down almost as fast, although it does take a while longer after an economic shock. In general though, the longer a global economic expansion runs, the more gold prices fall.

The Oldest Commodities Index

The commodities markets are much older than the stock markets. Some commodities prices go back thousands of years. The Commodity Research Bureau (CRB) index data used for this chapter go back more than 70 years.

The Bureau of Labor Statistics began the computation of a daily commodity price index in 1934. This eventually became the CRB Spot Market Price Index, a comprehensive measure of the price movements of 22 actively traded commodities. These commodities include cocoa beans, corn, steers, sugar, wheat, burlap, copper scrap, cotton, lead scrap, print cloth (spot), rubber, steel scrap, wool tops, butter, hides, hogs, lard, rosin, tallow, tin, zinc, and the basic energy-related items. Initially, the prices compiled to create the index were obtained from trade publications and government agencies. Today, prices are more readily available to everyone through electronic exchanges.

There are also numerous composite indexes that track all commodity prices. Some of those are new, and some have been around for a long time. Energy typically dominates the commodities markets by size, and it accounts for about 80 percent of the value of all commodities traded. Consequently, capitalization-weighted indexes are dominated by energy prices.

The CRB Index is an equally weighted index. This means that the price movement in cotton has the same impact as the price movement in oil. Equal weighting gives us a better picture of how

FIGURE 10-2

CRB Commodities Spot Prices, Inflation-Adjusted: Base of 100 in 1947

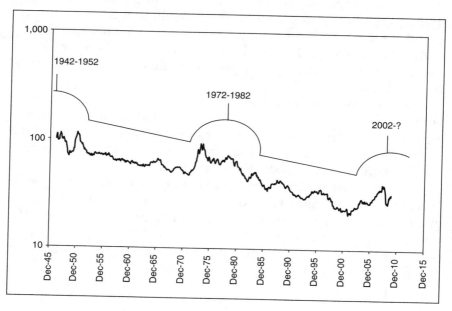

the average commodity price performed regardless of its footprint on the economy. Figure 10-2 is a graphical history of the inflation-adjusted CRB Spot Index since 1947.

The inflation-adjusted price of all commodities has fallen considerably over the past 63 years. The annual inflation-adjusted decline was about 1 percent per year. This is a result of many factors: productivity gains from technologies and innovations, increased foreign competition, substitutes for commodities paid for by governments, and government-imposed price controls and tariffs.

Some people believe that the world is destined for permanently higher commodities prices in the future. However, Figure 10-2 suggests that the recent boom may be short lived. The price pattern in Figure 10-2 shows that a commodities boom tends to happen every generation or so, with the last three boom periods starting almost exactly 30 years apart. Prices then fall to a lower level adjusted for inflation at the end of each boom.

Forward Contracts

Spot trading of physical commodities is not practical for most investors. A direct investment in grains is not possible unless you own a silo where you can store 10,000 bushels of corn. Buying oil on the spot market does not make sense for investors unless they own a tank to store 1,000 gallons of crude oil. There are a few exceptions to this rule. Physical gold and other precious metals can now be traded as an ETF.

Most people trade commodity futures rather than physical commodities. These are paper contracts that grant ownerships rights some time in the future. Futures contracts are based on a future delivery price rather then the current spot price. The contracts can be traded, like stocks, on a futures exchange.

Commodity futures represent an obligation to buy commodities in the months ahead based on a price that is negotiated today. A contract is a standardized agreement to buy or sell a specific commodity type and quantity at that future date and price. Only a small amount of money is needed to secure a futures contract, and this gives investors a huge amount of leverage.

Calculating Futures Prices

Futures prices can differ significantly from spot prices. Calculating the futures price begins with the current spot price, and then it adjusts for a variety of factors that may include seasonal changes in supply and demand, borrowing costs, storage expenses, and other costs-of-carry expenses. If futures prices are trading at a higher level than the current spot price, it is known as *contango.* When futures prices are trading lower than spot prices, it is known as *backwardation.*

Figure 10-3 is an example of the oil futures market in contango and backwardation. It is based on a $60-per-barrel expected spot price for oil.

There has been a long debate about the returns on commodities futures. Some studies suggest that the returns are comparable to stocks even though the long-term spot market has not achieved those results. Other academic studies show that futures returns tend to be closer to the inflation rate. The discrepancies revolve

FIGURE 10-3

Oil Futures Prices in Backwardation and Contango

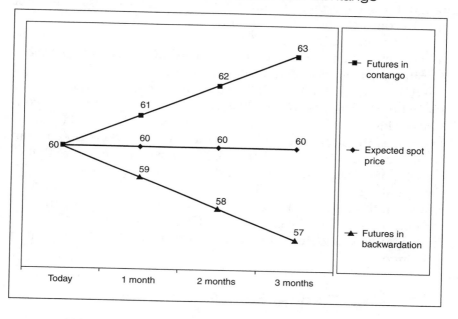

around the period studied, who conducted the study, and why it was conducted. Many studies that show abnormal returns have been done by people who have a vested interest in selling commodity investments. Neutral studies show far lower returns.

Logically, if commodities futures spend half their time in contango and half their time in backwardation, there should be no advantage to buying the spot or buying the futures. The total return should be the same whether you buy the physical asset and store it or buy the futures contract and invest your cash in short-term T-bills. This is essentially what has happened as we discuss later in this chapter.

Mutual funds and ETFs that invest in futures must roll contracts from one month to the next to avoid thousands of gallons of oil showing up at the company's doorstep on the futures' expiration date. The roll yield can be positive or negative, depending on the relationship of next month's futures prices to near-term futures prices. In a simplistic sense, if the commodity is in backwardation, the second month contract is less expensive than the first month contract, and buyers can earn a profit. If the commodity is in contango, the second month contract is more expensive than the first month contract, and buyers lose out.

For many years, energy futures buyers made money from an oil market stuck in backwardations. According to data from Barclays Capital, oil was in a state of backwardation about 57 percent of the time between 1983 and 2007. However, the gains earned during those times became losses in 2006 when the market went into contango. This hurt ETF investors. The United States Oil Fund (symbol: USO) was the first crude oil ETF on the U.S. market. USO began trading on April 10, 2006, at $68.25, a price roughly equal to that of a barrel of oil at the time. The fund closed one year later at $52.01, representing a decline of 23.8 percent. During that same period, however, the U.S. benchmark price of crude oil fell only a modest 6.5 percent. Much of the extra loss in USO was a loss resulting from the negative roll yield from an oil futures market that moved into contango.

Trading Futures Contracts

A futures contract is an agreement to buy or sell a set amount of a commodity on a designated date in the future and at an agreed-upon price. Futures are part of a class of securities called *derivatives*, so named because they derive their value from the worth of an underlying asset. In the case of commodities futures, a contract is priced in part on today's spot price for that commodity and in part on the anticipated spot price on the future delivery date.

Think of a futures contract as nothing more than buying a commodity on layaway. As a buyer, you agree on the price of a standardized commodity contract and holding amount for the contract known as margin. The balance on the contract is due on the delivery date of the commodity. A contract is an obligation, so it must be honored by both the buyer and the seller. However, you do not need to take delivery of the commodity. You are allowed to sell the contract any time before the delivery date and close out your position.

A standardized futures contract for a commodity has a preestablished size and settles on a preestablished date. It is traded on one of the established futures exchanges and is confirmed with a standard holding payment known as *margin*. Margin is typically 2 to 7 percent of the value of the contract, depending on the commodity. That money is placed in escrow until the contract expires.

Here is an example of how a commodities futures contract may be used. Assume that an oil refinery wants to lock in the price it pays for crude oil three months in advance. The refinery simply buys crude oil futures for delivery in three months and puts up a small amount of margin. Now the refinery knows the price that it will pay for crude three months in advance and can budget for it. In the same way, oil producers can sell oil futures to be delivered in three months, even though they do not have the oil on hand today. This allows the oil producers to know what price they will receive for the oil they sell three months from now and know how much they will need to produce.

The price of a futures contract depends on many factors. The most important factor is the spot price of the commodity. Typically, a near-term futures contract will be priced very close to the spot price. Other factors that influence price include the outlook for supply and demand, the cost of storage until delivery, and the level of interest rates between now and the delivery date. At times the futures price of a commodity contract may be higher than the spot price, and at other times it may be lower. This depends on the consensus price forecast. Figure 10-4 illustrates the historical difference in price between CRB spot prices and one-month CRB futures prices.

It is interesting to note that during the 1990s, near-term delivery futures prices lagged spot commodity prices by a considerable amount. During the decade, futures buyers were anticipating lower raw material costs as productivity gains and foreign competition drove prices down. A low point for commodities futures prices relative their spot prices occurred in the late 1990s. Futures prices rallied during the past decade. This caused the spread between spot prices and futures prices to disappear. For a while demand for futures-related products become so great that the return from futures was higher than the return from spot prices. This created a one-time excess gain for futures market investors that has since gone away.

FIGURE 10-4

CRB Commodities Spot Prices versus near Contract
Futures Prices

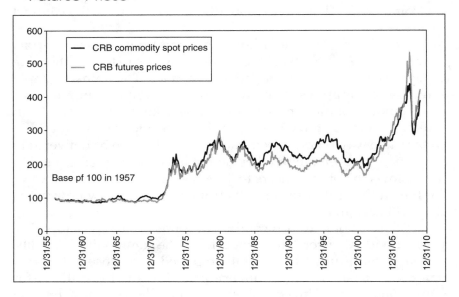

Commodities Total Return Indexes

The CRB Commodity Total Return Index in Figure 10-5 takes some explaining. The index is designed to replicate the return on an investible basket of commodities which cannot be invested in directly. Therefore, the way the index is calculated combines the price movement of commodities and the difference in price between old futures contracts near expiration and new futures prices on the day contracts are rolled to the next month, plus the income from Treasury bills.

As you recall, margin is required to buy a futures contract. Margin is about 5 percent of the value of the commodities that the futures contract represents. For example, a futures contract for $4,000 worth of gold for delivery in one month may require a 5 percent margin which is $200, which gains money market interest. Assuming that you have $4,000, this leaves $3,800 in your account that can be invested in something else while you wait for delivery. The total return on your investment for one month equals the price change on the gold futures contract plus the interest on the other 95 percent that

FIGURE 10-5

CRB Futures Total Return Index Assuming a T-Bill Return on the Cash Portion

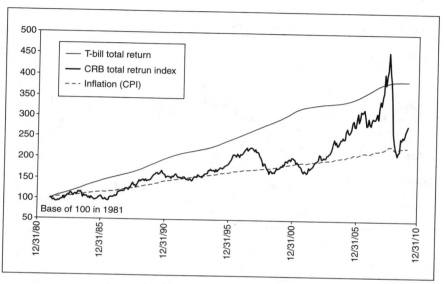

is sitting in your account. If you roll the contract to the next month, there will be another gain or loss based on the difference between near-term futures prices and one-month futures prices.

A total return commodities index includes the price change of the commodity, the price difference between near-term and one-month futures contracts, and the interest income earned overall on the cash and margin. The 95 percent cash portion is assumed to be invested in Treasury bills for the sake of calculating total return indexes. The one-month returns are linked together over an extended period of time to form Figure 10-5. As you can see, you make little to no money over T-bills if you do not time commodity purchases and sales correctly.

Commodities in a Portfolio

What makes commodities funds attractive to investors is their low correlation with stocks and bonds. This means that the traditional securities markets' going down does not affect the prices of

FIGURE 10-6

Rolling 36-Month Correlation of the CRB Total Return Index to U.S. Stocks and Intermediate-Term Treasury Bonds

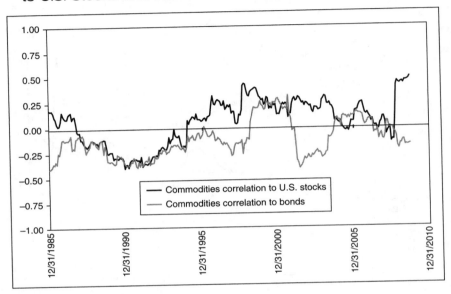

commodities. Figure 10-6 illustrates the correlation between the CRB Total Return Index, U.S. stocks, and Treasury bonds. Commodities total return indexes generally have a low correlation with stocks and bonds, and this should make them a good diversifier in a portfolio. But there are issues. One is the long-term low return from commodities, and the other is the tendency for high correlation with stocks when stocks are crashing.

Figures 10-5 and 10-6 represent a dilemma for investors. Commodities total return indexes have had at times low correlation with other asset classes, *but they also have historically low returns*. While low correlation is a great attribute for an asset class from a risk reduction perspective, *you cannot eat low correlation*. In addition, the correlation can become positive very quickly, and during periods when you don't want them to. When stocks tumble, commodities can also go into a steep decline. That was the case in 2008.

The purpose of investing is to achieve a long-term financial goal. Thus all investments in your portfolio should independently be expected to earn a real return over the inflation rate based in that asset class. Commodities fail this test. Although very volatile, commodities should not be expected to earn more than inflation over the long term. Even if the volatility of your portfolio is slightly lower with a commodities position, you are better off skipping this asset class and keeping your money in stocks and bonds that reward you with real returns.

If You Must Own Commodities

If you insist on owning commodities, then be sensible about how you invest. Buying individual commodities futures contracts is not a good idea. Individual contracts are very risky because of their high degree of leverage. You would need to invest in several different contracts on several different commodities to gain proper diversification. A better alternative is to get commodities exposure through a broadly diversified mutual fund. Another different approach is to invest through an industry-sector mutual fund that holds commodity-producing companies. A few reasonably priced mutual funds are listed in Table 10-4 at the end of this chapter.

Commodities mutual funds invest in derivatives of commodities total return indexes. Therefore, investors in those funds should understand how commodities indexes are constructed. There are several competing commodities total return indexes. Like stock indexes, each commodities index provider has its own methodology for calculating returns and its reasons for believing that its system is superior to everyone else's.

Three popular indexes are the Commodity Research Bureau Index (Reuters-CRB), the S&P GSCI (formally the Goldman Sachs Commodity Index), and the Dow Jones–UBS Commodity Index (DJ-UBS). The most important difference among these three indexes is their approach to weighting the different commodity groups; they include.

- Reuters-CRB is an equal-weighted index of 22 commodity prices. Equal weighting means that a 1 percent rise in the price of nickel has the same effect on the index as a 1 percent rise in the price of crude oil.
- The S&P GSCI considers the price of 24 commodities based on overall market value. Since the total value of oil produced globally dominates the commodities markets, the GSCI methodology generates an excessively heavy

energy weighting. In other words, a 1 percent rise in the price of crude oil has a significantly larger effect on the S&P GSCI than a 1 percent rise in the price of nickel.

- The DJ-UBS Commodities Index is derived from the value of 19 commodities. The DJ-UBS is also a market-weighted index, but with a twist: no commodity group in the index starts at over 33 percent (energy), and no single group component may be more than 15 percent (such as crude oil). The DJ-UBS is reweighted and rebalanced annually, with restrictions.

The difference in the three approaches to commodities indexes is explained in Table 10-1, which indicates the relative importance of different commodity groups in each of the three indexes.

Despite the differences in the group weights, the returns on the three commodity indexes have high correlation with one another and low correlations with U.S. equities and bonds. Table 10-2

TABLE 10-1

Commodity Index Weights in 2009

Commodity Group	Reuters-CRB Weight	S&P GSCI Weight	DJ-UBS Weight
Energy	18%	70%	33%
Grains	17%	9%	21%
Softs (sugar, cocoa)	23%	4%	9%
Base metals	12%	9%	18%
Precious metals	18%	3%	8%
Livestock	12%	5%	11%

TABLE 10-2

Commodities Total Return Index Statistics

2000–2009	Reuters-CRB	S&P GSCI	DJ-UBS	T-Bills
Annualized return	4.7%	5.0%	7.1%	2.9%

highlights the performance of the three popular methodologies from 2000 to 2009. The difference in return is based on the allocation of commodity sectors and the investment strategy that revolves around rebalancing the indexes.

There is no way to know which commodities index strategy will outperform the others in the future. In the long term, I anticipate that all the total return indexes are likely to result in similar performance, which should be something close to the return of Treasury bills.

Let's examine the feasibility of investing in the major commodities total return indexes. The published returns of the indexes do not reflect the return to. There are fees, tax issues. and fund capacity issues.

The cost of investing in commodities can be very high. Commodities and futures funds have management fees and perhaps sales commissions. The fees on some products reach 2 percent per year in addition to a sales charge that reach 5.75 percent. ETFs have helped drive down costs by introducing dozens of new products to the market during the last run-up in commodities prices. However, the cost of a commodities index fund is considerably more than the cost of an equity or bond index funds. Table 10-4 at the end of this chapter lists a few reasonably priced commodity mutual funds and ETFs.

Commodity funds are extremely tax inefficient. The amount of turnover in these funds generates a lot of distributable income. Much of the gains in a futures-related fund are treated as ordinary income for tax purposes. Gold and other precious metals are treated as a collectibles and are taxed at a higher capital gains rate than common stock gains. Investors in a high-income tax bracket should consider the after-tax returns before investing or hold these assets only in a tax-deferred retirement account.

One alternative to paying annual taxes on a commodities fund is to invest in an exchange-traded note (ETN). These debt-based investments issued by banks are designed to track the performance of commodities indexes without the burden of annual taxes. There are other risks with ETNs that are not found in mutual funds and

ETFs. You will need to read more about these products before investing because there is credit risk from the issuer.

There is an alternative to a direct investment in commodities mutual funds. Several low-cost industry-specific index funds concentrate their holdings on companies that are in a commodities business. These funds specialize in mining, energy, and other natural resources stocks. A partial list of commodities industry mutual funds is provided in Table 10-4 at the end of this chapter.

INVESTING IN HEDGE FUNDS

Hedge funds are not an asset class. They are a type of investment account. Hedge funds are pooled investment vehicles that are privately organized and administered by professional investment managers.

The hedge fund industry is not highly regulated, and that allows managers to skirt many regulatory requirements that mutual funds must follow. This limited disclosure has a couple of advantages for hedge fund managers. First, they are not required to disclose fund holdings to the public. Second, the secrecy is great for marketing. Fund managers tend to whisper loudly about their super-duper top-secret proprietary investment methods. But that is just marketing hoopla. There are thousands of hedge funds in existence. It is inconceivable that any more than a hundred or so have any special investment skill. And the few that do have proven skill are not interested in managing a few hundred thousand dollars for you. They are interested in hundred-million-dollar institutional clients.

A few years ago the Securities and Exchange Commission demanded more disclosure from hedge funds about their trading practices, and that includes conflicts of interest between fund managers and investors. But that was struck down in court, leaving hedge funds largely unregulated. Since hedge funds have assets of over $1 trillion and leverage that extends well beyond that amount, the sheer size and power of the hedge fund industry warrants a closer look by regulators. I believe there will be regulation in some way.

Hedge Fund Strategies

There is a wide range of hedge fund strategies. The managers may buy, or "go long," securities to take advantage of rising prices, and may "short" securities, or sell them without owning them, to take advantage of falling prices. Some hedge fund trading strategies are designed to earn a profit regardless of the direction of the financial markets. These include a market-neutral strategy, in which the managers go long and short in equal amounts, thus negating the effect of the overall market movement. The idea of market-neutral strategies is to capture value from underpriced and overpriced securities.

There are a few advantages and many disadvantages to hedge funds. Low correlation is one advantage. Several styles of hedge funds exhibit low correlation with major asset classes such as stocks and bonds. That makes these funds an attractive investment for diversification. In addition, several hedge fund managers have produced higher returns than the stock markets with less risk. On the negative side, hedge funds are very expensive. The average management fee for a single fund is 1.5 percent per year, plus there is a profit incentive averaging 20 percent. In addition, hedge fund performance is notoriously inconsistent. Good performance by a fund one year does not ensure or even predict good performance the next. Finally, there are high barriers to entry. Hedge funds are available only to high-net-worth investors. The minimum investment of some funds is $1 million or more.

There are three broad categories of hedge funds and several subcategories:

- *Arbitrage strategies.* Arbitrage is the practice of exploiting price inefficiencies in the marketplace. Pure arbitrage has no risk. The trades guarantee a return. Consider this very simple example. Assume XYZ stock is trading for $42 per share on the New York Stock Exchange and $41.90 on the London Stock Exchange. An investor can buy 1,000 shares in London for $41,900 and simultaneously sell 1,000 shares in New York for $42,000. The net gain to the investor is $100 risk free. There are hundreds of arbitrage opportunities that present themselves on a daily basis if you have access to the information and can trade very inexpensively.

- *Event-driven strategies.* Event-driven strategies take advantage of corporate transaction announcements and other one-time events. An example would be "distressed securities," which involve investing in companies that are in or near bankruptcy. Another type of event-driven strategy is an activist fund, which is predatory in nature. The managers of an activist fund take sizable positions in small, flawed companies and then use their influence to force management changes and restructuring. A third type of event-driven fund is venture capital. Venture funds invest in start-up companies.

- *Directional or tactical strategies.* The largest group of hedge funds uses directional or tactical strategies. An example of a directional fund is a commodities trading advisor (CTA). CTAs use charts and mathematical models to identify trends in global futures markets. CTAs may go long or short a market to profit from both rising and falling futures prices. A second example of a tactical fund is a macro fund. These are fundamentally driven "top-down," big-picture bets on currencies, interest rates, commodities, and global stock markets.

Table 10-3 lists the three major categories of hedge funds and the major strategies within each category. Table 10-3 represents only a sample of hedge fund types and strategies. The number of strategies is limited only by the imagination of people in the investment industry.

TABLE 10-3

Hedge Fund Categories and Strategies

Arbitrage Strategies	Event-Driven Strategies	Directional/Tactical Strategies
Fixed-income arbitrage	Mergers and acquisitions	Equity long/short
Convertible arbitrage	Distressed securities	Managed futures (CTA)
Special situations	Venture capital	Macro strategies

The Problem with Hedge Funds

Hedge funds have a certain sex appeal. The secretive nature of the business, the allure of high potential returns, and the low correlation with stocks and bonds—it is all very enticing. However, in this author's opinion, much of the hype surrounding the role of hedge funds in a portfolio is misplaced. For most individual investors, the disadvantages of high cost, low disclosure, lack of diversification, illiquidity of some funds, and poor consistency of performance far outweigh the benefits.

Since hedge funds are largely unregulated, the managers are not required to report their holdings or performance to the public. There are several companies that monitor the performance of hedge funds, although those published numbers are often biased. Some monitoring companies are paid by the hedge funds to promote the funds they report on. Other monitoring companies use flawed data collection methodologies. For instance, they do not include the performance of funds that have closed or merged. This produces an upward *survivorship bias* in the hedge fund indexes. When a hedge fund has a bad quarter, the managers may simply choose not to report the results. This leads to a *selection bias* in the index performance. Most monitoring companies allow a newly reporting fund to "backfill" performance with simulated historic returns that no investor actually earned. That creates a *backfill bias* in the indexes. Finally, most monitoring companies allow the hedge fund managers to price their own illiquid securities, thus introducing a *pricing bias* into the indexes.

When all the inconsistencies of the published hedge fund indexes are eliminated from the data, the total return of the indexes drops dramatically. Wholesalers of hedge funds claim that the returns on these funds are equal to the long-term return on the stock market, with less risk. However, after factoring out all inconsistencies in the indexes, the returns on hedge funds fall more in line with the return of intermediate-term government bonds, albeit with much greater risk than bonds.

If the flaws in hedge fund index performance do not stop you from investing in this hedge funds, the lack of consistency of performance should. The funds that performed well one year cannot be relied upon to deliver top returns in the following year, or in any year thereafter. In fact, after one good year, the probability of having a below-average second year is higher than that of having an above-average one.

Vikas Agarwal of Georgia State University and Narayan Naik of the London Business School wrote one of many published research reports documenting the erratic and unpredictable returns from hedge funds.[1] Agarwal and Naik found that persistence of return among hedge fund managers is short term in nature and that what little persistence there is disappears over a multiyear period. Thus, it is very unlikely that anyone can predict which hedge funds will perform well in the future and which ones will perform poorly.

In 1990, there were fewer than 300 hedge funds with assets totaling less than $30 billion. By 2007, the number approached 10,000 and total assets over $1 trillion. The recession in 2008 and 2009 led many funds to their doom. It was illogical to assume that the opportunities for gains have grown at the same rate.

A statistical analysis of the data from the 2003 edition of the *U.S. Offshore Funds Directory* shows that the closure rate of hedge funds has increased from roughly 2 percent per year for funds outstanding during the early 1990s to more than 12 percent of funds outstanding today. Many funds have already failed, and many, many more will fail. Consequently, many of the funds that exist today will not be around 10 years from now.

If You Must Invest in Hedge Funds

If you still believe that hedge funds are a good idea, please stop believing it. If you are compelled to invest in one, take some precautions. Investing in just one hedge fund can be a gamble. You simply cannot predict when a hedge fund's glory days are coming to an end.

Investors who are attracted to hedge funds need to diversify among many of them. The problem is that many funds have high minimums, so it is not possible for small investors to buy several funds at one time. A simple way to solve the diversification problem is with a fund of funds. A fund of funds is a limited partnership that invests in several hedge funds. Typically a fund of funds is diversified across multiple manager styles for added diversification.

The diversification benefit of a fund of funds is a plus, but the major disadvantage is that it adds another layer of annual management fees to the already high cost of the individual funds within the investment. In addition to another layer of management fees, some funds of funds collect a profit incentive on top of the management fee. After adding up all the fees and incentives paid to the individual fund managers and the fees and incentive fees paid to the fund of funds managers, the cost of owning one of these investments can easily eat up 50 percent of the profits—assuming there are profits.

The high cost of hedge fund participation, the lack of diversification ability, and poor performance consistency puts hedge funds in an investment category that this author does not consider appropriate for most individual investors. If you are interested in hedge funds, there are several easy-to-understand books available that will help, including *All About Hedge Funds*, written by veteran hedge fund manager Robert A. Jaeger (New York: McGraw-Hill, 2002).

INVESTING IN COLLECTIBLES

Investing in collectibles can be financially rewarding and an enjoyable hobby. Traditional collectibles include fine art, coins, stamps, gems, documents, antiques, and other such objects. However, profitability is not limited to traditional collectibles. Any rare or unusual item can be a better investment than a fine oil painting by a well-known artist.

There are a few disadvantages to investing in collectibles. The cost of acquiring, storing, and insuring the items can be high, and that takes away from long-term returns. In addition, the capital gains tax rate on collectibles is higher than it is for common stocks.

There are also limitations to investing in collectibles. Expertise is required in the items being collected, as well as a passion for details. If you do not have expertise, you would need to hire a professional consultant, which can add considerable cost. Another disadvantage of collectibles is that they can be illiquid assets. When you want to sell, there is not always a willing buyer at a fair price. You need to find a liquid market for buying and selling. Online auction companies such as eBay have helped tremendously in the search for liquidity and fair pricing.

On the positive side, the aesthetic value of collectibles may make up for most of the disadvantages. You can admire your collection with friends, relatives, and other collectors. In many cases, the social benefit from collecting outweighs the monetary benefits.

Collectibles Performance

Tracking the performance of collectibles is difficult at best. Most transactions are between private parties, and prices either are not disclosed or are not compiled in a single database. There are limited indexes that track collectibles.

New York University professors Jianping Mei and Michael Moses have created an index of the long-term return on fine art. The Mei Moses Fine Art Index tracks the sale prices of paintings, drawings, and sculpture auctioned in New York since 1875. Figure 10-7 illustrates the near 60-year compounded return of the Mei Moses Fine Art Index versus the U.S. stock market.

There was a big run-up in art prices that occurred from 1970 to 1990. Then the market started to trend sideways. The return indicated

FIGURE 10-7

Mei Moses Fine Art Index versus CRSP Total U.S. Stock Market

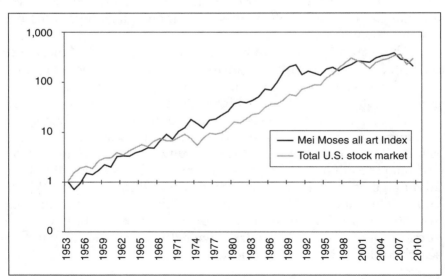

by the Mei Moses Fine Art was close to U.S. stocks over the period from 1954 to 2009. Art was slightly riskier than stocks during the period as measured by a slightly higher standard deviation.

Jianping Mei and Michael Moses have a free Web site with interesting research and periodic updates of their index. The Web site address is www.artasanasset.com. Registration is required. However, there is no cost to view the index results and read the online research of Mei and Moses.

Another interesting collectibles benchmark is the PCGS Coin Universe 3000 Index (CU3000). The Professional Coin Grading Service (PCGS) in Newport Beach, California, is a division of Collectors Universe, Inc. The CU3000 is an index that represents a broad list of 3,000 graded coins chosen by Coin Universe to represent the overall U.S. coin market. PCGS has several indexes on its Web site at www.pcgs.com. The data are free of charge.

Figure 10-8 compares the return on the CU3000 Index to the return on the total U.S. stock market since 1970. Like the Mei Moses Fine Art Index, between 1970 and 1989, the price of the collectible

FIGURE 10-8

PCGS Coin Universe 3000 Index versus the CRSP Total U.S. Stock Market

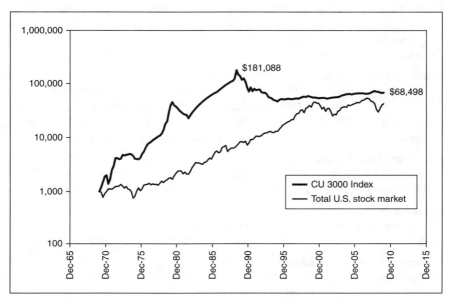

coin market jumped. The CU3000 increased in value by an amazing 181-fold, topping at 181,088 in 1989. Over the next five years, coin prices tumbled by nearly 75 percent and have recovered only slightly since the collapse.

The total return of the CU3000 Index collectible coins has been close to the return on the stock market since the index's inception in the 1950s in spite of the huge price surge and its ultimate collapse in price. Keep in mind that the coin index does not include acquisition costs, storage costs, or insurance.

ALTERNATIVE ASSET INVESTMENT LIST

Table 10-4 gives a partial list of mutual funds that invest in the alternative asset classes discussed in this chapter. Some funds

TABLE 10-4

Low-Cost Alternative Assets, Mutual Funds and ETFs

	Symbol	Benchmark
Commodities Funds		
iPath UBS-AIG Commodity ETN	DJP	UBS-AIG Commodity Index
iPath S&P GSCI Total Return ETN	GSP	S&P GSCI Total Return Index
GreenHaven Continuous Commodity	GCC	CRB CC Index-Total Return
PIMCO commodity real teturn	PCRAX	Dow Jones-AIG Commodity Index
Energy Mutual Funds		
iShares DJ Energy ETF	IYE	Dow Jones U.S. Energy Sector
iShares SP Global Energy ETF	IXC	S&P Global Energy Sector Index
Energy SPDR ETF	XLE	S&P U.S. Energy Select Sector Index
Vanguard Energy Fund	VGENX	Actively managed fund
Gold and Precious Metals Funds		
iShares COMEX Gold Trust	IAU	Gold and gold futures contracts
SPDR Gold Shares	GLD	Direct investment in gold bullion
Basic Materials		
iShares Basic Materials	IYM	Dow Jones U.S. Basic Materials
Vanguard Materials ETF	VAW	MSCI U.S. Investible Materials
Combined Natural Resources		
iShare Natural Resources	IGE	Goldman Sachs Natural Resources

invest in commodities using derivatives, and others invest in companies that are in the commodities business. The mutual funds listed in the table are presented as examples of alternative investments rather than as investment recommendations.

CHAPTER SUMMARY

Commodities and hedge funds do not make good investments in a long-term portfolio. The expenses associated with these alternative investments are high, and those costs outweigh the benefit of an increase in portfolio diversification. Money management companies are always seeking new ideas, and perhaps one day they will create a low-cost index or ETF that offers consistent low correlation with stocks and bonds and generates real return after inflation.

Collectibles are unique in that they have rarity value. The monetary rewards of collecting can also be enhanced by the aesthetic value from owning these investments. Collect what you enjoy collecting, and perhaps you will even make money doing it.

NOTE

[1]Vikas Agarwal and Naranyan Y. Naik, "Multi-Period Performance Persistence Analysis of Hedge Funds," *Journal of Financial and Quantitative Analysis,* vol. 35, no. 3, September 2000.

Managing Your Portfolio

CHAPTER 11

Realistic Market Expectations

KEY CONCEPTS

- Realistic market expectations are important to investment planning.
- Market volatility is more predictable than market return.
- There is a relationship between market risk and long-term expected return.
- Market forecasts are useful in the long term but not in the short term.

Several tools are used in the design, implementation, and maintenance of an asset allocation strategy. Part Three provides you with those tools so that you can design an asset allocation that fits your financial needs.

One important facet in the asset allocation process is for investors to have realistic market expectations. An investment plan works only if a person's expectations for market returns are in line with economic reality. In passing, some people say that market returns are not predictable, and I agree that that is true in the short term. However, the long-term return on markets can be estimated with a reasonable degree of accuracy, and those expectations should be used to assist in the investment planning process.

There are several methods used by investment analysts to forecast market returns. Some of these methods rely on a "top-down" picture of economic variables, which filter down into the expected returns on various asset classes. Other methods rely on a "bottom-up" strategy that builds from individual securities forecasts and cumulates in asset-class expected returns. Most analysts and economists agree to disagree on every element of market forecasting ranging from the methodology used to the modeling techniques to the input into those equations. Interestingly, despite differences of opinion and techniques, most long-term forecasts tend to fall within a narrow range of returns. At the end of this chapter is my own forecast of long-term market risk and return.

FORECASTING MARKET RETURNS

There are two basic market forecasting methodologies discussed in this chapter. The first method is a risk-adjusted return model that relies on historical price volatility in part to forecast the future performance of various asset classes relative to one another. The second method is an economic top-down model that relies on a long-term forecast of gross domestic product (GDP) to forecast various asset-class returns.

Forecasting a market's future return always involves the analysis of historical risk and return. While history does not repeat itself exactly, it casts a long shadow. There are important lessons to be learned from a study of economic history. Forecasting requires the confidence to extend some of those past characteristics into the future.

Analysis of market returns requires a long-term perspective. The past 30 years ending in 2009 have been generous to U.S. stock and bond investors despite a difficult equity environment over the past decade. The annualized return from stocks was approximately 11.2 percent between 1980 and 2009. During the same period the compounded return on the five-year Treasury bond was over 8.4 percent. Inflation was 3.5 percent during the period, meaning that the real return from stocks was over 7 percent and the real return from intermediate bonds was close to 5 percent.

Although the last 30-year period was profitable for stock and bond investors, there is little chance of those returns or better happening over the next 30 years. In fact, based on current economic conditions, the returns on U.S. stocks and bonds are likely to be considerably less than those during the 1980–2009 period, assuming that inflation remains low. The inflation rate was double digits in 1980, and it is in low single digits today. Accordingly, double-digit interest rates in 1980 have dropped to less than 3 percent today. Stock performance going forward will not be as high as it was in the past 30 years because inflation is a large factor in long-term market returns. High starting inflation means higher nominal returns, and low starting inflation means lower nominal returns. A realistic and conservative return for stocks over inflation is 5 percent annually.

MODEL 1: RISK-ADJUSTED RETURNS

The risk-adjusted return model relies on historical market volatilities to forecast the relative future performance for various asset classes. Market returns can vary considerably over different periods of time, although the volatility of those returns is more consistent. In the long term, the volatility of a market can be used to forecast its returns relative to those of other markets with different risks.

Depending on economic conditions, market returns can differ significantly from period to period. Table 11-1 lists the difference in returns during five independent decades starting in 1950.

TABLE 11-1

Compounded Returns by Decade

	S&P 500	5-year T-notes	T-Bills
1950–1959	19.4	1.3	1.9
1960–1969	7.8	3.5	3.9
1970–1979	5.9	7.0	6.3
1980–1989	17.5	11.9	8.9
1990–1999	18.2	7.1	4.9
2000–2009	−0.9	6.2	2.8

TABLE 11-2

Standard Deviation of Returns by Decade

	S&P 500	5-Year T-Notes	T-Bills
1950–1959	11.8	2.9	0.2
1960–1969	12.1	3.2	0.4
1970–1979	15.9	4.8	0.6
1980–1989	16.4	7.9	0.8
1990–1999	13.4	4.3	0.4
2000–2009	16.1	4.9	0.5

While the returns during different decades can vary considerably, the standard deviations of those returns during these independent 10-year periods tend to be more stable than the returns themselves. Table 11-2 highlights the standard deviation of market returns over the same decades starting in 1955.

Figure 11-1 compares the rolling 10-year annualized return of U.S. stocks to the rolling 10-year standard deviation of those returns. Notice that the volatility of the stock market is more consistent than the return on the market. Also note that the periods of highest volatility were also the periods of lowest return.

Bond market volatility has not been as consistent as stock volatility over the last 50 years. During the late 1970s and early 1980s, unusually high inflation caused an aberration in fixed-income prices. Interest rates surged with inflation to historic levels, and this caused an increased volatility of bond prices. By the late 1990s, bond market volatility had subsided to more moderate levels and remained there until 2007. Figure 11-2 illustrates the rolling 10-year standard deviation of various fixed-income investments.

Volatility is not risk in itself; rather, is it an indication of some economic risk in that it signifies rapid change in the attitude of investors toward making bets on that asset. Each asset class has its own unique financial risks that generate the price swings, and it may be subject to a greater overriding economic risk. For example, stock market volatility is an indication of a widespread change in corporate earnings estimates. Treasury bond market volatility is an indication of a widespread change in expected inflation. An increase in

FIGURE 11-1

The Relationship between Risk and Return, CRSP Total U.S.
Stock Market Index

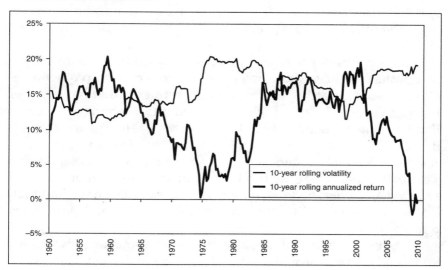

FIGURE 11-2

10-Year Rolling Standard Deviation of U.S. Fixed-Income
Securities

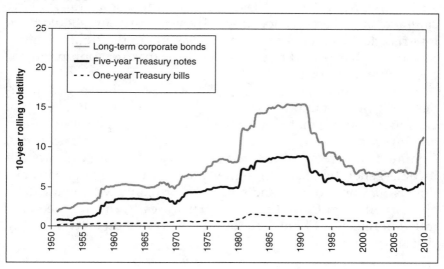

corporate bond volatility may result from higher expected inflation, a slowdown in economic activity, or both.

Spikes occur in volatility of asset-class returns on occasion and for many reasons. However, over time general asset-class return volatility remains relatively stable across the major asset classes.

Stable long-term volatilities allow an investor to develop a model that predicts future asset class returns *relative* to other asset classes using volatility differences. Investments that have higher volatility generally have higher expected returns, and investments that have lower volatility have lower expected returns. Accordingly, if you know the historical volatility of an investment, you can forecast its expected long-term return relative to all other asset classes. That being said, volatility itself is not a reason for higher expected returns. As we learned in Chapter 10, commodities have had high historic price volatility and have not generated high long-term returns.

Figure 11-3 illustrates the theoretical relationship between the known price volatility of several asset classes discussed in previous chapters, including the relationship of inflation to all investment returns. As the risk in an asset class increases, so does the expected return.

Figure 11-3 is divided vertically into two investment categories. To the left are asset classes that are appropriate for working capital cash and emergency funds. These investments should be in low-risk, low expected return asset classes. To the right are high-risk and high expected return asset classes that are appropriate for a long-term investment allocation.

The exceptions to the high-volatility discussion are commodities and gold. Commodities have high price volatility but have not paid investors for that risk. In the long term, the present value of any investment is the discounted sum of all long-term cash flows. Commodities are not like stocks and bonds because they are not income-generating. Consequently, the present value of $0 in cash flow is $0. Commodities and gold are worth only what you will be able to sell them for in the future. Historically, this has been the inflation rate. See Chapter 10 for more information on commodity risk and return.

FIGURE 11-3

Historic Market Volatility and Expected Return

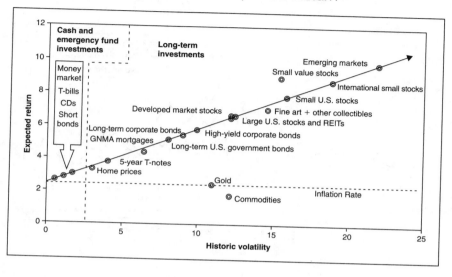

THE EFFECT OF INFLATION

The inflation rate is inherent in all market returns. Unfortunately, the returns generated by inflation are not "real" and do not buy extra goods and services. Nonetheless, our government taxes us as if inflation did add wealth.

Volatility-based models should factor out inflation expectations to derive a real return component for each asset class. Figure 11-4 illustrates the effect that inflation has on annual Treasury bill returns. The top line is the nominal return on Treasury bills for a one-year period, and the darker line below is inflation-adjusted real return. The average one-year Treasury bill yield since 1955 has been 5.1 percent, less inflation this has averaged 3.8, leaving a real gain of 1.3 percent.

Taxes are also an issue. Over the long term, the inflation-adjusted rate of return on T-bills has averaged about 1.3 percent. However, income taxes are due on the entire 5.1 percent return. The government does not factor out inflation when calculating how much interest you earned even though it was government policies

FIGURE 11-4

Annual Treasury Bill Returns, 1955–2009

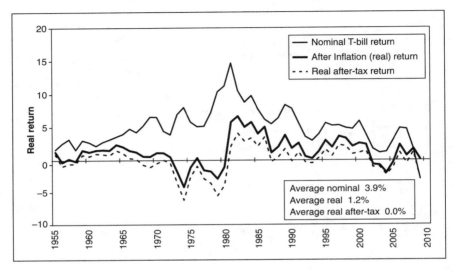

that created the inflation. The taxes on 5.1 percent interest are 1.3 percent, assuming a 25 percent tax rate. The real after-inflation, after-tax T-bills return was 0 percent—no return.

A return from T-bills of zero percent after taxes and inflation is not surprising and should be expected by investors. T-bills are risk-free. Any investment that is risk-free should also be return-free in an efficient market. There is truth to the saying "no pain, no gain." For all practical purposes, assume that, going forward, the after-tax inflation-adjusted return on T-bills will continue to average 0 percent.

Taxes are an expensive investment cost, and tax management should be part of every investor's plan. More information on taxes and management as it pertains to asset allocation and portfolio management is discussed in future chapters.

STACKING RISK PREMIUMS

All investments have risk. Even risk-free Treasury bills have inflation and tax risk if taxes and inflation go up before the T-bills mature. All other asset classes have additional risks on top of the inherent T-bills risks. By analyzing all the different unique risks inherent in an asset class that lead to price volatility and summing the expected return premiums for taking all those risks, you can estimate the expected total return on the investment. By "stacking" risks, the expected return of any asset class can be estimated. This section takes you through the process of stacking risk premiums to derive an expected return from an asset class.

Calculating an expected return for any asset class starts with T-bill risk and return because that is the safest investment you can own. The T-bill return can be divided into two parts: an expected inflation component and a real risk-free return component.

T-bill yields = expected inflation over the maturity period
+ real risk-free rate

Since Treasury bills are the safest investment available, all other investments must earn at least the T-bill's return. In addition, all other investments must have an extra return to compensate for the risks inherent in the particular investment. The extra return is known as a *risk premium.*

Asset class expected investment return = T-bill yield
+ risk premium

Every investment has an expected risk premium above and beyond T-bills that is based on that investment's unique risks. For example, 10-year Treasury bonds have term risk. That is the price risk that results from interest-rate changes that may occur after you buy a 10-year bond through its maturity date. If interest rates rise during that period, you lose out on the higher rates because your money will have been tied up in the 10-year note. Bonds with longer maturities have even greater term risk, and the greater the term risk, the higher the expected return of the bond. This is why long-term bonds yield more than short-term bonds.

Duration is an approximation of term risk in a bond. Basically, it is an estimate of price movement given a 1 percent move in general interest rates. Duration is calculated based on a bond's maturity date and its stated interest rate. Assume that a 10-year Treasury bond has a 7-year duration. This approximates a 7 percent loss in market value if interest rates go up by 1 percent.

Figure 11-5 highlights the term risk derived from Treasury Inflation-Protected Securities (TIPS) based on different maturities and durations. Since the inflation rate is already factored out of

TIPS Duration and Real Yield Spreads Premiums for Taking Term Risk

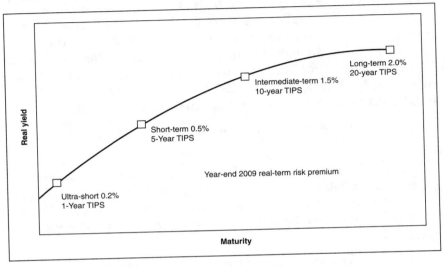

TIPS yields, the curve shown in Figure 11-5 represents pure term risk. See Chapter 8 for more information on TIPS.

Figure 11-5 shows the premium that investors will earn by changing the duration on their fixed-income portfolio across the bond maturity spectrum. Investors can increase or decrease this risk and return expectation by increasing or decreasing duration. For example, people can increase their expected return by about 0.5 percent by increasing their portfolio duration from about three years to about six years. This also increases fixed-income risk because there will be greater losses if interest rates rise.

$$\text{Treasury bond expected return} = \text{T-bill return} + \text{term risk premium}$$

All bonds have term risk. Corporate bonds, municipal bonds, and foreign bonds all have term risk that is reflected in their yields. In addition, those issues also have the risk of a credit downgrade or possible default. This credit risk will cause bond prices to fluctuate independent of term risk.

Investors who purchase bonds with credit risk expect to receive a premium for taking that risk. Table 11-3 represents

TABLE 11-3

Average Spreads for U.S. Corporate Bonds over U.S. Treasury Securities

Credit rating	Short Term (1–5 Years)	Intermediate Term (6–10 Years)	Long Term (11–30 Years)
Highest quality (AAA–AA) Minor credit risk premium	0.4	0.6	0.7
Good quality (A–BBB) Higher credit risk	0.8	1.0	1.1
Fair quality (BB–B) Credit risk and some default risk	2.4	2.6	2.7
Poor quality (CCC–C) Credit risk and high default risk	6.0–15.0	6.0–20.0	10.0–20.0

Source: Bloomberg, Federal Reserve, *Wall Street Journal*

the credit "spreads," which are the expected premiums across bond maturities and credit quality. AAA to BBB rated bonds are investment grade, and BB to C rated bonds are non-investment-grade, also known as high-yield bonds or junk bonds. As investors move further out in maturity, the premium for credit risk goes up because the uncertainty of interest payments goes up with time.

Corporate bonds = Treasury bonds + credit risk premium

Let's turn our attention to the equity market. Stocks have more risk than corporate bonds. There is no guarantee of income or gain from stocks; the shareholders are the last people to be paid in the event of a corporate bankruptcy, and the board of directors can cut common stock dividends without shareholder approval. This is all reflected in greater price volatility in stocks over bonds.

Figure 11-6 illustrates the rolling 10-year equity risk premium based on the 10-year return on stocks as measured by the CRSP 1–10 Total U.S. Stock Market Index over the 10-year return on long-term corporate bonds as measured by the Barclays Long-Term Corporate Bond Index. The figure reflects the extra amount of return (or loss) that U.S. common stock returned over corporate bonds in rolling 10-year periods.

FIGURE 11-6

Rolling 10-Year Equity Risk Premium over Corporate Bonds

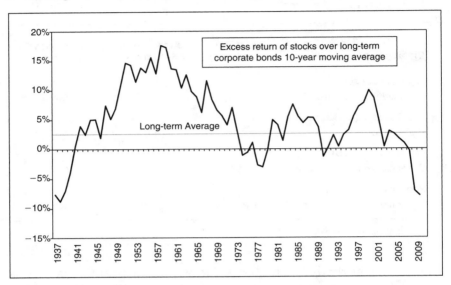

The equity risk premium is far from consistent. The difference between the 10-year annualized returns from stocks and bonds has varied from about minus 8 percent to plus 18 percent. If only there were a way to time these things! But there is not. Consequently, a long-term strategic position must be taken, with a long-term estimation of the risk premium. Given the risk of stocks and the current valuation of the market, a good prediction for the long-term equity risk premium going forward is about 3 percent annualized over long-term corporate bonds. I'll take a conservative view on the equity premium over corporate bonds and give it a 2 percent annualized expectation.

U.S. equity expectation = expected long-term corporate bonds
+ equity risk premium

There are other risk premiums that can be applied to the expected return on a portfolio in addition to the inherent risk of the equity market. For example, small-cap value stocks have a

FIGURE 11-7

Rolling 10-Year Small-Cap Value Premium FF Small-Cap
Value Stock Return Less the Total Stock Market Return

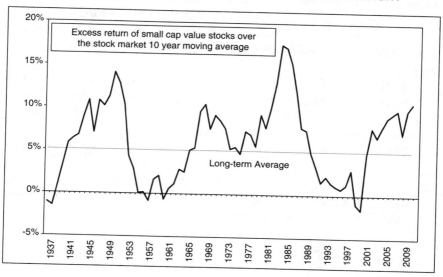

distinctive risk premium over large-cap stocks. There have
been extra risk premiums paid for investing in small companies
and for investing in less financially secure value companies.
Figure 11-7 illustrates the rolling 10-year small-value risk premium that small-cap value stocks earned over the return on the
total U.S. stock market.

The return premium for taking small-cap value risk has been
quite large and consistent over the years. The average has been
about 5 percent annualized. There have been only a few 10-year
rolling periods when small-cap value stocks have not performed
better than the total stock market. I'll take a conservative view on
the long-term small-cap value premium over the total stock market
and give it a 3 percent annualized expectation.

Small-cap value stocks = expected U.S. market return
+ small cap premium
+ value premium

AN ILLUSTRATION OF STACKING RISK PREMIUMS

Table 11-4 puts the entire stacking process into perspective. It is an example of layering risks to derive the expected long-term return for an asset class. The expected risk premiums in this chapter are the author's own estimates, which may or may not agree with other sources.

Both real and total expected returns are shown in Table 11-4 to highlight the inflation rate inherent in all asset-class returns. If inflation is higher than 3 percent, the total return on asset classes will be higher, and vice versa. Table 11-4 does not include all expected risk premiums for all the varied risks known in the markets. There are many other risks that are unique to individual investments that also deserve a return premium. Some of those risk premiums are used to calculate the long-term market return estimates at the end of this chapter.

TABLE 11-4

Examples of Expected Returns Derived by Layering Risk Premiums

	T-Bills	Intermediate-Term Treasury Notes	Intermediate-Term Corporate Bonds	Large-Cap Stocks	Small-Cap Stocks
Real risk-free rate	0.5	0.5	0.5	0.5	0.5
Term risk premium (intermediate)		1.5	1.5	1.5	1.5
Credit risk premium (intermediate)			1.0	1.0	1.0
Equity risk premium				2.0	2.0
Value stock risk premium					2.0
Small stock risk premium					1.0
Real expected return	**0.5**	**2.0**	**3.0**	**5.0**	**8.0**
Inflation	3.0	3.0	3.0	3.0	3.0
Total expected return	**3.5**	**5.0**	**6.0**	**8.0**	**11.0**

MODEL 2: ECONOMIC FACTOR FORECASTING

A second method for calculating expected market returns is through a "top-down" approach using an economic growth assumption. Gross domestic product (GDP) is the sum of all goods and services produced or sold in the United States. The Federal Reserve has a target for overall GDP growth, and it attempts to control that growth through changes in monetary policy. That growth number is about 3.0 percent after inflation.

About 10 percent of corporate-generated GDP eventually flows through to corporations as earnings. This number has been fairly consistent over time. Since corporate earnings are ultimately reflected in stock prices, economic growth forecasts can be used to forecast stock returns.

A simple formula for expected stock market returns using the earnings growth method is as follows:

$$\text{Equity return} = \text{earnings per share growth} + \text{cash dividends} + \text{valuation change}$$

To better understand this model, each variable needs to be explained:

1. *Earnings growth.* The primary driver of long-term stock market gains is corporate earnings. The more money companies earn, the higher the stock market goes relative to inflation. Earnings are a derivative of GDP growth.
2. *Cash dividends.* Many U.S. corporations pay out a portion of their earnings in the form of cash dividends. At the end of 2009, the dividend on the total U.S. stock market was about 2 percent. The growth of dividend payments has been about 3 percent per year, which is slightly less than the growth in earnings. The growth varies because of capitalization issues and decisions made in corporate boardrooms, which extends in part to government policies on taxation. Although higher dividends are attractive to income-seeking investors, there is no free lunch. Higher dividend payout means less cash for corporations to invest, consequently lower expected growth rates of earnings in the future. In addition, we have double

taxation of dividends in the United States. Corporate earnings are taxed once at the corporate level and again at the individual level if dividends are paid to shareholders.

3. *Valuation change.* The valuation is the price that investors are willing to pay for $1 worth of earnings. If investors believe that the growth in real corporate earnings will increase, they will pay more for the anticipated earnings stream. Thus, the ratio of price to earnings (P/E) increases. If economic conditions decline, the P/E of stocks typically falls as prices fall. The changing valuation affects overall investment return, but it does not have any effect on dividend payments.

Forecasting earnings growth can be accomplished using GDP per capita data. GDP per capita is the sum total of all goods and services produced in the United States during the year divided by the population. There is a direct and consistent relationship between GDP per capita growth and corporate earnings growth. Figure 11-8 clearly illustrates this relationship.

FIGURE 11-8

S&P 500 Earnings Growth is Highly Correlated with Per Capita GDP Growth

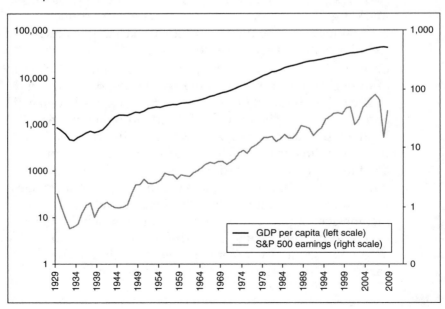

The long-term correlation between annual GDP per capita growth and S&P 500 earnings growth has been over +0.9. The correlation is higher if earnings are smoothed over 10 years to reduce the effect of recessionary earnings lulls.

THE FEDERAL RESERVE AND GDP GROWTH

The Federal Reserve has two primary mandates: first, to foster full employment by promoting controlled GDP growth, and second, to keep inflation in check. Basically, the Federal Reserve targets the economy to grow at about 3 percent per year (after inflation). This encourages steady job creation and holds inflation at a reasonable level. If the economy grows faster than the target, it can cause a supply-and-demand mismatch, which can lead to higher inflation.

The Federal Reserve controls economic growth with monetary policy decisions, mostly through the adjustment of the short-term interest rates that banks charge each other for overnight loans. Short-term rates can affect interest rates on mortgages and other lending rates. Those rates, in turn, have a direct impact on consumer and corporate borrowing behavior, which has a direct effect on economic activity. In a sense, the Federal Reserve is the tail that wags the dog.

It is difficult to envision real GDP growth at 3 percent in the United States given the mounting federal deficit, soaring state deficits, the trade deficit, the aging population, and potential tax increases to pay for all these deficits. On the other hand, earnings may increase at a faster rate than GDP in the foreseeable future resulting from productivity gains from technology, a leaner workforce, and a greater percentage of earnings coming from overseas ventures by U.S. multinational corporations. So, while 3 percent real GDP growth may be difficult to accomplish, a 3 percent real earnings growth may still happen, and that is the important number for stock price valuation.

DIVIDENDS AND MARKET VALUATION

The percentage of corporate earnings paid out in the form of cash dividends is less than 30 percent, although the number has risen slightly in recent years. Cash dividend payments can vary depending on current earnings, general economic outlook, stock buybacks, investment opportunities, tax law changes, and a variety of other factors. Over the long term, dividend payouts should grow in line

S&P 500 Earnings and Dividend Growth

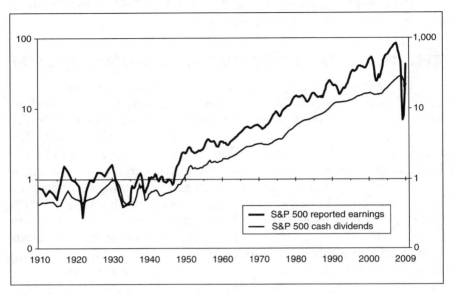

with earnings growth. Figure 11-9 represents the S&P 500 earnings and dividend growth since 1950.

A common measure of stock value is the price/earnings ratio, more commonly referred to as the P/E ratio. Many investors track the market P/E ratio in an attempt to determine when stocks are cheap and when they are expensive. Figure 11-10 illustrates the P/E ratio from 1950 to 2009 using a 10-year earnings average from Professor Robert Shiller's database that is available to be public at www.econ.yale.edu/~shiller/data.htm. There have been several periods when the ratio was high, although none quite match the speculative premium on stocks that existed in the late 1990s.

There are a couple of items that P/E ratio watchers should consider:

1. P/E multiples increase or decrease with changes in the inflation rate. If inflation increases, the present value of

FIGURE 11-10

Price/Earnings Ratio (P/E) using a 10-Year Earnings Average

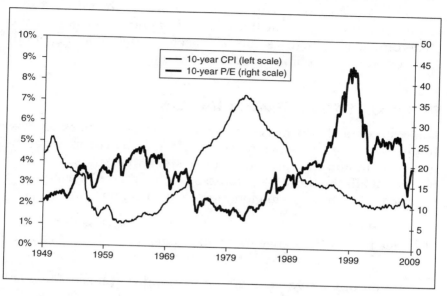

future earnings diminishes, and that causes the stock
market to go down and the P/E ratio to go down.
A decrease in inflation causes higher stock prices because
of the increase in the purchasing power of future
earnings. The effect of inflation on stock valuation is
clearly evident in Figure 11-9.

2. If most investors believe that corporate earnings will
increase faster and at a greater rate than the average, then
the prices of stocks will increase in anticipation of the
higher earnings forecast. The run-up in prices causes the
P/E ratio of the market to expand. This is the reason the
market kept going higher in the late 1990s. Earnings growth
was robust in the late 1990s, and investors believed that this
growth would continue as a result of rapid technological
advances. When earnings growth did not materialize, the
value of the stocks fell to a more normal level.

In the short run, speculation may drive stock prices, but in the long term, earnings growth is the real driver. Speculative moves are not predictable, so there is no sense in trying to put a speculation variable into a long-term forecast. Rather, for the forecasts that follow, it is assumed that the P/E ratio is held constant at the 18 percent level, which is a normal level for a low-inflation period. This constant helps eliminate speculative noise.

FORECASTING FIXED INCOME

Forecasting bond returns is simpler than forecasting stock returns. In the very long run, stock returns are driven by corporate earnings growth and the cash paid out as stock dividends. The only factor that affects future bond returns is interest rates. The formula for calculating the expected long-term return of bonds is:

Fixed-income return = yield at purchase + change in yield
Change in yield = change in inflation rate, the real risk-free rate
and credit spreads

If you buy a five-year corporate bond that has a 3 percent yield to maturity and interest rates do not change before the bond matures, then your annualized return after five years will be 3 percent. The example assumes that all interest payments are reinvested. If there is a change in interest rates, then your total return may be higher or lower depending on the direction of the change. That is due to differences in the reinvestment rate of the interest. If interest rates go higher while you own the bond, then your interest payments will be reinvested at higher rates, and you will achieve a higher return than 6 percent. The opposite is true if interest rates go lower—your return will be less than 6 percent.

Reported inflation and future inflation expectations are two primary drivers of interest rates. If actual inflation increases, interest rates go higher and bond prices fall. If there is lower inflation (disinflation), then interest rates go down and bond prices go up. Changes in anticipated inflation also move interest rates in the same way as actual inflation. However, if the forecasts do not prove

FIGURE 11-11

Interest Rates Track Inflation over Time

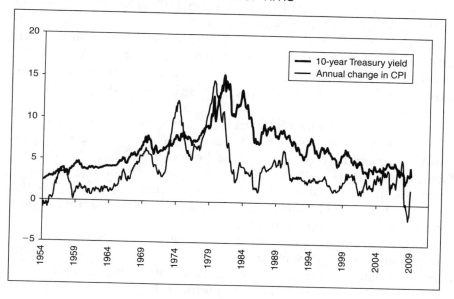

to be accurate, interest rates will revert back to their original level. Figure 11-11 illustrates the inverse relationship between the inflation rate and Treasury note yields.

Figure 11-11 highlights the most volatile interest-rate periods in U.S. economic history. From the early 1960s to the early 1980s, inflation soared to 15 percent. That created a huge sell-off in the bond markets. By 1982, inflation had dropped as fast as it accelerated, setting the stage for an historic rally in bonds. However, the rally was slow in developing because investors *anticipated* that the inflation rate would move higher again. But those fears were not justified. Since the early 1980s, inflation has fallen to low double digits, and in 2008 inflation was less than 0 percent, a phenomenon known as *deflation*. As a result, the yield on Treasury bonds hit its lowest level in 60 years.

A third driver of interest rates is a change in the real risk-free rate. The real return is the after-inflation yield of a bond. The easiest way to understand changes in the real risk-free rate is by observing changes in Treasury Inflation-Protected Securities (TIPS). One reason that the spreads on TIPS changes is taxes. As inflation forces interest rates higher, it is also adds to the principal value of TIPS. Since more taxes are due in high-inflation periods, the real yield on the bonds must be higher to pay the extra taxes. As we learned in Chapter 8, taxes are due on the total return of Treasury bonds, whether is it from inflation gains or interest.

There are several other drivers of interest rates that are specific to particular types of bonds. Corporate bonds have a risk premium for credit risk. The spread between Treasury bonds and corporate bonds will increase or decrease with changes in economic conditions. Mortgages have prepayment risk. The yield of a mortgage fund will vary with the amount of prepayments that occur in the mortgage market.

One problem in forecasting interest rates is that it is nearly impossible to predict changes in inflation or changes in credit spreads. That is where the Federal Reserve can help. The Federal Reserve tends to have an acceptable range for inflation that appears to be between 2 and 3 percent. An amount over 4 percent causes concern among the Federal Reserve Board members, and this generally leads the Fed to increase interest rates.

CREATING A FORECAST

We have analyzed several drivers of market returns, including asset risk, cash payments from interest and dividends, earnings growth, and economic considerations. These data were used to create Table 11-5. The 3 percent inflation rate was the average from 1980 to 2009. If the inflation rate is higher or lower, then the "With 3% inflation" column would be higher or lower as well.

Table 11-5 represents this author's conservative estimate of market returns over the next 30 years. There are no guarantees that any of these forecasts will be accurate. That being said, they are as good as any other market forecasts made using practical methods and done in a disciplined manner.

TABLE 11-5

Thirty-Year Estimates of Bonds, Stocks, and REITs
Assuming 3 Percent Inflation

Asset Classes	Real Return	With 3% Inflation	Risk*
Government-backed fixed income			
U.S. Treasury bills (1-year maturity)	0.5	3.5	1.5
Intermediate-term U.S. Treasury notes	1.5	4.5	5.0
Long-term U.S. Treasury bonds	2.0	5.0	5.5
GNMA mortgages	2.0	5.0	8.0
Intermediate tax-free municipal bonds (A rated)	1.5	4.5	5.0
Corporate and Emerging Market Fxed Income			
Intermediate-term high-grade corporate bonds (AAA–BBB)	2.3	5.3	5.5
Long-term investment-grade bonds (AAA–BBB)	2.8	5.8	8.5
Intermediate-term high-yield corporate bonds (BB–B)	4.0	7.0	15.0
Foreign government bonds (unhedged)	2.5	5.5	7.0
U.S. Common Equity and REITs			
U.S. large-cap stocks	5.0	8.0	15.0
U.S. small-cap stocks	6.0	9.0	20.0
U.S. microcap stocks	7.0	10.0	25.0
U.S. small-value stocks	8.0	11.0	25.0
REITs (real estate investment trusts)	5.0	8.0	15.0
International Equity (unhedged)			
Developed countries	5.0	8.0	17.0
Developed countries, small company	6.0	9.0	22.0
Developed countries, small value companies	8.0	11.0	27.0
All emerging markets including frontier countries	8.0	11.0	27.0

*The estimate of risk is the estimated standard deviation of annual returns.

CHAPTER SUMMARY

The acceptance of a market forecast is an important step in creating a proper asset allocation. No one knows exactly what the returns on the markets or the results of economic indicators will be over the next 30 years. However, there are stable factors that contribute to those market returns, and these factors are likely to persist into the future.

A forecast should always try to err on the conservative side. It is wiser to expect and plan for lower returns and then be pleasantly surprised if the forecast is too low rather than relying on a rosy forecast and possibly running out of money later in life. As the saying goes, it is better to be safe than sorry.

While the actual 30-year return on the markets cannot be known, the relationship between risk and return is predictable. Small stocks have more risk than large stocks and should outperform large stocks in the future. Corporate bonds have more risk than Treasury bonds and should outperform Treasury bonds in the future. With the order of investment risks and comparable returns in hand, you can move on to the next step to create an asset allocation that is right for your needs.

CHAPTER 12

Building Your Portfolio

KEY CONCEPTS

- A proper asset allocation is designed to match an investor's needs.
- The overall risk cannot be above one's tolerance for risk.
- The life-cycle method is a good place to start.
- A modified version of "your age in bonds" is also helpful.

A successful investment plan is one that is designed specifically for the person who intends to use it. While people's asset allocations will be broadly similar in some ways, each person's allocation will be uniquely different in others. This and the next two chapters offer guidance on designing an investment plan that is right for your needs.

Asset allocation books tend to have several examples of portfolios, and this one is no exception. The portfolios in this chapter are categorized into four generic groups based on different stages of life. The sample portfolios provided are general in nature and should be considered only as a guide when planning your portfolio.

"Your age in bonds" is a simplified method for determining the amount of risk to have in a portfolio. This method works well for younger people; however, it does not work as smoothly for all people nearing retirement or in retirement. Adjustments to the model are discussed that puts people's allocation age in line with their real life circumstances.

LIFE-CYCLE INVESTING

Your asset allocation will change several times as your circumstances and resources change over time. Investors' ages tend to have a meaningful impact on asset allocation decisions, not so much because they are aging but because over a career people convert their labor into assets and then live off those assets in retirement. In addition, people of different ages have different financial wants and needs, and that correlates with different perceptions on investment risk.

In my book, *Protecting Your Wealth in Good Times and Bad* (McGraw-Hill, 2003), I classify investors into four general groups based solely on where they are in life. These groups are early savers, midlife accumulators, transitional retirees, and mature retirees. The material in this chapter is a synopsis of the four stages and how people in different stages would approach the management of an investment portfolio.

The details of these four life phases are:

- *Early savers.* These are investors who are in the beginning stages of their careers and families. They start with few assets and a lot of ambition. This group generally spans ages 20 to 39.
- *Midlife accumulators.* These are investors who are established in their careers and family life. They are accumulators of many things, from cars to homes to appliances to children. From age 40 to 59, accumulators know where they stand on career and family and have a good sense of where they are going.
- *Transitional retirees.* This stage spans a group of people who are getting ready to retire, transitioning into retirement, and living an active lifestyle in retirement. The stage typically covers people ranging from age 60 to 79.
- *Mature retirees.* These fully retired investors are not as active as they used to be usually because of their own health concerns or those of a spouse. The needs for mature

retirees are different from the needs of any other group. Their needs range from health planning, to long-term care, to estate planning. At this stage, financial matters are often discussed with children, other family members, or a professional trustee.

Investors in all stages have some similar financial goals and similar concerns. Similar goals include a desire for financial security and the desire to pay less income tax. Similar concerns include the fear of running out of money and the fear of not having adequate health-care coverage when it is needed.

Investors at different ages have a wide range of differences. These include career challenges, family situations, risk tolerance based on investment experience, health issues, and personality strengths and weaknesses.

We can never know what the future holds in any aspect of life. This makes portfolio design a puzzle that is put together without all the pieces. We try to balance the correct technical solution based on the facts we do know with our assumptions about the future.

Behavior is also subjective input. The strange things that happen to us in life sometimes affect our behavior in ways we cannot predict. We can only guess how we will react to a sudden change in our social status, or martial status, or health status. The right asset allocation should have a high mathematical probability of achieving your financial goals while at the same time being compatible with what we estimate our emotional reaction will be to unexpected events. The goal of this chapter is to address the issues that drive the technical part of an asset allocation decision. Behavioral issues are discussed in Chapter 13.

TWO PORTFOLIOS FOR EACH STAGE

The remainder of this chapter is devoted to discussing the four stages of life-cycle investing. Asset allocations are suggested at each stage. They start with a broad recommendation for the amount to have in cash for living expenses and emergencies, long-term investment assets for future needs, and speculative investments. Figure 12-1 illustrates the three pyramid levels that are discussed. See Chapter 1 for a more detailed explanation of the investment pyramid.

FIGURE 12-1

Investment Pyramid of Liquid Assets

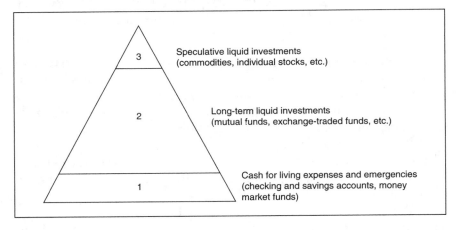

The middle of the pyramid holds your long-term investment portfolio, and that is the primary focus in this chapter. The pyramid base holds cash like investments and the top holds speculative investments. These are also mentioned briefly.

At the end of each stage, two sample portfolios are provided that cover the middle of the pyramid long-term investment section. Both sample portfolios offer broad diversification across several global asset classes. The first portfolio is a simple allocation utilizing four or five low-cost mutual funds or ETFs. The second portfolio is a more advanced multi-asset-class portfolio utilizing between 9 and 12 low-cost mutual funds or ETFs.

Either portfolio offers a good base from which to start—or end—in my opinion. You can begin with one of the portfolios and add or take away funds to suit your particular needs. You may want to limit the number of funds you have in your portfolio to 12 because after that you reach diminishing returns and higher costs.

The mutual funds and ETFs recommended in this chapter are low-cost examples. Substitutes are available in many investment categories from many different mutual fund companies. You may not have access to one or more of the mutual funds or ETFs listed in this book, as is the case with most employer retirement plans. In that case, you will have to substitute with the funds that are the closest fit available.

The sample portfolios provided should help you narrow your asset allocation decision, although they may not solve your situation completely. Other issues to consider are fees, taxes, and your tolerance for investment risk. Those topics are discussed briefly in this chapter and in more detail in other chapters.

STAGE 1: EARLY SAVERS

Three key components for accumulating wealth are savings habits, investment methods, and cost control. For early savers, the investment method and cost control are important, but it is not as important as developing a savings habit. Saving regularly will build an account faster than anything else a young person can do.

The biggest mistake that young people make is to not learn to save. Ideally, a young person will start saving at the same time he or she lands the first full-time job. The amount of saving at this stage does not need to be excessive. A rate of 10 percent of annual earnings per year is a good start. This can be done through an employer savings plan if one is available, or directly with money received from a paycheck.

Not having the discipline to stick to a savings plan is often the demise for young people. Incomes are typically entry-level pay, and expenses are mounting. Housing costs in some parts of the country are still high. Buying a house can demand a take of more than 40 percent of a person's income, including taxes and upkeep. In addition, the arrival of children adds considerable living expenses, not to mention the new need to save for college.

Career uncertainty is another distraction for early savers. Many young adults do not know the direction their career will take them, or what their true earnings will be. People change careers more often than they did in past generations, and this can result in the interruption of a savings plan.

With increasingly limited free cash and career uncertainty, what can a young person do to formulate a plan for the future? First, many employers have a company retirement plan that employees can contribute to on a pretax basis. Young investors should take full advantage of that opportunity, especially if the employer offers to match the amount contributed. Second, young people should develop an asset allocation that is within their tolerance for investment risk. Do not try to time the markets or chase last year's winners. Third, young people need to realize early that investment costs matter. Every dollar wasted on exorbitant mutual fund fees and high brokerage commissions is money down the drain. A consistent pretax savings plan that is invested in a sensible asset allocation of low-cost mutual funds is an excellent way to begin accumulating wealth for the future.

Early Savers—Asset Allocation

Young investors have the advantage of abundant human capital and time. Their asset is in their future labor that they will trade off for capital assets over the next 40 years of work. They can make investment errors and not be hurt much because they do not have a lot of money invested, and they have enough time to work and replace their losses.

Investors in their twenties and thirties should have about six months of living expenses in a bank checking account or money market equivalent to cover their living expenses and possible emergencies. They might also have a short-term bond or CD account where they are putting money away for a large purchase such as a new home.

Designing a long-term asset allocation for a young person is sometimes more difficult than designing one for someone at any other time in life. On the one hand, young investors have many years ahead of them, so they should choose an aggressive allocation. On the other hand, they have the least amount of investment experience and do not know what their risk tolerance level is. Consequently, while an aggressive asset allocation may be appropriate from a time perspective, early savers should guard against being too aggressive and losing control of themselves and their portfolios in a bear market.

Young savers have a lot of time to benefit from an aggressive allocation in their long-term investment portfolio. However, investing 100 percent in stocks is probably too aggressive. There are two reasons for not having an all-stock portfolio:

1. Most people cannot handle 100 percent in stocks 100 percent of the time. The volatility of a fully invested stock portfolio is too much to stomach in a bear market,

and this is true for everyone, not just early savers. There are two recent examples when this occurred. The first was after the "crash" of 1987, and the second was during the bear market of 2000 to 2003. During both of those periods, many investors both young and old who thought they had the tolerance to handle 100 percent in stocks did not finish with 100 percent in stocks. They reduced their position in the middle or end of the bear market, thereby locking in losses.

2. When stocks fall in value, investors should take that opportunity to buy more stocks. A 100 percent stock portfolio precludes this from happening. A 20 percent bond allocation will allow stocks to be purchased in a down market.

It is interesting to note that a misunderstanding of risk causes many early savers to not have enough equity in their portfolio and miss the potential for higher return. According to data available from the TIAA-CREF Institute, a surprisingly high percentage of young workers invest a significant portion of their self-directed employer pension assets in the low-interest-bearing fixed accounts.[1] As people progress into midlife, they seem to have a better understanding of their tolerance for risk and increase their equity exposure.

There is no one-size-fits-all asset allocation that early savers should use. Figure 12-2 highlights appropriate allocations for young investors who have some understanding of financial risk. Figure 12-2 represents an "either-or" allocation, not a "to-from" allocation. In other words, an investor chooses a fixed allocation of between 60 and 80 percent in stocks and stays with that fixed target. Investors should not be moving from 60 percent to 80 percent and back again based on their perception of market risk.

An appropriate median asset allocation for young people is about 70 percent in stocks and 30 percent in fixed income. The 70 percent stock and 30 percent fixed-income allocation provides significant risk reduction over a 100 percent stock portfolio and allows room for rebalancing. The result is a portfolio with acceptable risk that has the potential for gratifying long-term returns.

FIGURE   12-2

Early Savers Allocation Range

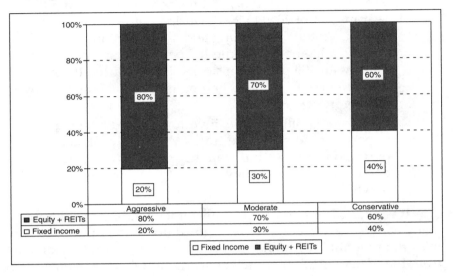

Early Savers—Asset-Class Categories

Once a strategic asset allocation between stocks and bonds has been decided on, the next step is category allocation. The two portfolios shown in Tables 12-1 and 12-2 highlight a basic asset allocation and

TABLE   12-1

Early Savers—Moderate Basic Portfolio (open-end mutual funds or ETF version)

Asset Class	Percent	Sample Low-Cost Funds and Symbols
U.S. equity	40%	Vanguard Total U.S. Stock Market Index (VTSMX) or Vanguard Total U.S. Stock Market ETF (VTI)
International equity	20%	Vanguard Total International Portfolio (VGTSX) or Vanguard FTSE All World ex-U.S. ETF (VEU)
Real estate	10%	Vanguard REIT Index Fund (VGSIX) or Vanguard REIT ETF (VNQ)
Fixed income	30%	Vanguard Total Bond Market Index Fund (VBMFX) or Vanguard Total Bond Market ETF (BND)

TABLE 12-2

Early Savers—Moderate Multi-Asset-Class Portfolio (open-end mutual funds or ETF version)

Asset Class	Percent	Sample Low-Cost Funds and Symbols
U.S. Equity		
Core equity	25%	Vanguard Total U.S. Stock Market Index (VTSMX) or Vanguard Total U.S. Stock Market ETF (VTI)
Small value	10%	Vanguard Small-Cap Value Index Fund (VISVX) or iShares S&P 600 Barra Value (IJS)
Microcap	5%	Bridgeway Ultra Small Company Market (BRSIX) or iShares Russell Microcap Index ETF (IWC)
Real estate	10%	Vanguard REIT Index Fund (VGSIX) or Vanguard REIT ETF (VNQ)
International Equity		
Pacific Rim—large	5%	Vanguard Pacific Stock Index (VPACX) or Vanguard Pacific Stock ETF (VLP)
Europe—large	5%	Vanguard European Stock Index (VEURX) or Vanguard European Stock ETF (VGK)
International small-cap value	5%	DFA International Small Cap Value* (DISVX) or WisdomTree International Small Cap Dividend (DLS)
Emerging markets	5%	DFA Emerging Markets* (DFEMX) or Vanguard Emerging Markets Stock ETF (VWO)
Fixed Income		
Investment-grade bonds	20%	Vanguard Total Bond Market Index Fund (VBMFX) or Vanguard Total Bond Market ETF (BND)
High-yield bonds	5%	Vanguard High Yield Bond Fund (VWEHX) or iShares iBoxx High Yield Corporate Bond (HYG)
Inflation-protected bonds	5%	Vanguard Inflation-Protected Securities (VIPSX) or iShares Barclays TIPS Bond Fund (TIP)

*DFA funds are available only through select investment advisors. Alternative funds are available to all investors.

a multi-asset-class allocation. All the investments listed are no-load low-cost mutual funds and ETFs.

All asset allocations recommended in this chapter should be adjusted to match an investor's needs, tax situation, and risk tolerance.

GROUP 2: MIDLIFE ACCUMULATORS

As we march through life, we mature physically, intellectually, emotionally, professionally, and financially. While waving good-bye to our thirties and facing midlife head on, we start to develop a more conservative attitude about money. That is because we real-ize that someday we may not be able to work anymore even if we wanted to. This prompts a rethinking about our methods of saving and investing, and perhaps a change in asset allocation to go along with this new way of thinking.

Most people concede that they are mortal some time during midlife. We also admit that there are ceilings to careers, our family income, and our lifestyle. In addition, people in midlife have seen a recession or two, they have watched the stock market and inter-est rates flip-flop over the years, and they have made a few bad investment decisions. These lessons make midlife accumulators well equipped to design a portfolio that fits their long-term needs.

Midlife investors form their first realistic vision of what retire-ment will look like, and they begin to mentally compute how much they might need in order to fulfill this vision. After those estimates are made logically and rationally, it is time for midlife accumula-tors to adjust their strategy so that their investments are in line with this vision.

There are two important realizations that midlife investors have that trigger a need for a portfolio adjustment. First, they realize that their productive years are about half over. Second, they start to see that a viable and sustainable investment policy is critical to reach-ing their retirement goal. Not only do savings have to be consistent, but the investment return on those savings start having an impact.

The investing experiments done by early savers must end in midlife. It is time to treat retirement investing as serious business. A sound investment policy must be created and maintained to help ensure that midlife accumulators attain their retirement goals.

Midlife Accumulators—An Investment Framework

During midlife, people begin to estimate how much money they will need in order to sustain their standard of living in retirement.

Granted, the estimate will be in rough form at best; however, it is a useful exercise.

Liability matching is a method of investing in which a person's asset allocation is matched to that person's future cash-flow needs. In other words, your portfolio is structured so that your investments match your retirement income needs. There are five basic steps in liability matching:

1. Estimate future living expenses. An estimate of future living expenses can be made by tracking current living expenses and making adjustments for expected changes to those expenses in the future. There are many different budgeting tools that can be found on the Internet and in books that can help you with a personal cash-flow analysis. You could also hire a professional financial planner to help you put those estimates together.

2. Estimate sources of noninvestment income during retirement. Sources of noninvestment income include Social Security and pension income. They do not include income from retirement accounts or personal savings.

3. Compare your noninvestment income to your expected living expenses during retirement. If there is an income gap, it will need to be filled with investment income.

4. Determine how much you need to accumulate to fill the annual income gap. Expect that you can withdraw a maximum of 5 percent from your investments, which means that you will need about 20 times the annual amount of income. For example, if you need an extra $12,000 per year in income, your portfolio at retirement should be at least $240,000.

5. Design, implement, and maintain a savings and investment plan that has the highest probability of growing your portfolio to the amount needed at retirement with minimum risk. Asset allocation is a major part of that investment plan.

These steps are a synopsis of the liability-matching process. To gain a more detailed understanding, acquire a copy of my previous book, *Protecting Your Wealth in Good Times and Bad* (New York: McGraw-Hill, 2003) There is also an explanation in my free online book, *Serious Money, Straight Talk about Investing for Retirement*, which is available as a free download at www.PortfolioSolutions.com.

Midlife Accumulators—Asset Allocation

During midlife, investors reach the halfway mark in their careers. It is a period when salaries are on the rise, and this means that the amount allocated to savings should also be increasing. It is a point in life where investors can see the future with more clarity and can use that vision to develop a strategic asset allocation that matches future retirement needs.

At this stage, the cash savings set aside for living expenses and emergencies should be extended out to 12 months, if possible. A larger emergency fund will help cover those unanticipated needs that seem to occur all too often with growing families.

Speculative investments should not grow any larger then they have been during the early-saver years and probably should start to wind down. It is dangerous to think that you will find a way to make money by speculating at this point in your life if you did not make any money by speculating when you were young.

During midlife, long-term investment accounts are growing larger, and working years are growing shorter. A balanced asset allocation is appropriate. Figure 12-3 highlights the range of asset allocations that is typical for midlife accumulators. Like asset allocations for all groups, Figure 12-3 represents an either-or allocation, not a to-from allocation. Do not try to shift between stocks and bonds at what seem like appropriate times. No one can time the markets.

The median asset allocation for people in midlife is 60 percent in stocks and 40 percent in fixed income. Tables 12-3 and 12-4 give basic and multi-asset-class portfolios for midlife accumulators.

During midlife, people begin to reach higher levels of earnings, which may affect their investment choices. Taxes can play a considerable role in asset allocation. If a person's income places him or her in an income tax bracket of 30 percent or more, that person should consider tax-free municipal bonds. The after-tax return from tax-free bonds will be higher than having taxable bonds and paying the taxes. More information on how taxes affect asset allocation can be found in Chapter 15.

FIGURE 12-3

MidLife Allocation Range

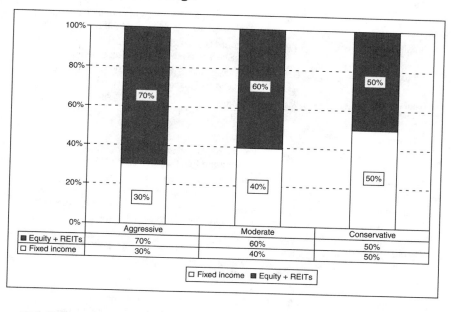

TABLE 12-3

Midlife Accumulators—Moderate Basic Portfolio (open-end mutual funds or ETF version)

Asset Class	Percent	Sample Low-Cost Funds and Symbols
U.S. equity	35%	Vanguard Total U.S. Stock Market Index (VTSMX) or Vanguard Total U.S. Stock Market ETF (VTI)
International equity	17%	Vanguard Total International Portfolio (VGTSX) or Vanguard FTSE All World ex-US ETF (VEU)
Real estate	8%	Vanguard REIT Index Fund (VGSIX) or Vanguard REIT ETF (VNQ)
Fixed income	40%	Vanguard Total Bond Market Index Fund (VBMFX) or Vanguard Total Bond Market ETF (BND)

TABLE 12-4

Midlife Accumulators—Moderate Multi-Asset-Class Portfolio (open-end mutual funds or ETFs)

Asset Class	Percent	Sample Low-Cost Funds and Symbols
U.S. Equity		
Core U.S. equity	20%	Vanguard Total U.S. Stock Market Index (VTSMX) or Vanguard Total U.S. Stock Market ETF (VTI)
Small value	10%	Vanguard Small-Cap Value Index Fund (VISVX) or iShares S&P 600 Barra Value (IJS)
Microcap	5%	Bridgeway Ultra Small Company Market (BRSIX) or iShares Russell Microcap Index ETF (IWC)
Real estate	8%	Vanguard REIT Index Fund (VGSIX) or Vanguard REIT ETF (VNQ)
International Equity		
Pacific Rim—large	4%	Vanguard Pacific Stock Index (VPACX) or Vanguard Pacific Stock ETF (VLP)
Europe—large	4%	Vanguard European Stock Index (VEURX) or Vanguard European Stock ETF (VGK)
International small-cap value	5%	DFA International Small Cap Value* (DISVX) or WisdomTree International Small Cap Dividend (DLS)
Emerging markets	4%	DFA Emerging Markets Core* (DFEMX) or Vanguard Emerging Markets ETF
Fixed Income		
Investment-grade bonds	20%	Vanguard Total Bond Market Index Fund (VBMFX) or Vanguard Total Bond Market ETF (BND)
High-yield bonds	10%	Vanguard High Yield Bond Fund (VWEHX) or iShares iBoxx High Yield Corporate Bond (HYG)
Inflation-protected bonds	10%	Vanguard Inflation-Protected Securities (VIPSX) or iShares Barclays TIPS Bond Fund (TIP)

*DFA funds are available only through select investment advisors. Alternatives are available to all investors.

GROUP 3: TRANSITIONAL RETIREES

Transitional retirement covers the period from preretirement though active retirement. A person typically enters the preretirement phase from three to five years before leaving full-time employment.

Preretirement is not a formal announcement of impending retirement; rather, it is a thought process. During this period, many people become perplexed about questions such as when to retire, whether they have enough money to retire, and what amount of money they can safely withdraw from savings so that they do not run out of money in retirement. It is probably the most conservative period in a person's life.

Most people who are nearing retirement tend to be in their peak earning years and peak savings years. They are at or close to their highest level of career advancement and are earning top wages. On the home front, household expenses have stabilized and are possibly going down. Children are either self-sufficient or only a few years away from becoming self-sufficient. It is a nice time because you actually have money that is all yours.

The transition from full-time work to retirement signals a new investment phase in a portfolio. The portfolio will convert from accumulation to distribution. That means that investors will soon stop putting money in and start taking some out.

People who are closing in on a retirement date think and act in the most conservative manner of their lives during these transition years. They tend to shift their portfolios to the asset allocation that they will use during retirement. The shift does not happen overnight. Rather, it tends to be gradual as the retirement year approaches.

Brand-new retirees are uncertain about how their cash flow in retirement is going to work out or whether they have a good retirement plan. That causes some people to be very defensive with their asset allocation by reducing risky investments to a small percentage of their portfolio and by hoarding cash.

There is little reason to be overly conservative in a portfolio during the transition phase. Some extra cash in a short-term bond fund is appropriate because it helps the cash-flow jitters go away after about a year or two. I generally recommend at least one year and up to two years in living expenses in a cashlike account or short-term bond fund during retirement.

The tip-of-the-pyramid speculative investments should be avoided as you transition into retirement. If you have not made money speculating by now, you are not going to do it in retirement. Let the urge go. Now is the time to be businesslike with your wealth.

Handling Pensions and Social Security

Most retirees will receive some income from Social Security and perhaps a defined-benefit pension plan. How do these incomes work into an asset allocation? Do you treat them as a bond or something else? If you treat them as a bond, how do you price them?

Income that flows from Social Security and defined-benefit plans do not have par values, and they do not have maturities. They pay as long as you are alive. In addition, there is a risk that the cash flows from a pension and Social Security will diminish or stop. Your employer may have to cut pension distributions because of bankruptcy, and no one can possibly predict what Social Security benefits will be paid in the future. I think we can all agree that future benefits are not going to be up to the current level. This makes putting a bond valuation on a pension or Social Security difficult, if not impossible.

Another aspect of these assets is the lack of control. You cannot change the rules, and you cannot "opt out" of the programs. It is wishful thinking to believe that some day you will be able to call the Social Security office and say, "I don't want to be in the Social Security program anymore. Please send that $200,000 present value of Social Security benefit to my IRA rollover account, and I'll manage the money myself." That is not going to happen in our lifetime. With a defined-benefit plan, your employer may get into financial trouble and a judge from bankruptcy court will decide how much you will get. You have no control over these assets.

Should we view the income streams from these assets as bonds? It does not appear that way to this financial advisor. The variables are too great, and any valuation error can be too large to label these cash-flow streams as fixed income in a portfolio. That being said, retirees have liabilities that have to be paid every month. These liabilities include cash payments for food, shelter, clothing, insurance, automobiles, and a range of other regular expenses. A typical retiree may have about $72,000 in nondiscretionary expenses each year, which is $6,000 per month. For the sake of this discussion, let's assume that the cash flow from a pension and Social Security covers $30,000 of those expenses, which is $2,500 per month. That is less than half the monthly cash liability that a person needs who is spending $72,000 per year.

With a pension and Social Security covering a portion of a retiree's monthly cash liabilities, the rest must come from personal savings, investments, and self-directed retirement accounts. In this case it is $42,000 per year, or $3,500 per month. If pension income and Social Security benefits change, so would the amount needed from investments. In addition, any discretionary spending such as travel and gifting will also come from savings and investments.

Now that we have reduced monthly liabilities based on the cash flow from pensions and Social Security as we know them today, we can create a rational asset allocation to match the remaining monthly cash liabilities. The liability reduction method appears to be the best way to handle income from pensions and Social Security. The method takes into consideration cash flows from these illiquid and uncontrollable assets, without trying to calculate a present value of these assets, call them bonds, and uncomfortably try to cram them into an asset allocation decision.

Cash Flows in Retirement

Expenses will vary during retirement, but over time they will not be as high as they are when you were working. Early on, you will be traveling more, eating out more, fixing up the house, spending more time shopping, possibly joining a gym, and taking care of small medical concerns that you didn't have time for when you were working full time. As time passes and you grow accustomed to being retired, you'll spend less on clothes, less on travel, less on food, and less on housing, and you'll stop spending so much for automobiles. If you have two automobiles, you may decide to cut back to one.

Your home may become a source of cash if needed. The house you own may become too big, so you will downsize. That will release equity from your house, which can be used to generate more income. If you keep your house, you can always tap into the equity in your home by using a mortgage, a home equity loan, or a reverse mortgage that pays monthly income.

Social Security is another source of revenue, and the system will not be disappearing any time soon. All those who are eligible to receive payments will get something, even if the benefits are reduced. Changes in payout amounts and retirement ages will undoubtedly be made for younger people, but not for those already collecting benefits.

If you have living parents who have an estate or other persons who have named you as a beneficiary of an estate, your net worth will increase upon their passing. No one likes to talk about or count on the money he or she will eventually get from an inheritance. Nonetheless, it is a fact that the money will eventually come to you.

All these items plus more are important when forecasting cash flow in retirement. If you need help figuring all this out, it would help to contact a reputable fee-only financial planner. To find a financial planner located in your area, contact the Garrett Planning Network at (866) 260–8400. Two other sources of financial planner referrals are the Financial Planner Association at (800) 322–4237 and the National Association of Personal Financial Advisors at (800) 366–2732. All three organizations have Web sites.

Withdrawal Rates in Retirement

One question asked by most people in preretirement is how much they can safely withdraw from their portfolios without touching the principal. There have been several in-depth studies on this question, and they all point to about a 4 percent withdrawal rate.

However, there are many factors that need to be considered before you limit your rate to 4 percent or less. Several are:

- At what age are you retiring? Younger retirees should probably limit their withdrawal rate to 4 percent or less because they have a long time horizon. Older retirees can afford to have a higher withdrawal rate because their time horizon is shorter.
- How much do you want to leave behind when you are gone? Retirees who want to leave their children or other heirs as much as possible should withdraw less than those who do not wish to leave so much behind.
- How long do you believe you will be an "active" retiree? Everyone eventually slows down as a result of age or health. Spending during the mature retirement years is typically less than in the active retirement years. This means that it is okay if you spend a little more in your active years.

Cash for withdrawals can be produced in a portfolio in many ways. Interest and dividend income are two sources. There is also annual rebalancing in a portfolio. You can easily calculate the amount of income your investments will give you and then take any shortfall during a rebalancing.

Transitional Retirees—Asset Allocation

Figure 12-4 highlights an appropriate asset allocation for people transitioning into retirement and already in an early retirement stage.

The transition from working to retirement is an uncertain time. Accordingly, a retiree's portfolio should be managed with stability and safety of principal as its primary objectives. However, a retirement portfolio still needs growth. A person at age 65 is likely to live for 20 more years, according to IRS Publication 590. As such, the median asset allocation for people in early retirement is 50 percent in stocks and 50 percent in fixed income.

Tables 12-5 and 12-6 give basic and multi-asset-class portfolios for investors in this stage.

FIGURE 12-4

Transitional Retirees' including Active Retirees' Allocation Range

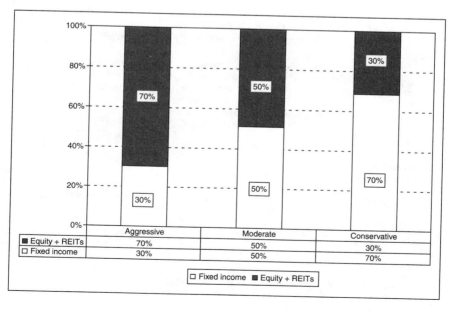

	Aggressive	Moderate	Conservative
■ Equity + REITs	70%	50%	30%
□ Fixed income	30%	50%	70%

□ Fixed income ■ Equity + REITs

TABLE 12-5

Transitional and Active Retirees—Moderate Basic Portfolio (open-end mutual funds or ETFs)

Asset Class	Percent	Sample Low-Cost Funds and Symbols
U.S. equity	30%	Vanguard Total U.S. Stock Market Index (VTSMX) or Vanguard Total U.S. Stock Market ETF (VTI)
International equity	15%	Vanguard Total International Portfolio (VGTSX) or Vanguard FTSE All World ex-US ETF (VEU)
Real estate	5%	Vanguard REIT Index Fund (VGSIX) or Vanguard REIT ETF (VNQ)
Fixed income	48%	Vanguard Total Bond Market Index Fund (VBMFX) or Vanguard Total Bond Market ETF (BND)
Cash equivalent	2%	Low-cost money market fund with checking

TABLE 12-6

Transitional including Active Retirees—Moderate Multi-Asset-Class Portfolio (open-end mutual funds or ETFs)

Asset Class	Percent	Sample Low-Cost Funds and Symbols
U.S. Equity		
Core U.S. equity	18%	Vanguard Total U.S. Stock Market Index (VTSMX) or Vanguard Total U.S. Stock Market ETF (VTI)
Small value	8%	Vanguard Small-Cap Value Index Fund (VISVX) or iShares S&P 600 Barra Value (IJS)
Microcap	4%	Bridgeway Ultra Small Company Market (BRSIX) or iShares Russell Microcap Index ETF (IWC)
Real estate	7%	Vanguard REIT Index Fund (VGSIX) or Vanguard REIT ETF (VNQ)
International Equity		
Pacific Rim—large	3%	Vanguard Pacific Stock Index (VPACX) or Vanguard Pacific Stock ETF (VLP)
Europe—large	3%	Vanguard European Stock Index (VEURX) or Vanguard European Stock ETF (VGK)
International	4%	DFA International Small Cap Value* (DISVX) or small-cap value WisdomTree International Small Cap Dividend (DLS)
Emerging markets	3%	DFA Emerging Markets* (DFEMX) or Vanguard Emerging Markets Stock ETF (VWO)
Fixed Income		
Investment-grade	24%	Vanguard Total Bond Market Index Fund (VBMFX) bonds or Vanguard Total Bond Market ETF (BND)
High-yield bonds	12%	Vanguard High Yield Bond Fund (VWEHX) or iShares iBoxx High Yield Corporate Bond (HYG)
Inflation-protected bonds	12%	Vanguard Inflation-Protected Securities (VIPSX) or iShares Barclays TIPS Bond Fund (TIP)
Cash		
Cash equivalent	2%	Low-cost money market fund with checking

*DFA funds are only available through select financial advisors. Alternatives are available to all investors.

GROUP 4: MATURE RETIREES

The good news is that Americans are living longer; the bad news is that we do not live forever. The average life expectancy of a 65-year-old is 86, which is about 10 years longer than it was in 1940 according to the Department of the Treasury. Today's seniors are also healthier and more active. They eat better, get more exercise, and smoke less than they did in prior generations. Longevity trends are so strong that new life insurance tables recently introduced by the Society of Actuaries go out to age 120.

Alas, the Fountain of Youth is still yet to be discovered. No one lives forever. At some point, we all need to get our financial house in order and prepare for the afterlife. This means that someone else will be handling your financial affairs eventually. That may occur while you are still alive, and it will definitely occur after you're gone.

It is a common for mature retirees to do detailed estate planning. One of the decisions to make is who will manage their affairs when they are no longer able too. This chore is normally taken over by the healthy spouse while both husband and wife are still living. When there is only one person, the job is typically taken on by a son or daughter, a relative, or a professional representative.

I highly recommend that if you choose a son or daughter to handle your finances, you give them fair warning far in advance. Once a helper has been chosen, that person will need to become informed of your financial situation. This includes an understanding of your estate plan, your investment accounts, and your insurance documents, including knowing where all these things are located in your home.

Any financial planner will tell you that the transition of financial responsibility from parents to children can work out either very well or very poorly. There are steps you can take to avoid cost and confusion and to ensure that the transition occurs smoothly. The following list pertains to your investment accounts and contains steps you can take to ensure a smooth transition:

1. Write down where all your documents are and who your representatives are and give this to whoever is going to be responsible for your affairs.
2. Consolidate all your investment accounts with one or two custodians, such as Charles Schwab, Vanguard, or

Fidelity. This will make management of the investments easier and will help your heirs settle the estate when you pass away.

3. Write a detailed statement, in your own words, describing how your portfolio is being managed and how you expect it to be managed in the future. The document should include a general investment strategy as well as points of contact.

4. Insist that the person you choose to manage your estate understand basic financial principles including asset allocation and why you are using low-cost mutual funds.

Mature Retirees—Asset Allocation

The asset allocation of a mature retiree's portfolio can vary depending on who is going to use the money. There should be two years of living expenses in cash and short-term bonds, and there should not be any tip-of-the-pyramid speculative investments. However, the allocation of the long-term liquid investments can vary considerably.

On the one hand, a portfolio should be conservatively managed to carry a retiree through the remainder of his or her life. On the other hand, the allocation could favor the needs and ages of the beneficiaries if a retiree is not going to need all of his or her money. Generally, a portfolio is managed based on a combination of both scenarios. Figure 12-5 highlights suggested asset allocation for mature retirees.

As in the other stages, the range of allocations presented in Figure 12-5 is three separate portfolios. Trying to time markets by moving between allocations is not a prudent strategy. Tables 12-7 and 12-8 give sample portfolios for investors in this stage.

The asset allocation recommendations outlined in Tables 12-7 and 12-8 represent that portion of the portfolio that will be used by a mature retiree during his or her lifetime. More than likely, a majority of the assets are not going to be used by the retiree. Rather, they will be passed on to heirs. Therefore, a portion of the portfolio should be allocated based on the needs of those inheriting the assets.

FIGURE 12-5

Mature Retiree Allocation Range

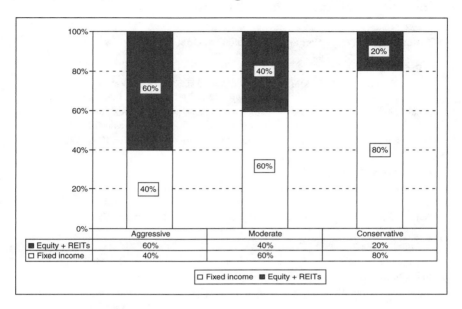

	Aggressive	Moderate	Conservative
■ Equity + REITs	60%	40%	20%
□ Fixed income	40%	60%	80%

□ Fixed income ■ Equity + REITs

TABLE 12-7

Mature Retirees—Moderate Basic Portfolio (open-end mutual funds or ETFs)

Asset Class	Percent	Sample Low-Cost Funds and Symbols
U.S. equity	25%*	Vanguard Total U.S. Stock Market Index (VTSMX) or Vanguard Total U.S. Stock Market ETF (VTI)
International equity	10%	Vanguard Total International Portfolio (VGTSX) or Vanguard FTSE All World ex-US ETF (VEU)
Real estate	5%	Vanguard REIT Index Fund (VGSIX) or Vanguard REIT ETF (VNQ)
Fixed income	40%	Vanguard Total Bond Market Index Fund (VBMFX) or Vanguard Total Bond Market ETF (BND)
Short-term bonds	18%	Vanguard Investment Grade Short-Term (VFSTX) or Vanguard Short-Term Bond ETF(BSV)
Cash equivalent	2%	Low-cost money market fund with checking

TABLE 12-8

Mature Retirees—Moderate Multi-Asset-Class Portfolio
(open-end mutual funds or ETF version)

Asset Class	Percent	Sample Low-Cost Funds and Symbols
U.S. Equity		
Core U.S. equity	20%	Vanguard Total U.S. Stock Market Index (VTSMX) or Vanguard Total U.S. Stock Market ETF (VTI)
Small value	5%	Vanguard Small-Cap Value Index Fund (VISVX) or iShares S&P 600 Barra Value (IJS)
Real estate	5%	Vanguard REIT Index Fund (VGSIX) or Vanguard REIT ETF (VNQ)
International Equity		
Pacific Rim—large	4%	Vanguard Pacific Stock Index (VPACX) or Vanguard Pacific Stock ETF (VLP)
Europe—large	4%	Vanguard European Stock Index (VEURX) or Vanguard European Stock ETF (VGK)
Emerging markets	2%	DFA Emerging Markets* (DFEMX) or Vanguard Emerging Markets Stock ETF (VWO)
Fixed Income		
Investment-grade bonds	30%	Vanguard Total Bond Market Index Fund (VBMFX) or Vanguard Total Bond Market ETF (BND)
Short-term bonds	18%	Vanguard Investment Grade Short-term (VFSTX) or Vanguard Short-Term Bond ETF (BSV)
Inflation-protected bonds	10%	Vanguard Inflation-Protected Securities (VIPSX) or iShares Barclays TIPS Bond Fund (TIP)
Cash		
Cash equivalent	2%	Low-cost money market fund with checking

*DFA funds are only available through select financial advisors. Alternatives are available to all investors.

YOUR AGE IN BONDS: THE MODIFIED VERSION

A simple way to decide on a stock and bond allocation is to use a rule of thumb called "your age in bonds." Age plays an important part in determining asset allocation. The consensus is that the older you get, the less risk you should take. This makes sense for two reasons: first, you have less time to make up losses, especially if you are in the distribution phase of life; and second, if you are still working, you have only a few years to replace those losses from savings.

Very simply, whatever a person's age is, that is the allocation he or she should have in bonds. The remainder of his or her portfolio would be invested in riskier assets such as stocks. For example, a 55-year-old may have 55 percent of savings in bonds and the rest in a diversified stock portfolio. This allocation would change every year or every few years as the investor ages.

The concept of age in bonds has the appeal of simplicity. It is easy to understand and appears to solve a difficult financial planning question about asset allocation. However, is it practical to apply this rule of thumb to all investors? No, it is not. Let's look at two age groups: 30-year-olds and 55-year-olds. We are going to test how well "your age in bonds" works for each of these groups.

Most 30-year-olds are still at the beginning of their careers or perhaps making their first career change. They all have many years of work and savings ahead. Thirty-year-olds typically have very little in savings, which means that the market gyrations have only a minor impact on their net worth. Accordingly, 30-year-olds should concentrate more on formulating a regular savings plan, and whatever money they do save should be largely invested in equity as long as the allocation does not exceed their tolerance for risk. Consequently, 70 percent in equity and 30 percent "your age in bonds" works fine for most 30-year-olds.

The range of financial situations for people at the age of 55 is much broader than when they were 30 years old. There are 55-year-olds who have accumulated significant wealth, while others have accumulated very little. Some people are close to vesting in an employer pension, while others are relying 100 percent on their own savings for retirement. Family status is quite diverse also. Some people are married, others divorced, others remarried, and still others never married. There are those caring for large families, some with small families, some with no family, and some with extended families including helping out aging parents or other relatives. Consequently, there is no typical 55-year-old. Their situations are all unique, and their asset allocation needs to take into account a host of life situation variables.

In general, it's more appropriate to create generic, all-purpose portfolio models for younger people and less appropriate to propose generic asset allocation models for older investors. Life has a way of introducing lots of sticky details as we grow older—and those details should have a bearing on our investment portfolio. Very simply, it is possible to aggregate the asset allocation needs of 30-year-olds without doing too much violence to their individual circumstances. But investors over the age of 55 have other issues. The plot has thickened, and their individual circumstances need to be factored into their portfolio design.

We speak of age as an important portfolio determinant, and we looked at your age in bonds as a proxy for asset allocation. Is the model useless? No, but adjustments should be made, and the adjustment can be in determining the "allocation age" of an investor. This concept was articulated in an article titled "What's Your Asset Allocation Age?" This article was coauthored by Brigham Young University professor Craig L. Israelsen and me in *Financial Planning Magazine*, November 2009 issue.

A person's allocation age may be higher or lower than a person's chronological age, depending on the individual investor. In a sense, your age in bonds is a reasonable place to begin forming an asset allocation, and then adjustments should be made up or down based on factors unique to each individual.

Here is a simple example using an allocation age adjustment to chronological age. Assume a 65-year-old couple has accumulated $2 million in liquid investment assets. Both people are 65. The couple has two grown children ages 33 and 37 who do not need financial support. The couple spends about $100,000 per year, of which $60,000 comes from pensions and Social Security. Only $40,000 comes out of savings.

Let's split the $2 million into two accounts, if only on paper. The first account is $1 million. This account is to provide the couple with $40,000 for living needs for their rest of their life, which is reasonable based on a 4 percent distribution rate. The second $1 million is in savings and will likely not be used at all by the couple. It will all go to the children.

In view of this scenario, what is an appropriate allocation for each $1 million account and what is appropriate for the total $2 million? The $1 million to be used primarily for income for the couple can be invested based in the couple's age in bonds, which would make that account 65 percent bonds and 35 percent stocks. The other $1 million could be invested according to the two children's ages. Since the children's average age is 35, let's use age in bonds again and make that account 35 percent bonds and 65 percent stocks. The two accounts can be managed separately with two separate allocations, or they can be combined and make one combined allocation. A combined account of $2 million would be allocated as 50 percent in stocks and 50 percent in bonds. The couple's 50-year commingled allocation age is quite different from their chronological age; however, it may be more appropriate for their situation.

Another example: assume the case of two 55-year-old female investors. How do we differentiate the special needs of each person? The questions to ask cover a wide range of issues, such as income needs, retirement needs, pensions, current and forecasted living expenses, bequeathing goals, passive income sources, the degree of detachment (i.e., risk tolerance), and so on. These real-life variables will dramatically affect each woman's asset allocation. The chronological age-based allocation of 55 percent in bonds may be a good starting point or baseline allocation model. There are a number of life variables that will ultimately determine the allocation age of the investor.

Assume that one of the 55-year-old women is barely getting by financially and that the other is doing very well. The first woman has a small amount she saved in her 401(k) and that is all. She has some housing debt and is caring for her aging parents who are both in their eighties. In her case, an age-in-bond association would put her portfolio at 45 percent in stocks. The may be too aggressive, and an adjustment should be made. A more appropriate allocation age is 70 based on her life situation because she has very high cash-flow risk and is caring for elderly parents. She cannot afford to lose any sizable amount of her savings. The second 55-year-old has a healthy and generous pension plan, no housing or consumer debt, and a large Roth IRA account balance which is positioned very conservatively. In addition, she is expected to inherit a sizable estate in the next few years. Her allocation age is closer to 40 because she has little cash-flow risk, no debt, and no foreseen future liabilities.

For both women the age-in-bonds rule is too restrictive. Recall that both investors have a chronological age of 55. However, the first investor will have a 70 percent allocation to bonds because of her tight financial situation, with the balance of the allocation (in this case 30 percent) invested in the equity portfolio. The second investor will have a 40 percent allocation to bonds and a 60 percent equity allocation because she is in a much better financial situation.

CHAPTER SUMMARY

Selecting an appropriate asset allocation during all phases of life is essential to your long-term investment plan. A successful investment plan incorporates the basic necessities of broad diversification, stability, tax management, and growth, while also including special styling that makes a portfolio unique to the person who intends to use it.

While all investors are alike in some ways, they are different in many others. Accordingly, most investment portfolios will be broadly similar in some ways and unique in others. If you manage your portfolio well over the years and do not become emotional about investment decisions, then it should pay dividends to you through retirement and eventually be passed on your heirs.

A life-cycle methodology is one strategy for beginning your quest to discover an appropriate asset allocation. The asset allocation and investment selections for the four stages of life provided here are only guides. You will need to adjust the portfolios to fit your specific situation as you age, and your "allocation age" in bonds may be a good solution.

NOTE

[1]Jacob S. Rugh, "Premium and Asset Allocations of Premium-Paying TIAA-CREF Participants as of March 31, 2004," TIAA-CREF Institute, www.tiaa-crefinstitute.org.

How Behavior Affects Asset Allocation Decisions

KEY CONCEPTS

- Behavioral finance is the study of investor decision making.
- Staying below your maximum tolerance for risk is critical to investment success.
- Asset allocation stress testing helps refine investor risk tolerance.
- Rebalancing keeps your portfolio in line with your investment policy.

Investor behavior is the second leg of asset allocation. A well-developed plan works only when the investor sticks to the plan through good markets and bad. This means being brutally honest about your ability to handle risk.

Modern portfolio theory (MPT) assumes that all investors have access to all available information about securities at the same time and that they act rationally on this information when making investment decisions. It presupposes that investors also understand the nature of risk and return in various markets, including the correlations between each market, when creating an asset allocation. Once an investment plan has been designed and implemented, the theory expects that rebalancing will occur in a disciplined manner to capture a diversification benefit and control risk.

Theory is theory. This is not how all investors act. Investors do have the intention of maximizing profit while minimizing risk; however, no individual can know what all market participants know in aggregate; and no individual investor will act unemotionally in every phase of portfolio management. The end result of these human tendencies is that most people have portfolio performance that is below the markets they are investing in.

Researchers have uncovered a surprisingly large amount of evidence showing that irrational behavior and repeated errors in judgment explain a significant portion of this known shortfall in individual investment performance. These human flaws are consistent, predictable, and widespread.

The financial markets are not the cause of investment plan failure; rather, it is the investors themselves who cause their own demise. I have seen this over two decades of experience working with individual investors. A sensible investment plan never fails an investor; the investor fails the plan. The abandonment of a good plan usually occurs either during a deep bear market or a strong bull market.

A successful asset allocation strategy requires that individuals understand the dynamics behind diversification and reallocation. It also demands that investors be on the alert for flaws in their own judgment that can cause the plan to collapse.

Underestimating market risk is a major culprit in behavioral errors. If an investor takes too much risk in a portfolio without knowing or understanding the risk, that investor will become emotional when steep losses occur; and that investor will make mistakes. It is unavoidable. Overextended investors become anxious about their asset allocation in poor markets, and they will abandon their long-term investment plan eventually and opt for the safety of low returning short-term investments. It is critical that each investor know how much risk there is in an asset allocation *before* implementing that plan to ensure that they will not blow out of an allocation prematurely. Emotional decision making is not part of a viable investment plan.

BEHAVIORAL FINANCE

Behavioral finance is an academic field that attempts to understand and explain how psychology influences an investor's decision-making process. A fledgling field of study in the early 1960s, behavioral finance has grown to be an important area of research at several influential institutions. Professors recognized as experts in the field include Daniel Kahneman (Princeton), Meir Statman (Santa Clara), Richard Thaler (University of Chicago), Robert J. Shiller (Yale), and Amos Tversky. Tversky is frequently cited as the forefather of the field. He died in 1996.

The following list touches on a few observations made by behavioral finance researchers. Unfortunately, the list only scratches the surface. Much more information about this fascinating field is available on the Internet and in your local library:

- People tend to be more optimistic about stocks after the market goes up and more pessimistic after it goes down.
- Investors give too much weight to recent information, such as one quarter's earnings, and too little weight to long-term fundamentals.
- People tend to buy investments that have recently had a large run-up in performance. Over 80 percent of new mutual fund purchases go into the funds that have the best one-year return.
- Investors label investments as "good" or "bad" based on where the current price is relative to the price they paid rather than on the underlying fundamentals of the investment.
- People are reluctant to admit an error in judgment. Consequently, many people pay high commissions and fees to brokers and advisors so that they have someone to blame.
- The confidence investors have in the future earnings of high-priced companies is often too high, and the confidence they have in the earnings growth of low-priced companies is often too low.
- Overconfident investors generally believe that they have more knowledge and information than they actually have. As a result, they tend to trade too much and underperform the market.
- The profile of an overconfident investor is male, professional, with at least one advanced academic degree.
- Women tend to have a longer-term view of the markets than men do. They maintain an investment plan longer, and as a result they generally perform better.

Asset allocation strategies are based on rational decisions and the discipline to maintain those decisions. Unfortunately, individual investors can become quite irrational when it comes to investment decisions, especially during large swings in the markets. Successful investors understand the limitations of the markets as well as their own limitations, and they develop a proper asset allocation that accommodates both.

MORE INTERESTING INFORMATION

One surprising aspect of behavioral finance research is that a majority of individual investors surveyed know that they don't invest well. According to a Vanguard Group survey of 401(k) participants, a sizable 85 percent of employees consider themselves to be unskilled investors and would rather hire a professional manager.

Interestingly, the Vanguard Group found that the poorest-performing investment accounts in 401(k) plans belong to those participants who have the most education, have the highest incomes, and consider themselves skilled investors. Researchers Olivia Mitchell and Stephen Utkus at the University of Pennsylvania's Wharton Pension Research Council studied why a high-paid professional might have low returns.[1] They found that individuals who earn more are likely to be higher up the management hierarchy, making them feel more in control of their destiny. Utkus found that the overconfidence of higher-income participants caused them to trade more often. This was a major factor leading to lower investment performance.

Professor Meir Statman (Santa Clara) is an expert in a behavior known as the *fear of regret*. People tend to feel sorrow and grief after having made an error in judgment. Investors are typically emotionally affected when a security was bought for more than the current price. Some psychologists have concluded that investors typically consider the loss of $1 twice as painful as the pleasure from a $1 gain.

Statman's findings have a direct impact on investors using asset allocation strategies. Rebalancing a portfolio requires that investors sell part of a winning investment and buy more of a losing one. It is hard for investors to sell what makes them happy and buy more of what makes them sad, especially during a deep bear market when everyone is gloomy.

The research on behavioral finance is wide and deep. In recent years there have been dozens of books published on the subject. Most of these books can be checked out at your local library. There is also a significant amount of information available on the Internet for free. A virtual clearinghouse of behavioral finance studies can be found at www.behaviouralfinance.net.

DISCOVERING YOUR RISK TOLERANCE

After formulating an appropriate asset allocation based on your assets and your future liabilities, the other side of the coin is your tolerance for investment risk. Risk tolerance is a measure of the amount of price volatility and investment loss you can withstand before changing your behavior. The ideal portfolio may give you concern during a bear market, but it does not have enough volatility to lead you to change your investment strategy. A portfolio with too much risk will cause a change in behavior during a volatile period, which results in a change or abandonment of an investment plan.

An emotional decision to change or abandon an investment plan as a result of market risk ultimately *increases* portfolio risk and reduces return. People become emotional only after they lose money. If an investor has been in a bad market long enough to lose money, that investor doesn't want to be out of the market when it turns around. That becomes a strategy of all risk and no return.

An emotional decision does not necessarily result in the sale of risky investments. It could simply mean not investing new money in the markets at the time when you intended to, or delaying portfolio rebalancing into stocks while you "wait and see" what happens to the market.

If by chance an investor happens to time the market correctly in the short term, it may lead to large losses in the long run. Investors who guess correctly one time tend to attribute their good fortune to their investment skill rather than to luck. Once people believe that they are able to "read" the markets, they set themselves up for big and costly mistakes in the future.

HOW BEHAVIORAL FINANCE AFFECTS YOU

Finding your personal risk tolerance can be a tricky business. People understand that investing requires risk; however, it is common for people to overestimate the amount of risk they can handle. This is especially true during a prolonged bull market.

During the late 1990s, almost every investor was making money in the stock market. Investing seemed like a one-way street of high returns with little risk. Every time stock prices hiccuped, all that was said was, "Buy the dips." It was difficult to find an active investor who didn't think he or she was smart. The television media reinforced that belief by keeping investors informed through continuous "live" market broadcasts. Stock chat rooms on the Internet were filled with homespun stock analysts who had no formal training. Favorite clichés of the period were "This time it's different," and "We are in a new paradigm of stock valuation."

Opportunistic authors were not going to miss out on the action. In early 1999, James Glassman and Kevin Hassett published their highly acclaimed bestseller *Dow 36,000* (New York: Three Rivers Press, 2000). The two used historical data to show that there was no risk in the stock market over long periods. They argued that when the world understood this fact, the Dow Jones Industrial Average (DJIA) would triple in value. Not to be outdone, in September of 1999, Charles W. Kadlec published *Dow 100,000: Fact or Fiction* (Upper Saddle River, NJ: Prentice Hall Press, 1999). He predicted that the DJIA would increase 10 times in value by the year 2020.

Time proved painful to those who chose to ignore risk or rationalize it away. Between March 2000 and March 2003, the DJIA fell by 40 percent and the tech-heavy Nasdaq Index fell by 80 percent. There was blood in the streets as investors slashed their stock holdings and tried to preserve what little they had left. Needless to say, both *Dow 36,000* and *Dow 100,000* can now be found at most flea markets priced at less than $1.

By 2007, the S&P 500 had crawled back and was hitting new highs in October. Then an economic tsunami hit the U.S. housing market causing a domino effect that tore apart financial markets throughout the world. Too-big-to-fail financial institutions ruptured at their base. First Bear Sterns went under and then Lehman Brothers and AIG. The entire U.S. banking industry was in peril.

The financial industry might have come to a screeching halt if not for the innovation of the Federal Reserve along with the Treasury Department. With Congress's permission, hundreds of billions of dollars in taxpayer money was pumped into the banking system to stabilize the markets by providing liquidity.

Over an 18-month period, the S&P 500 collapsed by more than 57 percent from an October 12, 2007, high of 1,562 down to an intra-day low of 666 on March 9, 2009. Bank stocks fell by about 70 percent over the same period. It was a terrifying time for many equity investors and a real test of their tolerance for financial risk.

When a person overestimates his or her tolerance for risk, a bear market like the one in 2008 will expose this misjudgment. This will always be an expensive and painful lesson that is not forgotten for years. The two bear markets that occurred between 2000 and 2009 created too much pressure for overextended investors, and many sold near market bottoms.

Only those investors who have an asset allocation at or below their tolerance for risk survive deep bear market. Finding an investment allocation that will survive during all market cycles is not easy, but it is worth the effort.

RISK TOLERANCE QUESTIONNAIRES

Risk tolerance questionnaires are common in the investment industry. Questionnaires are available through all mutual fund companies, brokerage firms, and private investment advisors. In addition, you can find them in financial planning books and in some investment-related magazines.

The goal of risk tolerance questionnaires is to find the maximum level of risk that an investor is capable of handling. In doing so, they ask various questions about your investment experience and try to model your risk-and-return profile. Some go as far as recommending an appropriate mix of investments based on your answers. If you are curious, there are sample questions from one questionnaire at the end of this chapter.

Questionnaires are one place to begin your inquiry into your risk tolerance; however, they should not be relied on for accuracy. One problem with this approach is that most questionnaires are too vague. They don't ask for enough information. Since each answer is important to the numeral risk score, a short list of questions means an unreliable result. In addition, if you took the same questionnaire several times over a one-year period, the results would be different each time you answered, depending on how you felt and your recent stock market experience.

Another concern with questionnaires is that the information is misused. The purpose of a questionnaire is to determine your *maximum* level of risk. They are not designed to determine your *appropriate* level of risk based on your financial needs. Nevertheless, sellers of investment products use the results to guide people into portfolios that have the maximum level of risk whether they need it or not. Why? Risky investments pay the advisor more money. Stock mutual funds have higher fees than bond mutual funds and pay brokers bigger commissions.

The timing of taking the questionnaire does have a significant impact on the answers you give. If the stock market has been in an upward trend and volatility is low, people tend to be optimistic, and this is reflected in the amount of risk they are willing to take. But that is not the point of a questionnaire. The idea is to see how you will react in bear markets. Accordingly, I do recommend taking a risk tolerance questionnaire only after a sharp decline in stock prices of 10 percent or more and you are not feeling good about it.

Despite the problems surrounding investment questionnaires, they do get people thinking about the maximum level of risk they can handle, and that is a start. These tools are just one arrow in your quiver to help guide you into an appropriate portfolio.

THE ASSET ALLOCATION STRESS TEST

Once you believe that you have an asset allocation that is appropriate for your needs, there is another tool that can help you determine if it is at or below your risk tolerance level. The asset allocation stress test is a simple form of market simulation that will help you understand how you might react during the next downturn in the financial markets.

The technique involves asking "what if" questions, and the investor answering them honestly. Here is a simple example of such a question:

Assume that you invested half of your life savings in a total U.S. stock market index fund and the other half in a total U.S. bond market index fund. By the end of the year, the stock fund had collapsed by 30 percent, while the bond fund was up by 10 percent. You planned to rebalance the portfolio back to a 50 percent stock and 50 percent bond position annually. However, given the large loss in the stock portion, what action would you take?

1. Rebalance the portfolio back to the 50 percent stock and 50 percent bond target.
2. Do nothing until you have a clearer picture of market direction.
3. Sell part of the stock fund and buy more of the bond fund to reduce your risk.

If the 50 percent stock and 50 percent bond allocation was at a level below your risk tolerance, you would choose answer 1—sell bonds and buy stocks to rebalance back to the original target. On the other hand, you're above your tolerance for risk if you let the portfolio remain out of balance (answer 2) or if you were inclined to sell stocks (answer 3). If this is how you would act, then a 50 percent stock and 50 percent bond allocation is beyond your tolerance for risk.

I also find that most people have an *actual* risk tolerance that is lower than their *declared* tolerance for risk. In other words, people do not want other people to think they cannot handle a loss, because that might be seen as a personality flaw.

A macho attitude doesn't help you in investing. It doesn't matter how low your level of risk is, as long as you know what it is. Understanding your limit for financial loss will guide you to a proper allocation, and that will increase the probability that you will maintain your investment plan through good times and bad.

AN EXAMPLE OF THE STRESS TEST

The following is a detailed example of an asset allocation stress test. It suggests an initial asset allocation to an investor and then stress-tests the allocation to observe how the investor reacts to a volatility shock. If an emotional reaction to loss occurs, a change in asset allocation is needed to bring the portfolio into line with the investor's true tolerance for risk.

Consider a single woman in her midfifties who decides to retire after being offered early retirement from her employer. The woman will receive a small monthly pension as well as a $300,000 IRA rollover from a 401(k). She meets with a financial planner to ask for assistance in investing the $300,000 IRA rollover.

The planner concludes that the woman will not make enough from the pension to cover her living expenses and travel plans. She will need to withdraw $1,000 per month from the IRA to supplement her pension income. After determining the woman's cash-flow needs, the conversation turns to asset allocation. The advisor explains the historical returns and risks of each asset class, how modern portfolio theory works, and the necessity for annual rebalancing. The advisor asks the woman to complete a risk tolerance questionnaire to find the maximum level of risk she can deal with.

The woman completes the risk tolerance questionnaire, and the financial planner calculates the results. He concludes that the woman has the risk tolerance to handle an aggressive portfolio. The advisor suggests an asset allocation of 70 percent in stocks and 30 percent in bonds.

Before recommending individual investments, the planner wishes to ensure that a 70 percent stock and 30 percent bond portfolio is not above the woman's risk tolerance. Therefore, he asks her to take an asset allocation stress test.

A hypothetical portfolio is created to simulate the month-by-month value of a 70 percent stock and 30 percent bond portfolio between the years 2000 and 2002. Two investments are selected for the study: the Vanguard Total Bond Market Index fund and the Vanguard Total U.S. Stock Market Index fund.

The planner assumes that the woman starts with $300,000 in December 1999, withdraws $1,000 per month starting at the end of January 2000, and rebalances the portfolio back to a 70 percent stock and 30 percent bond mix at the end of each year. Table 13-1 is a summary of the investment results over the three-year period.

As the financial planner works through the year 2000 results with his client, the woman is relatively accepting of the results. Although the loss in 2000 is $11,745 and the withdrawals are $12,000 during the period, she is comfortable with the performance and with rebalancing the portfolio at the end of 2000.

TABLE 13-1

Stress Test 1: 70 Percent Stocks and 30 Percent Bonds, 2000–2002; Start with $300,000

Quarter End	Vanguard Total U.S. Stock Fund	Vanguard Total Bond Fund	70% Stocks	30% Bonds	Total Investment Gain/Loss	Total Withdrawn @ $1,000/ Month	Ending value
Dec. 1999			210,000	90,000			300,000
Mar. 2000	3.84%	2.42%	216,564	90,678	10,242	(3,000)	307,242
June 2000	-4.39%	1.48%	205,557	90,520	2,077	(6,000)	296,077
Sept. 2000	0.27%	3.07%	204,612	91,799	5,411	(9,000)	296,411
Dec. 2000	-10.17%	3.98%	182,303	93,953	(11,745)	(12,000)	276,255
Mar. 2001	-12.27%	3.24%	168,151	84,062	(32,787)	(15,000)	252,213
June 2001	7.47%	0.79%	179,212	83,226	(19,562)	(18,000)	262,438
Sept. 2001	-15.93%	4.29%	149,164	85,296	(44,540)	(21,000)	234,460
Dec. 2001	12.32%	-0.08%	166,041	83,728	(26,231)	(24,000)	249,769
Mar. 2002	0.97%	0.06%	175,034	73,476	(24,490)	(27,000)	248,510
June 2002	-12.69%	2.80%	151,322	74,033	(44,645)	(30,000)	225,355
Sept. 2002	-16.84%	3.71%	124,340	75,279	(67,381)	(33,000)	199,619
Dec. 2002	7.82%	1.47%	132,563	74,886	(56,551)	(36,000)	207,449

The year 2001 starts with a rebalanced target allocation of 70 percent in stocks and 30 percent in bonds. However, in 2001 the stock market continues lower. By the end of that year, the woman has $249,769 in her portfolio, which is $50,231 below its starting value of $300,000. The woman is no longer smiling. She acknowledges that $24,000 has been withdrawn from the portfolio over the last two years, and she reluctantly agrees that she will still rebalance the portfolio back to the target of 70 percent in stocks and 30 percent in bonds for the start of 2002.

As the financial planner works through 2002, a flag goes up that ends the exercise. In June 2002, the portfolio value falls to $225,355, and the woman becomes very concerned. By September, the portfolio value falls below $200,000 to $199,619. That is a breaking point for the woman. She becomes emotional about the 70 percent stock and 30 percent bond allocation, which is evident when she comments, "At this rate I will be broke in five years."

When answering questions on a questionnaire, it is easy for people to mistakenly assume that they can handle more risk than they are capable of handling. Despite the woman's young retirement age and her desire to take risk, she is not capable of handling the risk of a 70 percent stock and 30 percent bond portfolio.

The financial planner explains to the woman that if she is inclined to abandon her investment plan after losing money, then the 70 percent stock and 30 percent bond portfolio asset allocation is too aggressive. A less aggressive asset allocation should be implemented from the start. The financial planner suggests a moderate allocation using a 40 percent stock and 60 percent bond portfolio.

Table 13-2 is a replay of the stress test. This time it is benchmarked to a 40 percent stock and 60 percent bond portfolio. The woman starts with $300,000 in December 1999, withdraws $1,000 per month, and the portfolio is expected to be rebalanced back to a 40 percent stock and 60 percent bond target allocation at the end of each year.

At its low point in September 2002, the market value of the 40 percent stock and 60 percent bond portfolio is $249,585. However, only $17,415 of the reduction is due to poor market conditions. The rest is the cumulative withdrawals from the portfolio. The woman is more comfortable with the portfolio and decides that a 40 percent stock and 60 percent bond mix is appropriate for her risk tolerance.

TABLE 13-2

Stress Test 2: 40 Percent Stocks and 60 Percent Bonds, 2000–2002; Start with $300,000

Quarter End	Vanguard Total U.S. Stock Fund	Vanguard Total Bond Fund	40% Stocks	60% Bonds	Total Investment Gain/Loss	Total Withdrawn @ $1,000/ Month	Ending Value
Dec. 1999			120,000	180,000			300,000
Mar. 2000	3.84%	2.42%	123,108	182,856	5,964	3,000	302,964
June 2000	–4.39%	1.48%	116,204	184,062	3,266	6,000	297,266
Sept. 2000	0.27%	3.07%	115,017	188,213	9,230	9,000	300,230
Dec. 2000	–10.17%	3.98%	101,820	194,204	5,024	12,000	293,024
Mar. 2001	–12.27%	3.24%	101,328	180,011	(6,661)	15,000	278,339
June 2001	7.47%	0.79%	107,397	179,933	2,330	18,000	284,330
Sept. 2001	–15.93%	4.29%	88,789	186,152	(7,059)	21,000	271,941
Dec. 2001	12.32%	–0.08%	98,228	184,503	3,731	24,000	279,731
Mar. 2002	0.97%	0.06%	111,478	166,439	1,917	27,000	274,917
June 2002	–12.69%	2.80%	95,831	169,599	(7,570)	30,000	262,430
Sept. 2002	–16.84%	3.71%	78,193	174,391	(17,415)	33,000	249,585
Dec. 2002	7.82%	1.47%	82,808	175,455	(8,737)	36,000	255,263

Would the 40 percent stock and 60 percent bond portfolio decision have saved the women from selling stocks some time during the 57 percent market decline that took place between October 2007 and March 2009? That is hard to say. I can only speak from experience with my own clients when I say that the *probability* of capitulation was much lower with a 40 percent stock allocation then if she had invested 70 percent in stocks. A 70 percent stock allocation would have created too much stress, and the woman would have sold at some point in the bear market, and she would have less wealth today because of it.

Effective investing involves having realistic expectations about market volatility and then coupling those expectations with an understanding of your tolerance for risk. If you assume too much risk in a portfolio, there is a high probability that you will abandon your investment strategy during severe market downturns. In contrast, investors who have taken the stress test and are emotionally prepared for the risk they have elected will be able to maintain their allocation during all market conditions. Discipline in maintaining strategy is an essential element of investment success.

REBALANCING FINANCIAL RISK

Portfolio rebalancing is a fundamental part of asset allocation. Rebalancing reduces portfolio risk and creates a diversification benefit in the form of a higher long-term return.

There are many methods of rebalancing although they all do the same thing. A portfolio's fixed target allocation is compared to its current allocation, and a rebalancing occurs when the asset classes are off target by a predefined percent.

The most common type of rebalancing works on a regular time interval, such as monthly, quarterly, or annually. Another method is based on percentage bands around asset classes. Other strategies for rebalancing are available and can become quite complex. They involve a sophisticated mix of differential percentages and time elements that take a long time to implement and involve more trading costs.

I recommend that individual investors avoid sophisticated rebalancing strategies. For simplicity, annual rebalancing is practical and the one used throughout this book. Annual rebalancing captures most of the diversification benefit that other options provide without having you spend a lot of time or money on the process.

There are other situations in which your portfolio will be rebalanced using cash. When money is added to a portfolio, this is an ideal time to check the asset allocation and invest the additional cash where it is needed. If you are taking withdrawals from your portfolio, this creates another opportunity to rebalance. You could also have interest and dividends from investment flow into a money market fund rather than being automatically reinvested (see Chapter 14). Cash income created by current investments can be reinvested where needed if it is not withdrawn.

Being consistent with rebalancing is also a good test of risk tolerance. Investors will rebalance at the appropriate time without hesitation if their portfolio is within their risk tolerance. A portfolio's asset allocation may be too aggressive if an investor hesitates on rebalancing in a bear market. If you are hesitant when stocks are suffering, it may be time to rethink your plan and make a permanent adjustment to the stock and bond mix.

WHEN TO USE RISK AVOIDANCE

Risk avoidance is a different concept from risk tolerance. Risk avoidance is a conscious decision not to invest up to your known risk tolerance level. This is a risk control measure. You take only the amount of risk that you need to accomplish a financial objective. In short; know your pain threshold and know when to avoid it.

There are many good reasons not to hold a risky portfolio. There is no need to invest at your peak risk tolerance level once you have accumulated enough assets to easily reach your investment objectives with lower risk. Keeping a higher level of risk in a portfolio when there is no need for that risk could lead to disastrous results. There is nothing worse than having enough money to retire and then losing it because you did not take the risk level down.

Many former employees of bankrupt companies know firsthand the dangers of taking risk needlessly. As you recall from Chapter 2, it is common for employees to invest in their company stock. However, if that company collapses, these people not only lose their jobs but also could lose most of their savings.

TABLE 13-3

Low-Risk Asset Allocation Example

Investment Class	Percent
Diversified U.S. stock fund	12%
Diversified foreign stock fund	5%
REIT mutual fund	3%
Intermediate-term bond fund	40%
Short-term bond fund	35%
Money market fund	5%

The risk avoidance pendulum can swing too far in the conservative direction as well. It is not prudent to eliminate all potential risk from a portfolio when you have enough, because you might need higher returns to beat inflation in the future. All investments face the corrosive effects of inflation and taxes. Retaining some risky assets in the portfolio has the advantage of earning an inflation adjustment after taxes. Also, most people do not spend all their money while they are alive, and at least some assets will go to younger heirs. An appropriate asset allocation may go beyond your lifetime to include children or other heirs.

Table 13-3 is an example of a low-risk portfolio. There is a position in short-term bonds and intermediate-term bonds. Unless you are cashing in a portfolio within a few years, at least half of the fixed-income portion should be in intermediate-term bonds to capture a higher return. The portfolio should still have at least a 20 percent allocation to growth investment, such as common stock and real estate. A 20 percent allocation to growth assets and 80 percent to fixed income is more efficient than 100 percent in a fixed-income portfolio.

Risk avoidance should be based on your known assets and an assessment of your future liabilities. Reducing risk when the time is appropriate ensures that the markets will not take away the financial security you have worked so hard to achieve.

CHAPTER SUMMARY

Successful asset allocation requires that you act rationally and methodically when managing your portfolios. The best asset allocation is one that an investor is comfortable with during all market conditions and will have the discipline to maintain even during prolonged downturns. That is easier said than done. Most investors are not entirely rational in their decision-making process. Researchers in the field of behavioral finance have uncovered a large number of irrational behaviors and errors in judgment that lead to lower investment returns.

Many portfolio failures occur when investors take on more risk than they are capable of handling. Too much portfolio risk results in adverse investor behavior during market downturns. The right amount of risk is a level where an investor does not become emotional about the portfolio when the markets are poor.

There are several personality tests that investors can take in an attempt to find their true tolerance for investment risk and an appropriate asset allocation. One assessment of maximum risk is the use of risk assessment questionnaires. A portfolio stress test can help investors find an appropriate asset allocation that is right for their needs. Finally, portfolio management is as much common sense as mathematics. Erring on the side of prudence never sent anyone to the poorhouse.

Once a portfolio asset allocation has been set, rebalancing will occur on a regular basis to capture the diversification benefits and to control risk. Rebalancing strategies can be simple or elaborate. Rebalancing once per year is simple and provides good diversification benefits.

SAMPLE RISK TOLERANCE QUESTIONS

(This is not a complete questionnaire)

1. When making a long-term investment, I plan to hold the investment for

❑ 1–2 years
❑ 3–4 years
❑ 5–6 years
❑ 7–8 years
❑ 9–10+ years

2. During 2008, stocks fell by more than 20 percent in a short period. If I owned an investment that suddenly fell by 20 percent, I would:

❑ sell all of the remaining investment.
❑ sell a portion of the remaining investment.

❑ hold onto the investment and sell nothing.

❑ buy more of the investment.

3. My previous investment experience in asset classes is (check all the apply):

❑ short-term assets (cash, money markets).

❑ U.S. government/corporate bonds or bond mutual funds.

❑ large stocks and stock funds.

❑ small-company stocks and funds.

❑ international stocks and stock funds.

4. Generally, I prefer investments with little or no fluctuation in value, and I'm willing to accept the lower return associated with these investments.

❑ Strongly disagree

❑ Disagree

❑ Somewhat agree

❑ Agree

❑ Strongly agree

5. During market declines, I tend to sell portions of my riskier assets and invest the money in safer assets.

❑ Strongly disagree

❑ Disagree

❑ Somewhat agree

❑ Agree

❑ Strongly agree

6. I would invest in a mutual fund based solely on a brief conversation with a friend, coworker, or relative.

❑ Strongly disagree

❑ Disagree

❑ Somewhat agree

❑ Agree

❑ Strongly agree

7. In the first quarter of 2009, some bond investments fell by more than 6 percent. If I owned a "safe" investment that fell by 6 percent over a short period, I would:

❑ sell all of the remaining investment.

❑ sell a portion of the remaining investment.

❑ hold onto the investment and sell nothing.

❑ buy more of the investment.

8. My current and future income sources (for example, salary, Social Security, pension) are:

❑ very unstable.

❑ unstable.

❑ somewhat stable.

❑ stable.

❑ very stable.

The answers to these questions will help you develop a general asset allocation based on your tolerance for risk. However, more work will be required to develop an appropriate portfolio for your needs.

NOTE

[1]Olivia S. Mitchell and Stephen P. Utkus, *Lessons from Behavioral Finance for Retirement Plan Design*, Wharton School and Vanguard Center for Retirement Research, November 24, 2003.

CHAPTER 14

When to Change Your Asset Allocation

KEY CONCEPTS

- Asset allocation decisions are typically not permanent.
- Life changes lead to asset allocation changes.
- Too much risk in a portfolio should be managed downward.
- Estate planning needs eventually set asset allocation.

Asset allocation changes can take two forms. The first is based on changing needs, and the second is the result of an assessment mistake.

Asset allocation changes based on changing needs should be done only after careful consideration. Adjustments are needed as we go through life with the intent to balance our assets to our changing long-term liabilities. Most of the time these changing liabilities are our own, although some may belong to people who occasionally rely on us for financial help.

We have all made an asset allocation mistake during our lives. These mistakes tend to manifest themselves in a bull market or bear market when we realize that our portfolio is not in line with who we are emotionally. When an asset allocation mistake becomes obvious, an adjustment should be made to bring the portfolio in line with our true feelings. These changes should be controlled rather than made as the result of a knee-jerk reaction. Haphazard asset allocation changes are not in your best interests because they are mostly driven by fear or greed.

THE THREE REASONS TO CHANGE YOUR ALLOCATION

Changing your asset allocation is a major decision and can be compared to changing careers. There are several good reasons to change your asset allocation along life's journey. These changes require deep thinking and even-handed judgment, and they should not be made in a time of duress. Following are three prominent reasons I believe a person has a legitimate reason to make an asset allocation change. These are:

1. Your financial goal is well within reach.
2. You realize that you will not need all your money during your lifetime.
3. You realize that your tolerance for risk is not as high as you thought it was.

The above reasons are three of the most common triggers for an asset allocation change, although there are many other reasons. For example, starting a new business may prompt people to become more conservative in their asset allocation because they are now taking business risk in other ways as well as needing extra liquidity. A divorce could change both spouses' asset allocation as each party looks to his or her financial future as a single person rather than as a couple. A serious medical issue may change long-term goals, and this may affect asset allocation. Finally, the death of a spouse may also affect asset allocation decisions because one person has lower liabilities than two.

Whatever the reason for an asset allocation review, it should be done with as much care and diligence as your initial allocation. Any change to an asset allocation should be long term and with the intent to match long-term liabilities and savings goals.

YOUR FINANCIAL GOALS ARE WITHIN REACH

Consider a reduction to risk when you are within reach of your financial goal. At some point in the employment rat race, you realize that you may have enough money and will be looking for the exit ramp. This would be the time to take your foot off the gas pedal and move into the right-hand lane where you can prepare for the next road in life should you decide to take that exit.

Assume that you wish to retire in three years with $2 million in retirement savings. If you already have $1,800,000 in savings, then the rate of return you need is to achieve your $2,000,000 goal does not require a high-risk allocation. You may decide to lower your equity exposure because you no longer need to take as much risk to meet your future liabilities and goals.

Figure 14-1 illustrates the idea of reducing risk. There are two value projections in the figure: (1) a projected account value for an

FIGURE 14-1

Reducing Risk as an Investment Goal Becomes More Easily Attainable

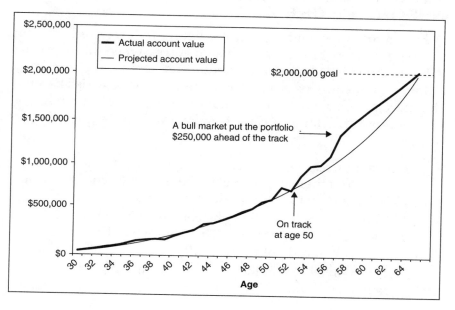

investor who starts at age 30 with $30,000 and assumes savings of $1,000 per month and a 7 percent annual growth rate, (2) the actual account value of the investor based on actual financial market returns.

The projected account value in Figure 14-1 is the same as the actual account value at age 52. However, a bull market in stocks over the next five years drove the actual account value $250,000 above the projected account value by age 57. This gives the investor the option to significantly reduce risk in the portfolio and still meet his or her $2 million goal by age 65. If an investor was using 60 percent stocks through age 57, he or she could cut that in half to 30 percent in stocks and still make the $2 million number.

A bull market will propel a portfolio well ahead of its growth schedule. Depending on where people are in their careers, the bull market could give them the option to reduce risk and coast into their retirement goal. It does not necessarily mean that every person should reduce risk, but anyone approaching retirement should at least do the analysis and consider this option.

WHAT TO DO IN A BEAR MARKET JUST BEFORE RETIREMENT

A bear market can put a portfolio below its projected account value right before retirement. What do you do when this happens? A bear market is not a reason to reduce risk even if it occurs right before retirement. This is also not the time to increase risk because that may put you over your tolerance for risk. Here are five dos and don'ts for dealing with a bear market for people close to retirement:

1. Don't increase risk. It would be a mistake to increase risk close to retirement in an effort to make up what you lost. Doubling up to catch up does not work.
2. Don't decrease risk. Stay the course with your portfolio allocation and wait it out. There has never been a bear market that did not recover fully.
3. Try to save more in the final years or months before retirement.

4. You could also work a year or two longer. An extra year or two in the accumulation phase means an extra year or two less in the withdrawal phase. This can increase your retirement savings longevity by more than a decade.

5. If you decide to go ahead with retirement on your planned date, you may have to reduce your spending until a recovery pushes your account value higher. Try spending only the interest and dividend income your portfolio generates. This income is relatively stable even though the portfolio value is temporarily down.

YOU'RE NOT INVESTING IT ALL FOR YOURSELF ANYMORE

A change to your allocation may be appropriate if you conclude that you will not be the only one who will benefit from your money. In this case, you are investing part of your portfolio for yourself and another part for those who will receive a portion of your wealth. Your overall asset allocation should then reflect the needs of all parties concerned.

Assume you have $2 million in retirement savings. Your needs may be covered by $1 million, and this amount is allocated to 30 percent stock and 70 percent bonds. The second $1 million will be passed on to your heirs. Since heirs tend to be younger, they can be more aggressive. So that portion receives a 70 percent stock and 30 percent bond allocation. Put together, an appropriate allocation for your portfolio is 50 percent stock and 50 percent bonds.

When you are no longer investing only for yourself, does your age still matter? Perhaps you should be considering the age of your beneficiaries, or perhaps a combination of ages based on your age and the age of those who will inherit the money. This goes against conventional thinking which says that you should be decreasing risk in the later stages of life. However, it makes sense to increase the risk to accommodate the needs of your beneficiaries if you are not going to need the money, because your heirs may well need the money.

"Your age in bonds" is a simple asset allocation method that suggests whatever a person's age is, that is the percentage allocation he or she should have in bonds. When more than one person is going to benefit from your assets, a combination of ages should be used. This concept is discussed in detail in Chapter 12 and in an article titled "What's Your Asset Allocation Age?" The article was coauthored by Brigham Young University professor Craig L. Israelsen and me and appeared in *Financial Planning Magazine*, November 2009.

YOU'RE IN OVER YOUR HEAD

I start this section by talking about the problems that can arise with using historic market data to determine an asset allocation. Market return data are typically presented using annual, quarterly, and monthly returns. These periods are fine for measurement, but they often miss what is really happening day to day, especially the "terrifying moments" that occur over a few days or even intraday. It is these anxious periods when sleepless nights occur and when investors make emotional decisions. These moments are missed in the periodic market data.

Annual returns miss the really big moves that happen during a year. Consider 1987, the year of the market crash. The stock market was down by over 20 percent on a single day. That day was October 19, and it is known as Black Monday. Does this crash occur if you looked only at the total return for the year? No. The total return for the S&P 500 in 1987 was positive 5.1 percent. Black Monday did not happen if you considered only the annual return.

Quarterly and monthly returns are deceiving also. The S&P 500 was down by 22 percent from January 1, 2009, through March 9, 2009. However, that loss was cut to less than 11 percent by the end of March, so the quarterly return was only about half as bad as what the market experienced. By the end of the year the S&P 500 was up by more than 26 percent. Monthly returns can also mask extreme volatility. It is not unusual for the stock market to be up or down 10 percent intermonth.

Daily and intraday returns are what we live and breathe, and this is when the terrifying moments occur. We can see this movement in measures of daily and intraday price volatility. Figure 14-2 illustrates the CBOE Volatility Index (VIX) level from 2007 through 2009 to provide a picture of this emotion-creating phenomenon.

FIGURE 14-2

High Market Volatility Signals Terrifying Moments in Investors' Lives

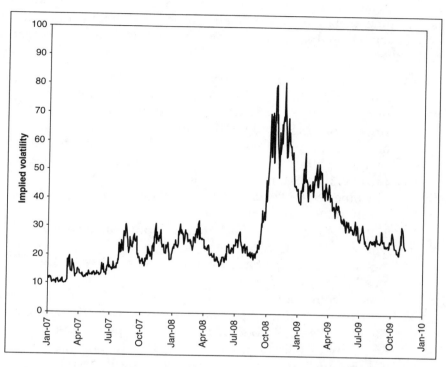

Spikes in price volatility create fear and uncertainty in the financial markets. Typically, a VIX reading above 30 means that investors are fearful. During late 2008 and early 2009, the VIX was consistently over 50 and hit 80 on more than one day.

There are a few days during every bear market when we all wonder how low the market can go. Those are the days when you cannot flip on the television, the radio, or even check your e-mail without in-your-face bad news about stock prices. Those are the days when you can be certain the headlines on the six o'clock news and in the newspapers will highlight the money you are losing, and they will feature abundant numbers of gurus who are forecasting deeper losses.

WHAT TO DO WHEN YOU DON'T KNOW WHAT TO DO

All this pressure may put you in a high-anxiety situation. If you are not sleeping at night because you are worried sick about your portfolio and you are on the verge of making an emotional decision to "Sell it all!" then action needs to be taken. Here is what you should do:

1. Look at the amount of income you are getting from your current investments. The income coming from your investments generally does not go down even though prices do. Stocks and bonds continue to pay dividends and interest. When your annual expenses can be covered by the cash flows from dividends, interest, and outside income, it makes it easier to ride out a bear market. This "income reality check" helped a lot of my clients get through the 2008 bear market.

2. If the income reality check does not put you at ease and you are still sick to your stomach about the future of your portfolio, then you have too much stock exposure and need to permanently reduce it. How do you do that? Lower your equity position by 10 percent. For example, if you are at 60 percent stocks, go to 50 percent. If you are at 40 percent stocks, go to 30 percent. A 10 percent reduction in equity usually reduces investor anxiety long enough for the stock market to recover. Once the 10 percent reduction in stock is completed, keep the allocation as is through the bottom of the market and beyond. Don't go back to the risk level you once had in your portfolio because you may be setting yourself up for another emotional sell during the next bear market. This small reduction will likely have only a small effect on the long-term return of your portfolio and a huge effect on your short-term psyche.

3. If you are still having an emotional reaction after a 10 percent stock reduction in your portfolio, then you still have too much risk. Reduce your portfolio by another 10 percent in equity. This should allow you to think clearly and get past the bear market. Once you get to this level of risk, stay there, even when the market recovers.

By all means, do not sell because you are experiencing panic if you cannot stand the heat anymore. Emotional investing is a lose-lose-lose proposition. Panic sellers almost always capitulate near a market bottom in prices, and then they lose again when they don't get back in during the recovery, and then again because their own actions create a life-long bias against Wall Street, banking, and the American economic system. That is not a good way to invest.

CHAPTER SUMMARY

Asset allocation drives your portfolio risk and return. A decision to change your allocation should be well thought out. Any change should be made with the care and diligence that you applied the first time you created your portfolio.

Allocation changes occur for many reasons. Three common reasons are (1) a change in your financial situation, (2) a decision to share your wealth with other people, and (3) investing over your tolerance for risk. The first two reasons for an allocation change can be done over time with the benefit of calmness and reflection. The third allocation can become emotionally charged unless you recognize the symptoms of too much risk early and deal with the situation appropriately.

Fees Matter in Asset Allocation Planning

KEY CONCEPTS

- Expenses have a direct impact on investment returns and should be low.
- Taxes can be controlled through proper management.
- Discipline is the key to investment success.
- Professional investment advisors can provide assistance.

Successful asset allocation is all about planning, implementation, and investment discipline. It involves proper investment selection based on your needs and regular maintenance. Effective cost controls including tax management also play a major part in investment success. All these elements together form a no-nonsense, businesslike approach to managing your money.

The purpose of this chapter is twofold: first, to discuss cost controls including tax management, and second, to introduce methods for seeking professional help when needed. The more you pay in fees and commissions, the less you earn in return. Controlling costs is an important part of any investment strategy, and that includes a good tax strategy. Some people opt to hire a professional investment manager to help with this asset allocation process and to stay on track. The final part of the chapter discusses the advantages and disadvantages of hiring an investment advisor.

INVESTMENT COSTS

"A penny saved is a penny earned." That old axiom applies particularly well to investing. Every penny spent on unnecessary mutual fund fees, custodial charges, commissions, advisor's fees, and other expenses is one penny less that you have for retirement. One simple way to increase your investment performance is to lower your investment costs. Investors should scrutinize their portfolio and rid it of high-priced investment products that erode long-term performance.

How does investment cost affect investment performance? High costs could take thousands of dollars in income away from you every year. Consider this example.

Assume that a young man of age 24 starts saving 10 percent of his $36,000 salary. Over his 40-year career, the man receives a 3 percent annual pay increase and saves 10 percent of that increase. He then retires at age 65 and begins to withdraw 4 percent of his retirement savings each year. Assume that he can invest in either a low-cost mutual fund family or a high-cost fund family. The low-cost funds have expenses of 0.5 percent per year, and the high-cost funds have expenses of 1.5 percent per year.

Assume that the markets earn 7.5 percent per year. Table 15-1 shows the difference between a low-fee mutual fund portfolio that earns 7.0 percent after fees and a high-fee mutual fund portfolio that earns only 6.0 percent.

In this example, the lower-expense funds accumulated 32 percent more money in 40 years. The cash benefit that resulted was over $472,000. That is an enormous amount for someone in

TABLE 15-1

One Percent in Fees Makes a Big Difference in Your Wealth

	6% Return	7% Return	Difference	% Increase
Retirement account value	$1,471,394	$1,943,699	$472,305	32%
Annual withdrawal at 4%	$58,856	$77,748	$18,892	32%
Monthly withdrawal	$4,905	$6,479	$1,574	32%

retirement. The extra money increased this person's annual retirement income by almost $19,000 per year based on a 4 percent withdrawal rate.

COMPARING FUND EXPENSES

In 2009, Morningstar Principia database listed over 20,000 mutual funds that had a minimum initial purchase amount of less than $10,000. This list included exchange-traded funds and all share classes of open-end funds. It did not include money market funds. About 70 percent of those funds were equity-based investments, and the remaining were bonds funds, balanced funds, currency and commodity funds. The average annual expense ratio for all funds was 1.4 percent. Slightly less than half the listed funds were pure no-load, which means that they charge no front-end sales charge, back-end sales charge, or level loads charged each year. Only about 4,500 funds were no-load and also had no 12b-1 fee. A 12b-1 fee is part of the expense ratio that is paid out to a brokerage firm or financial advisor. It frequently substitutes for a commission in no-transaction fee brokerage account programs such as Schwab's Mutual Fund Marketplace.

Fund expenses have a direct and negative effect on fund performance. It does not matter how you pay the fee; in aggregate, fees are bad. The more you pay, the less you will earn in return. Don't pay a lot of money for the hope of high returns. It is not worth the cost.

Figure 15-1 compares the fee savings and five-year annualized return advantage of several Vanguard index funds compared to their representative Morningstar category averages. The average fee for the Vanguard index funds was 0.2 percent, and the average fee for the categories ranged between 1.0 and 1.4 percent. In every category, the no-load index funds saved a considerable amount in fees over the category average, and this led to higher returns for index funds in every category.

Index funds have no sales commissions. However, many funds in the categories listed do charge a sales commission. In Figure 15-1 commissions have not been deducted, from the five-year average. Index fund returns would have faired even better had the commissions been included in the analysis.

FIGURE 15-1

Index Fund Fee Savings and Return Advantage

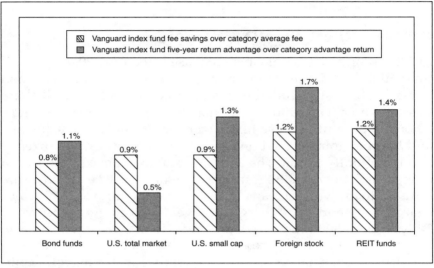

Source: Morningstar Principia, January 2010

It is clear to even the most casual observer that low-cost stock and bond index funds have a significant advantage over other funds that charge average fees. Virtually every study of mutual fund performance done by every pure academic has come to the same conclusion: Mutual fund fees not only matter but they matter a lot. Don't pay high fees or sales loads when investing your portfolio.

About 6 percent of all mutual funds reported expenses below 0.5 percent per year. These are the funds you should be selecting from. There are several low-cost, no-load fund companies available to people who have less than $10,000 to invest. One such company is the Vanguard Group, located in Valley Forge, Pennsylvania. Vanguard has over 90 low-cost, low initial investment funds listed in the Morningstar database. The average expense for a Vanguard funds and ETFs is less than 0.3 percent. This is huge cost advantage for investors.

Many people are unaware of the fees they are paying, and this is not entirely the fault of the investor. Fund companies cleverly hide mutual fund costs. For example, mutual fund companies routinely pay for research, computers, and software through "soft dollars" and "rebates" that are backroom deals with brokerage firms. These extra costs are typically not reported to investors, but they do show up in subpar fund performance.

TAXES ARE AN EXPENSE

Investors who buy mutual funds in a taxable account may incur a cost that can dwarf all others—the cost of taxation. There are four different events that can trigger a tax on mutual fund shareholders. Three of these events are created by cash distributions by a mutual fund. Investors trigger the fourth taxable event by selling mutual fund shares.

Mutual fund companies distribute ordinary interest and dividend income to shareholders on a regular basis. Interest income is subject to ordinary federal income taxes at an individual's rate, and dividends incur a lower tax rate.

Capital gains distributions by fund companies are also common, and they are a taxable event. Realized capital gains are divided into short-term gains on investments held one year or less and long-term gains on investments held for more than one year. Like dividends, long-term capital gains are taxed at a lower tax rate than ordinary income. Short-term gains are taxed as ordinary income. Mutual fund distributions are subject to income taxes even if a shareholder automatically reinvests the cash in more shares.

Mutual fund managers do not hesitate to distribute all income and realized capital gains. If the fund manager did not distribute the income and gains, the fund itself would have to pay a 35 percent tax on those amounts.

ETFs have certain tax advantages over traditional mutual funds when it comes to distributing capital gains. Basically, ETF managers are able to eliminate the realized gains in a fund because of the way ETF trading operations are structured. More detail on ETF structure is discussed later in this chapter.

Mutual fund and ETF income and capital gains distributions are reported to taxable shareholders annually on Form 1099-DIV. The report is sent in late January for the previous tax year. Not all cash distributions shown on Form 1099-DIV represent taxable income. Municipal bond funds distribute mostly tax-free interest income that is not taxable at the federal level. The exceptions are certain municipal bonds that pay taxable income, and possibly bonds subject to the alternative minimum tax (ATM). In addition, some mutual funds return capital each year. This is your own investment coming back to you. Both tax-free income and capital distributions are also listed on Form 1099.

The fourth event that triggers a tax liability is the personal sale or exchange of mutual funds and ETFs that have an unrealized capital gain. All investors are required to track the purchase and sale price of their mutual fund shares and report realized gains or losses to the IRS on Schedule D of their tax returns. If you exchange one fund for another fund within the same fund family, you are required to report the sale of the first fund and pay a tax on any realized gain.

The IRS has ruled that it is your responsibility to track the gains and losses on the sale of mutual fund shares. At a minimum, you should keep a separate ledger for each fund, and at the end of each year match up any share sales with a purchase price. Mutual fund companies and brokerage firms may provide you with gain and loss information, but it is still your responsibility to ensure that the data are correct and to report this information to the IRS.

ASSET LOCATION REDUCES TAXES

Asset *allocation* is the percentage of your overall portfolio that you invest in different investment categories. Asset *location* is the type of account in which each investment is placed. Some types of accounts are taxable, some are tax-deferred, and at least one is tax-free. Different categories of investments are taxed at different tax rates. Therefore, with proper placement of your investment choices in the various types of accounts, you can reduce the tax burden on the overall portfolio.

The proliferation of tax-deferred and tax-free savings opportunities has added a new dimension to the traditional asset allocation equation. Tax-deferred accounts include, but are not limited to, individual retirement accounts (IRAs), 401(k) plans, Keogh plans, and 403(b) plans. The investments in tax-deferred accounts are subject to taxation only when the money is withdrawn.

Roth IRAs allow tax-free growth and tax-free withdrawals. They can also be passed on to future generations without incurring an income tax. Roth IRA accounts are always funded with after-tax contributions.

Some investments are less tax-efficient than others. Corporate bond interest is taxed at a higher rate than stock dividend income. Short-term capital gains are taxed at a higher rate than long-term capital gains. Since different investments and different types of accounts are taxed differently, investors can reduce their annual tax burden by placing appropriate investments in the right accounts. Investments that distribute a high level of taxable income should be placed in tax-deferred or tax-free accounts, and investments with low-tax dividend distributions and long-term capital gains should be placed in taxable accounts.

Examples of investments that you should consider placing in a tax-deferred or tax-free account include:

- Corporate bonds and bond funds
- Certificates of deposit, agency bonds, and mortgages
- Mutual funds that have a high turnover of securities
- REITs and REIT mutual funds
- Commodities funds

Examples of investments that you should consider placing in a taxable account include:

- Low-turnover equity funds, including equity index funds
- Broad market equity exchange-traded funds
- Municipal bonds and municipal bond funds

Saving on taxes is a good idea; however, nothing is as easy as it seems. Tax location strategies have side effects that may hinder investment strategy. Here are issues to consider:

- Tax location strategies make rebalancing difficult. Having different investments stretched across several accounts creates a rebalancing quagmire.
- Your personal tax rate is not consistent. The ideal tax location strategy today may not be the ideal strategy five years from now.
- Tax rates today are not likely to be the tax rates in the future. Any change may affect your strategy.

One more concern with asset location that is worth mentioning deals with human behavior. Investors sometimes compare the performance of the accounts they own to one another rather than looking at the entire picture from the top down. By mistakenly focusing on the performance of each account separately, investors can turn an asset location strategy into a ticking bomb. When one account performs badly compared to another, an investor may decide to switch investments in the underperforming account without considering the overall asset allocation. Investors who practice asset location need to remember that it is the big asset allocation picture that matters, not each individual account.

TAX SWAPS FOR HIGHER AFTER-TAX RETURNS

Stock and bond prices change every day. Occasionally, there will be a loss in one of the mutual funds in a taxable account. When a loss occurs, "swapping" mutual funds can increase after-tax performance. Tax swapping involves selling one investment and incurring a tax loss while simultaneously buying another investment that is very similar to the one sold but not "substantially identical" to it. That keeps your overall asset allocation on target while harvesting the loss. The tax loss can then be used to offset gains from other parts of the portfolio, to offset mutual fund distributions, or to offset up to $3,000 per year in ordinary income. Harvesting tax losses when they are available helps turn lemons into cherries.

Here is an example. Assume that you hold the Vanguard Total U.S. Stock Market ETF (ticker symbol: VTI) fund at a loss. Sell VTI and buy the iShares Russell 3000 ETF (ticker symbol: IWV). Figure 15-2 illustrates the tracking between the two funds.

The two funds have nearly identical returns, but they are not substantially identical because they are managed by different mutual fund companies and are benchmarked to different stock indexes; VTI tracks the MSCI U.S. Broad Market Index, and IWV tracks the Russell 3000 Index. A swap from VTI to IWV allows you to capture the loss while staying 100 percent invested in the stock market.

FIGURE 15-2

Weekly Closing Prices of VTI and IWV

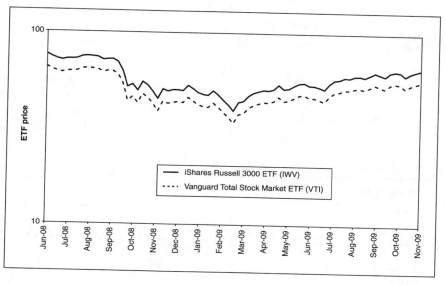

ESTABLISH TAX LOTS BY DOLLAR COST AVERAGING

Most people buy mutual funds over time when they have excess capital. I recommend saving your taxable dollars and making regularly scheduled quarterly investments. This strategy is commonly known as dollar cost averaging. One reason dollar cost averaging makes sense is that it establishes different "tax lots" for your shares. Each quarter you buy shares at a different price, thereby establishing different tax positions. For example, instead of investing $1,000 one month, $500 the next, and $1,500 the next, invest $3,000 once per quarter on a regular basis. That makes tax swapping much easier.

Let's look at an example to see how tax swapping works. Assume that you are buying $3,000 worth of VTI each quarter on the first day of the quarter. You bought two lots in January and April at $50 per share and a third lot in July at $60 per share. In July, the purchases would be those shown in Table 15-2.

TABLE 15-2

Purchases for January through July

Purchase Date	VTI Price	Number of Shares	Cost	Value on July 1
January 1	$50	60	$3,000	$3,600
April 1	$50	60	$3,000	$3,600
July 1	$60	50	$3,000	$3,000
Account shares and value, July 1		170	$9,000	$10,200

TABLE 15-3

Values on August 1

Purchase Date	Cost	Number of Shares	Value on August 1	Gain (Loss)
January 1	$3,000	60	$3,240	+240
April 1	$3,000	60	$3,240	+240
July 1	$3,000	50	$2,700	(300)
Account shares and value, August 1		170	$9,026	+180

Assume that during the third quarter the stock market suffers a 10 percent correction. On August 1, VTI is trading down at $54 per share from $60 in July. Your account value and tax lot values are now those shown in Table 15-3.

The overall account has a gain of $180, but the 50 VTI shares bought on July 1 have a loss of $300. If you track specific tax lots, you can take a $300 loss by designating on Schedule D the liquidated 50 shares where the ones bought on July 1. This loss would create a tax savings. If you do not designate the July 1 tax lot, the IRS will assume that the shares being sold were the first ones bought, which were the January 1 shares. Consequently, you will owe tax on a short-term capital gain of $240.

By designating on Schedule D the tax lot sold as the one bought on July 1, the portfolio would realize a loss of $300 rather than a short-tem gain of $240. A capital loss can be deducted from ordinary income for up to $3,000. This means that the loss would reduce your tax liability for the year by about $105, assuming a 35 percent tax bracket. The total difference in taxes between selling short-term shares at a $240 gain and selling short-term shares at a $300 loss is $189 ($84 + $105).

On the same day you sell VTI, you buy $2,700 of IWV to maintain a consistent asset allocation. The net result of the transaction is to harvest a tax loss of $300 that you can write off against income taxes while remaining 100 percent invested in a broad market index fund.

There are a couple of issues surrounding tax-swapping that you should consider before you try this strategy. First, depending on where you trade, commissions and other fees may reduce the effectiveness of a tax swap. Second, since the IRS has not addressed tax swapping in mutual funds and ETFs, there is no clear definition of what "substantially identical" means to fund investors. Accordingly, consult your tax advisor before using tax swaps in a portfolio. His or her interpretation of the tax code may differ from mine.

INDEX FUNDS—LOW FEES AND LOW TAXES

Throughout this book, I have made numerous references to index mutual funds and exchange-traded funds (ETFs). An index fund is a mutual fund or ETF that seeks to replicate the return of a particular market index. Index funds have low expenses compared to actively managed funds and have lower turnover of securities in the portfolio, which also keeps costs low.

Index funds and ETFs have a large following among institutional investors such as pension funds and insurance companies. Ironically, one of the most vocal advocates of index funds for individual investors is Warren Buffett, self-made billionaire and chairman of Berkshire Hathaway, Inc. Although Buffett made his fortune through individual stock selection, in the 2004 annual report of Berkshire Hathaway, he explains in no uncertain words why individual investors should be buying and holding index funds:

> Over the [past] 35 years, American business has delivered terrific results. It should therefore have been easy for investors to earn juicy returns: All they had to do was piggyback Corporate

America in a diversified, low-expense way. An index fund that they never touched would have done the job. Instead many investors have had experiences ranging from mediocre to disastrous.

There have been three primary causes for poor experiences: first, high costs, usually because investors traded excessively or spent far too much on investment management; second, portfolio decisions based on tips and fads rather than on thoughtful, quantified evaluation of businesses; and third, a start-and-stop approach to the market marked by untimely entries (after an advance has been long underway) and exits (after periods of stagnation or decline). Investors should remember that excitement and expenses are their enemies. And if they insist on trying to time their participation in equities, they should be fearful when others are greedy and greedy only when others are fearful.

Index funds and ETFs are available in a variety of asset classes and categories. There are many U.S. stock funds, international stock funds, bond funds, and even commodities and gold funds. If you are considering an investment in a particular asset class, chances are that there is an index fund or ETF available, or that one will be available shortly.

The Morningstar Principia database lists over 1,150 index funds and index-based ETFs that trade in the United States, and many new funds are being added each year. These funds cover a wide variety of markets and are issued by several competing companies. The Standard & Poor's 500 is the most commonly used index. There are 25 funds listed in the Principia database that attempt to replicate the performance of the S&P 500 Index.

There are three reasons that index mutual funds and ETFs are an ideal choice for those pursuing an asset allocation strategy in your portfolio:

1. *Low tracking error with the indexes.* The data used in almost all asset allocation analysis come directly from the return on the market. Accordingly, market-matching index funds and ETFs are a logical investment choice for people who want to make the most of asset allocation analysis. Any deviation from index funds adds an element of risk that was not captured in the asset allocation analysis.

2. *Low expense ratios.* In general, stock and bond index funds and ETFs have the lowest investment fees in the industry. The lowest-cost index funds and ETFs charge about 0.1 percent per year, which is well below the industry average of 1.4 percent. One word of caution: Not all index funds have low fees. Some investment companies charge over 1.0 percent to invest in exactly the same indexes as very low-cost funds. Let the buyer beware.

3. *Low tax liability.* Index funds generally have very low turnover of securities compared to actively managed funds. Low turnover results in low capital gains distributions to taxable shareholders. This means low tax liability. In addition, ETFs have a special tax benefit in that the fund manager can rid the portfolio of low-cost stock by distributing it to a third party.

For more information about index funds and ETFs, including a detailed analysis of indexes and their construction, see my previous books, *All About Index Funds,* 2nd edition (McGraw-Hill, 2007) and *The ETF Book,* 2nd edition (John Wiley, 2009). The marketplace for index funds and ETFs is growing rapidly. New funds are being added weekly as fund companies expand into new and exciting markets. Check for current news on index funds by going to the www.Morningstar.com Web site. Two good sources for current information on new ETFs are www.IndexUniverse.com and www.ETFguide.com.

HIRING A LOW-FEE ADVISOR

The process of asset allocation can be difficult for some investors and an unwelcome chore for others. The design, implementation, monitoring, rebalancing, tax management, and occasional reassessment of strategy can take a lot of effort, and that is not how many people want to spend their free time.

If an investor would rather not manage his or her own portfolio, or cannot manage the account for health or legal reasons, one solution is to hire a professional investment manager. A competent manager can help you formulate an asset allocation, implement the plan, monitor the results, rebalance when needed, and modify the asset allocation when your needs dictate that it is appropriate to do so.

There are several benefits to employing the services of a low-fee investment manager if you believe you should have one. Here is a partial list of the benefits:

1. *Planning and implementation.* Managers can help clients understand their cash-flow needs and then design, implement, and maintain a specific asset allocation to meet those needs. As a person's situation changes, the manager will suggest appropriate changes in the asset allocation.

2. *Consistency of strategy.* Discipline is critical to investment success. Investors need to follow their plan and rebalance their portfolios on a regular basis. It is the job of an investment manager to ensure that this process happens.

3. *Create a circuit breaker.* During uncertain market conditions, some investors need to talk with someone about their concerns. A call to an advisor or financial planner usually calms an investor's nerves and stops the investor from making an emotionally incorrect decision.

4. *Place someone on duty 365 days per year.* There are times when all investors get sidetracked. An investment manager is there to do the investment chores for you all day, every day.

The biggest challenge when hiring an investment manager is finding a good one. Advisors come in all sizes, levels of competence, and investment philosophies. You'll likely be satisfied with your advisor if he or she is of like mind and charges reasonable fees. All else tends to be about style rather than substance.

Be careful about advisors who have ulterior motives. Many people in the business claim to be on your side, but they are actually selling investment products as a company rep. By definition, anyone who is compensated by commissions is not an advisor; such a person is selling. It is unrealistic to think that you will be offered unbiased investment advice under these circumstances.

Make sure you check the background information on a potential advisor on the Securities and Exchange Commission Web site at www.SEC.gov. If you have any question in your mind as to what a particular advisor's competence level is, go on to the next one.

Find out *exactly* how an advisor is paid and what that fee is. Advisors' fees should be fair, and there should be no conflicts of interest with the investments they use in client portfolios. An advisor should put all cost information in writing. Don't hire an advisor who will not line-item your costs. Are you are getting investment services; how much is that? Are you getting financial planning advice; how much is that? Are your tax returns prepared; how much is that?

Advisors generally charge a fee based on a percentage of the account's value. The fee can range from reasonable to expensive. Make sure you are not paying too much to have your portfolio managed. There is nothing to gain from paying a lot of money for investment management services when those services are available elsewhere for far less. My company, Portfolio Solutions, LLC, charges 0.25 percent of assets subject to a minimum quarterly household fee. This is a fair fee for investment management services.

CHAPTER SUMMARY

Low investment fees and tax control play an important role in the success of an investment plan. The more you pay in fees and taxes, the lower your long-term investment performance. How you allocate your investments across different accounts goes a long way toward keeping taxes low. In addition, swapping out of losing funds and harvesting losses can increase your after-tax return.

The heart of a successful asset allocation strategy relies on the investor's confidence that a multi-asset-class, low-cost approach to portfolio management is right for him or her. With confidence comes a commitment to maintaining an asset allocation during all market conditions. A properly designed portfolio of low-cost investments that is within an investor's tolerance for risk will help ensure that the plan is followed in good times and bad.

All About Asset Allocation has covered a lot of ground. The tools and strategies discussed in this book provide a no-nonsense, businesslike approach to managing your portfolio effectively. Learn the principles of asset allocation, design an investment plan that fits your needs, implement and maintain that plan, and keep your costs low. You will be further ahead in the future for doing so.

APPENDIX A

Research Web Sites

Bogleheads.org   Bogleheads was inspired by the writings and actions of John C. Bogle, founder and former chairman of the Vanguard Group. This unbiased online community of investors will help answer the questions you have about asset allocation and investment selection.

DFAfunds.com   Dimensional Fund Advisors offers unique index funds through advisors. Its three-factor approach to portfolio construction is gaining acceptance worldwide.

DowJones.com   Dow Jones offers great information on the markets and has a wonderful historical section featuring charts that include major economic and world events.

ETFguide.com   In-depth information on exchange-traded products including proprietary research, fundamental databases, and a variety of interesting topics.

IndexUniverse.com   This Web site provides news, information, and analysis of markets, index funds, and the latest inside talk about exchange-traded funds.

iShares.com   You can learn about exchange-traded funds and use the helpful portfolio management tools on the iShares Web site.

Morningstar.com   This Web site is full of free information and analysis on mutual funds, stocks, bonds, ETFs, financial planning, and a range of other investment-related topics.

MSCIbarra.com   MSCI Barra provides investment decision tools to investment institutions worldwide including indices and portfolio risk and performance analytics for use in managing equity, fixed income, and multi-asset-class portfolios.

PortfolioSolutions.com   The main Web site of my firm, Portfolio Solutions, LLC. We are a leading investment advisor specializing in asset allocation and low-cost investing.

Russell.com   This site provides comprehensive information about all the Russell indexes and methodologies.

Spglobal.com   Standard & Poor's offers comprehensive analyses of and commentary on all of its global indexes.

Ssga.com   State Street Global Advisors manages many exchange-traded funds around the world. Its site offers tools and information.

Vanguard.com   Vanguard has an "education, planning, and advice" section that is one of the best on the Web. There is lots of good information in the "Plain Talk Library."

Wilshire.com   Wilshire indexes are explained, with past returns available.

APPENDIX B

Recommended Reading

All About Index Funds, by Richard A. Ferri, CFA. A guide to low-cost index fund investing that complements this book. 2nd edition, published in 2007 by McGraw-Hill.

The Art of Asset Allocation, by David M. Darst. Asset allocation information for intermediate to advanced investors. 2nd edition, published in 2008 by McGraw-Hill.

Asset Allocation: Balancing Financial Risk, by Roger C. Gibson. Asset allocation concepts made understandable. 4th edition, published in 2007 by McGraw-Hill.

The Bogleheads' Guide to Investing, by Taylor Larimore, Mel Lindauer, and Michael LeBoeuf. This book provides sound advice on a variety of issues including mutual funds, bonds, diversification, and taxes. Published in 2006 by Wiley.

The Coffeehouse Investor, by Bill Schultheis. An asset allocation book for those who want to keep their life simple. 2nd edition, published in 2009 by Portfolio Hardcover.

Common Sense on Mutual Funds, by John C. Bogle. A low-cost mutual fund icon shares his views on investing. 2nd edition, published in 2009 by Wiley.

The ETF Book, by Richard A. Ferri, CFA: All you need to know about exchange-traded products. 2nd edition, published in 2009 by Wiley.

The Four Pillars of Investing: Lessons for Building a Winning Portfolio, by William J. Bernstein. An easy-to-read guidebook on asset allocation for all levels. Published in 2002 by McGraw-Hill.

The Intelligent Asset Allocator, by William J. Bernstein. An analysis of sensible asset allocation strategies for intermediate and advanced investors. Published in 2000 by McGraw-Hill.

Mutual Funds: Profiting from an Investment Revolution, by Scott Simon. An investment advisor shares his views on the asset allocation of low-cost index funds. Published in 1998 by Namborn.

Protecting Your Wealth in Good Times and Bad, by Richard A. Ferri, CFA. A sensible life-long saving and investing handbook for all investors. Published in 2003 by McGraw-Hill.

A Random Walk Down Wall Street, by Burton G. Malkiel. A comprehensive look at today's market and what is driving it. 9th edition, published in 2007 by W. W. Norton & Company.

Stocks for the Long Run, by Jeremy Siegel. A classic book about investing, with market data going back 200 years. 4th edition, published in 2007 by McGraw-Hill.

Winning the Loser's Game, by Charles Ellis. A classic book on how to increase returns and decrease risk through investment policy and indexing. 5th edition, published in 2009 by McGraw-Hill.

Wise Investing Made Simple, by Larry Swedoe. Knowing how modern financial markets work helps investors make more informed and better investment decisions. Published in 2007 by Charter Financial Pub Network.

GLOSSARY

12b-1 Fee   An annual fee charged by some mutual funds to pay for marketing and distribution activities. The fee is taken directly from fund assets, which reduces a shareholder's total return.

Active Management   An investment strategy that seeks to outperform the average returns on the financial markets. Active managers rely on research, market forecasts, and their own judgment and experience in selecting securities to buy and sell.

Alternative Minimum Tax (AMT)   A separate tax system designed to ensure that wealthy individuals and organizations pay at least a minimum amount of federal income taxes. Certain securities that are used to fund private, for-profit activities are subject to the AMT.

Annualize   To make a figure for a period of less than a year apply to a full year, usually for purposes of comparison. For instance, a portfolio turnover rate of 36 percent over a six-month period could be converted to an annualized rate of 72 percent.

Ask Price   The price at which a security is offered for sale. For a no-load mutual fund, the ask price is the same as the fund's net asset value per share. Also called *offering price*.

Automatic Reinvestment   An arrangement by which the dividends or other earnings from an investment vehicle are used to buy additional shares in the investment vehicle.

Average Coupon   The average interest rate (coupon rate) on all the bonds in a portfolio.

Average Effective Maturity   A weighted average of the maturity dates for all securities in a money market fund or bond fund. (The maturity date is the date when the buyer of a money market instrument or a bond will be repaid by the security's issuer.) The longer the average maturity, the more a fund's share price will move up or down in response to changes in interest rates.

Back-End Load   A sales fee charged by some mutual funds when an investor sells fund shares. Also called a *contingent deferred sales charge*.

Benchmark Index   An index that correlates with a fund; used to measure a fund manager's performance.

Beta   A measure of the magnitude of a portfolio's past share-price fluctuations in relation to the ups and downs of the overall market (or an appropriate market index). The market (or index) is assigned a beta of 1.00, so a portfolio with a beta of 1.20 would have seen its share price rise or fall by approximately 12 percent when the overall market rose or fell by 10 percent.

Bid-Ask Spread   The difference between what a buyer is willing to bid (pay) for a security and the seller's asking (offer) price.

Blue Chip Stocks   Common stocks of well-known companies with a history of growth and dividend payments.

Bond Covenant   The contractual provision in a bond indenture. A positive covenant requires certain actions, and a negative covenant limits certain actions.

Book Value   A company's assets, minus any liabilities and intangible assets.

Broker/Broker-Dealer   An individual or firm that buys or sells mutual funds or other securities for the public.

Capital Gain/Loss   The difference between the sale price of an asset—such as a mutual fund, stock, or bond—and the original cost of the asset.

Capital Gains Distributions   Payments to mutual fund shareholders of gains realized during the year on securities that the fund has sold at a profit, minus any realized losses.

Cash Investments   Short-term debt instruments—such as commercial paper, banker's acceptances, and Treasury bills—that mature in less than one year. Also known as *money market instruments* or *cash reserves*.

Certified Financial Planner (CFP)   An investment professional who has passed exams administered by the CFP Board of Standards on subjects such as taxes, securities, insurance, and estate planning.

Certified Public Accountant (CPA)   An investment professional who is licensed by a state to practice public accounting.

Chartered Financial Analyst (CFA)   An investment professional who has met competency standards in economics, securities, portfolio management, and financial accounting as determined by the Institute of Chartered Financial Analysts.

Closed-End Fund   A mutual fund that has a fixed number of shares, usually listed on a major stock exchange.

Commodities   Unprocessed goods, such as grains, metals, and minerals, traded in large amounts on a commodities exchange.

Consumer Price Index (CPI)   A measure of the price change in consumer goods and services. The CPI is used to track the pace of inflation.

Correlation Coefficient   A number between -1 and 1 that measures the degree to which two variables are linearly related.

Cost Basis   The original cost of an investment. For tax purposes, the cost basis is subtracted from the sale price to determine any capital gain or loss.

Country Risk The possibility that political events (e.g., a war, national elections), financial problems (e.g., rising inflation, government default), or natural disasters (e.g., an earthquake, a poor harvest) will weaken a country's economy and cause investments in that country to decline.

Coupon/Coupon Rate The interest rate that a bond issuer promises to pay the bondholder until the bond matures.

Credit Rating A published ranking, based on a careful financial analysis, of a creditor's ability to pay the interest or principal owed on a debt.

Credit Risk The possibility that a bond issuer will fail to repay interest and principal in a timely manner. Also called *default risk*.

Currency Risk The possibility that returns for Americans investing in foreign securities could be reduced because of a rise in the value of the U.S. dollar compared to foreign currencies. Also called *exchange-rate risk*.

Custodian Either (1) a bank, agent, trust company, or other organization responsible for safeguarding financial assets or (2) the individual who oversees the mutual fund assets of a minor's custodial account.

Declaration Date The date when the board of directors of a company or mutual fund announces the amount and date of the entity's next dividend payment.

Default Failure to pay principal or interest when it is due.

Depreciation A decrease in the value of an investment.

Derivative A financial contract whose value is based on, or "derived" from, a traditional security (such as a stock or bond), an asset (such as a commodity), or a market index (such as the S&P 500 Index).

Discount Broker A brokerage firm that executes orders to buy and sell securities at commission rates lower than those of a full-service brokerage.

Distributions Either (1) withdrawals made by the owner from an individual retirement account (IRA) or (2) payments of dividends and/or capital gains by a mutual fund.

Dividend Reinvestment Plan The automatic reinvestment of shareholder dividends in more shares of the company's stock.

Dividend Yield The annual rate of return on a share of stock, determined by dividing the annual dividend by the current share price. In a stock mutual fund, this figure represents the average dividend yield of the stocks held by the fund.

Dollar Cost Averaging Investing equal amounts of money at regular intervals on an ongoing basis. This technique ensures that an investor buys fewer shares when prices are high and more shares when prices are low.

Earnings per Share A company's earnings divided by the number of common shares outstanding.

Efficient Market The theory that stock prices reflect all market information that is known by all investors.

Enhanced Index Fund An index fund that is designed not only to generally track an index but also to outperform that index through the use of leverage, futures, trading strategies, capital gains management, and other methods.

Equivalent Taxable Yield The yield needed from a taxable bond to give the same after-tax yield as a tax-exempt issue.

Exchange Privilege A shareholder's ability to move money from one mutual fund to another within the same fund family, often without additional charge.

Exchange-Traded Fund (ETF) A mutual fund that trades like a stock on a stock exchange. The fund's approximate NAV is calculated every 15 seconds by the exchange it trades on. ETF shares trade close to the calculated price because of an arbitrage process that involves a third party called an *authorized participant*.

Exchange-Traded Note An unsecured debt security issued by a bank or finance company that acts like an exchange-traded fund in that it tracks an index and also has the credit risk of the issuer.

Ex-dividend Date The date when a distribution of dividends and/or capital gains is deducted from a mutual fund's assets or set aside for payment to shareholders. On the ex-dividend date, the fund's share price drops by the amount of the distribution (plus or minus any market activity). Also known as the *reinvestment date*.

Expense Ratio The percentage of a portfolio's average net assets used to pay its annual expenses. The expense ratio, which includes management fees, administrative fees, and any 12b-1 fees, directly reduces returns to investors.

Federal Reserve The central bank that regulates the supply of money and credit throughout the United States. The Fed's seven-member board of governors, appointed by the president, has significant influence on U.S. monetary and economic policy.

Fee-Only Advisor An arrangement in which a financial advisor charges a set hourly rate or an agreed-upon percentage of assets under management for a financial plan.

Financial Industry Regulatory Authority (FINRA) This is the largest independent regulator for all securities firms doing business in the United States dedicated to investor protection and market integrity through regulation and complementary compliance.

First-In, First-Out (FIFO) A method for calculating taxable gain or loss when mutual fund shares are sold. The FIFO method assumes that the first shares sold were the first shares purchased.

Front-End Load A sales commission charged at the time of purchase by some mutual funds and other investment vehicles.

Full Faith and Credit A pledge to pay interest and principal on a bond issued by the government.

Fund Family A group of mutual funds sponsored by the same organization, often offering exchange privileges between funds and combined account statements for multiple funds.

Fundamental Analysis   Examining a company's financial statements and operations as a means of forecasting stock price movements.

Futures/Futures Contracts   Contracts to buy or sell specific amounts of a specific commodity (such as grain or foreign currency) for an agreed-upon price at a certain time in the future.

Global Fund   A mutual fund that invests in stocks of companies in both the United States and foreign countries.

Gross Domestic Product (GDP)   The value of all goods and services provided by U.S. labor in a given year. One of the primary measures of the U.S. economy, the GDP is issued quarterly by the Department of Commerce.

Hedge   A strategy in which one investment is used to offset the risk of another.

High-Yield Fund   A mutual fund that invests primarily in bonds with a credit rating of BB or lower. Because of the speculative nature of high-yield bonds, high-yield funds are subject to greater share price volatility and greater credit risk than other types of bond funds.

Indexing   An investment strategy designed to match the average performance of a market or a group of stocks. Usually this is accomplished by buying a small amount of each stock in a market.

Index Providers   Companies that construct and maintain stock and bond indexes. The main providers are Standard & Poor's, Dow Jones, Barclays Capital, Morgan Stanley, Russell, and Wilshire.

Inflation Risk   The possibility that increases in the cost of living will reduce or eliminate the returns on a particular investment.

Interest-Rate Risk   The possibility that a security or mutual fund will decline in value because of an increase in interest rates.

International Fund   A mutual fund that invests in securities traded in markets outside of the United States. Foreign markets present additional risks, including currency fluctuation and political instability. In the past, these risks have made the prices of foreign stocks more volatile than those of U.S. stocks.

Investment Advisor   A person or organization that makes the day-to-day decisions regarding the investments in a portfolio. Also called a *portfolio manager.*

Investment Grade   A bond whose credit quality is considered to be among the highest by independent bond-rating agencies.

Junk Bond   A bond with a credit rating of BB or lower. Also known as a *high-yield bond* because of the rewards offered to those who are willing to take on the additional risk of a lower-quality bond.

Large Cap   A company whose stock market value is generally in excess of $10 billion, although the amount varies among index providers.

Liquidity   The degree of marketability of a security; that is, how quickly the security can be sold at a fair price and converted to cash.

Load Fund   A mutual fund that levies a sales charge, either when shares are bought (a front-end load) or when they are sold (a back-end load).

Long-Term Capital Gain   A profit on the sale of a security or mutual fund share that has been held for more than one year.

Management Fee   The amount a mutual fund pays to its investment advisor for the work of overseeing the fund's holdings. Also called an *advisory fee*.

Market Capitalization   A determination of a company's value, calculated by multiplying the total number of shares of the company's stock outstanding by the price per share. Also called *capitalization*.

Maturity/Maturity Date   The date when the issuer of a money market instrument or bond agrees to repay the principal, or face value, to the buyer.

Median Market Cap   The midpoint of the market capitalization (market price multiplied by the number of shares outstanding) of the stocks in a portfolio. Half the stocks in the portfolio will have a higher market capitalization, and half will have a lower market capitalization.

Midcap   A company whose stock market value is between $2 billion and $10 billion, although the range varies among index providers.

Municipal Bond Fund   A mutual fund that invests in tax-exempt bonds issued by state, city, and/or local governments. The interest obtained from these bonds is passed through to shareholders and is generally free of federal (and sometimes state and local) income taxes.

Mutually Exclusive   A situation in which the occurrence of one event excludes the possibility of another event. If an investment is a member of one index, this precludes membership in others.

Negative Correlation   A situation in which the value of one of two investments moves opposite to the value of the other.

Net Asset Value (NAV)   The market value of a mutual fund's total assets minus its liabilities, divided by the number of shares outstanding. The value of a single share is called its *share value* or *share price*.

No-Load Fund   A mutual fund that charges no sales commission or load.

Nominal Return   The return on an investment before adjustment for inflation.

Noncorrelation   A situation in which the changes in the value of two different investments are completely independent of each other.

Open-End Fund   An investment entity that has the ability to issue or redeem the number of shares outstanding on a daily basis. Prices are quoted once per day, at the end of the day, at the net asset value (NAV) of the fund.

Operating Expenses   The amount paid for asset maintenance or the cost of doing business. Earnings are distributed after operating expenses are deducted.

Option   A contract in which a seller gives a buyer the right, but not the obligation, to buy or sell securities at a specified price on or before a given date.

Overlap   The situation that arises when two indexes or mutual funds are not mutually exclusive. The degree to which two funds or indexes have similar holdings, as measured in percentage of market value.

Payable Date   The date when dividends or capital gains are paid to shareholders. For mutual funds, the payable date is usually within two to four days of the record date. The payable date also refers to the date on which a declared stock dividend or bond interest payment is scheduled to be paid.

Portfolio Transaction Costs   The expenses associated with buying and selling securities, including commissions, purchase and redemption fees, exchange fees, and other miscellaneous costs. In a mutual fund prospectus, these expenses would be listed separately from the fund's expense ratio. They do not include the bid-ask spread.

Positive Correlation   A situation in which the value of one of two investments moves in unison with the value of the other.

Premium   An amount by which the price of a security exceeds the face value or redemption value of that security or the price of a comparable security or group of investments. It may indicate that a security is highly favored by investors. Also refers to a fee for obtaining insurance coverage.

Price/Book (P/B) Ratio   The price per share of a stock divided by the stock's book value (i.e., its net worth) per share. For a portfolio, the ratio is the weighted average price-to-book ratio of the stocks it holds.

Price/Earnings (P/E) Ratio   The share price of a stock divided by its per-share earnings over the past year. For a portfolio, the weighted-average P/E ratio of the stocks in the portfolio. The P/E ratio is a good indicator of market expectations about a company's prospects; the higher the P/E ratio, the greater the expectations for a company's future growth in earnings.

Prospectus   A legal document that gives prospective investors information about a mutual fund, including discussions of its investment objectives and policies, risks, costs, and past performance. A prospectus must be provided to a potential investor before he or she can establish an account and must also be filed with the Securities and Exchange Commission.

Proxy   Written authorization by a shareholder giving someone else (such as fund or company management) authority to vote his or her shares at a shareholders' meeting.

Quantitative Analysis   In securities, an assessment of specific measurable factors, such as cost of capital; value of assets; and projections of sales, costs, earnings, and profits. Combined with more subjective or qualitative considerations (such as management effectiveness), quantitative analysis can enhance investment decisions and portfolios.

Real Estate Investment Trust (REIT)   A company that manages a group of real estate investments and distributes at least 90 percent of its net earnings annually to its stockholders. REITs often specialize in a particular kind of property. They can, for example, invest in real estate, such as office buildings, shopping centers, or hotels; purchase real estate (an equity REIT); or provide loans to building developers (a mortgage REIT).

Real Return   The actual return received on an investment after factoring in inflation. For example, if the nominal investment return for a particular period was 8 percent and inflation was 3 percent, the real return would be 5 percent (8 percent − 3 percent).

Record Date   The date used to determine who is eligible to receive a company's or fund's next distribution of dividends or capital gains.

Redemption   The return of an investor's principal in a security. Bond redemption can occur at maturity or before maturity; mutual fund shares are redeemed at net asset value when an investor's holdings are liquidated.

Redemption Fee   A fee charged by some mutual funds when an investor sells shares within a short period of time after their purchase.

Registered Investment Advisor (RIA)   An investment professional who is registered—but not endorsed—by the Securities and Exchange Commission (SEC), who may recommend certain types of investment products.

Reinvestment   Use of investment income to buy additional securities. Many mutual fund companies and investment services offer the automatic reinvestment of dividends and capital gains distributions as an option to investors.

Return of Capital   A distribution that is not paid out of earnings and profits. It is a return of the investor's principal.

Risk Tolerance   An investor's ability or willingness to endure declines in the prices of investments while waiting for them to increase in value.

R-Squared   A measure of how much of a portfolio's performance can be explained by the returns on the overall market (or a benchmark index). If a portfolio's total return precisely matched the return on the overall market or benchmark, its R-squared would be 1.00. If a portfolio's total return bore no relationship to the market's returns, its R-squared would be 0.

Sector Diversification   The percentage of a portfolio's stocks that is placed in companies in each of the major industry groups.

Sector Fund   A mutual fund that concentrates on a relatively narrow market sector. These funds can experience higher share-price volatility than diversified funds because sector funds are subject to issues specific to a given sector.

Securities and Exchange Commission (SEC)   The federal government agency that regulates mutual funds, registered investment advisors, the stock and bond markets, and broker-dealers. The SEC was established by the Securities Exchange Act of 1934.

Sharpe Ratio   A measure of risk-adjusted return. To calculate a Sharpe ratio, an asset's excess returns (its return in excess of the return generated by risk-free assets such as Treasury bills) is divided by the asset's standard deviation. It can be calculated compared to a benchmark or an index.

Short Sale The sale of a security or option contract that is not owned by the seller, usually to take advantage of an expected drop in the price of the security or option. In a typical short sale transaction, a borrowed security or option is sold, and the borrower agrees to purchase replacement shares or options at the market price on or by a specified future date. Generally, this considered a risky investment strategy.

Short-Term Capital Gain A profit on the sale of a security or mutual fund share that has been held for one year or less. A short-term capital gain is taxed as ordinary income.

Small Cap A company whose stock market value is less than $2 billion, although the amount varies among index providers.

Spread For stocks and bonds, the difference between the bid price and the ask price.

Standard Deviation A measure of the degree to which a fund's return varies from its previous returns or from the average return for all similar funds. The larger the standard deviation, the greater the likelihood (and risk) that a security's performance will fluctuate from the average return.

Style Drift When a fund moves away from its stated investment objective over time.

Swap Agreement An arrangement between two parties to exchange one security for another, to change the mix of a portfolio or the maturities of the bonds it includes, or to alter another aspect of a portfolio or financial arrangement, such as interest-rate payments or currencies.

Taxable Equivalent Yield The return on a higher-paying but taxable investment that would equal the return on a tax-free investment. The determination depends on the investor's tax bracket.

Tax Deferral Delaying the payment of income taxes on investment income. For example, owners of traditional IRAs do not pay income taxes on the interest, dividends, or capital gains accumulating in their retirement accounts until they begin making withdrawals.

Tax-Exempt Bond A bond, usually issued by a municipal, county, or state government, whose interest payments are not subject to federal tax and in some cases state and local income taxes.

Tax Swapping Creating a tax loss by the simultaneous sale of one investment or fund and purchase of a similar investment or fund that is not substantially identical to it.

Total Return A percentage change, over a specified period, in a mutual fund's net asset value, with the ending net asset value adjusted to account for the reinvestment of all distributions of dividends and capital gains.

Transaction Fee/Commission A charge assessed by an intermediary, such as a broker-dealer or a bank, for assisting in the sale or purchase of a security.

Treasury Security   A negotiable debt obligation issued by the U.S. government for a specific amount and maturity. Income from Treasury securities is exempt from state and local taxes but not from federal income tax. Treasury securities include Treasury bills (T-bills; 1 year or less), Treasury notes (T-notes; 1 to 10 years), and Treasury bonds (T-bonds; over 10 years).

Turnover Rate   An indication of trading activity during the past year. Portfolios with high turnover rates incur higher transaction costs and are more likely to distribute capital gains (which are taxable to nonretirement accounts).

Unit Investment Trust (UIT)   An SEC-registered investment company that purchases a fixed, unmanaged portfolio of income-producing securities and then sells shares in the portfolio to investors, usually in units of at least $1,000. Usually, it is sold by an intermediary such as a broker.

Unrealized Capital Gain/Loss   An increase (or decrease) in the value of a security that is not "real" because the security has not been sold. Once a security is sold by the portfolio manager, the capital gains/losses are "realized" by the fund, and any payments to the shareholder are taxable during the tax year in which the security was sold.

Volatility   The degree of fluctuation in the value of a security, mutual fund, or index. Volatility is often expressed as a mathematical measure, such as a standard deviation or beta. The greater a fund's volatility, the wider the fluctuations between its high and low prices.

Wash Sale Rule   The IRS regulation that prohibits a taxpayer from claiming a loss on the sale of an investment if that investment or a substantially identical investment is purchased within 30 days before or after the sale.

Yankee Dollars/Bonds   Debt obligations, such as bonds or certificates of deposit, bearing U.S. dollar denominations and issued in the United States by foreign banks and corporations.

Yield Curve   A line plotted on a graph that depicts the yields of bonds of varying maturities, from short term to long term. The line, or "curve," shows the relationship between short-term interest rates and long-term interest rates.

Yield-to-Maturity   The rate of return an investor would receive if the securities held in his or her portfolio were held until their maturity dates.

INDEX